STRIKE FROM THE SEA

STRIKE FROM THE SEA

THE DEVELOPMENT AND DEPLOYMENT OF STRATEGIC CRUISE MISSILES SINCE 1934

Norman Polmar and
John O'Connell

Naval Institute Press
Annapolis, Maryland

Naval Institute Press
291 Wood Road
Annapolis, MD 21402

Library of Congress Cataloging-in-Publication Data

Names: Polmar, Norman, author. | O'Connell, John F. (John Francis),
    1930–2018, author.

Title: Strike from the sea : the development and deployment of strategic
    cruise missiles since 1934 / Norman Polmar, and John O'Connell.

Other titles: Development and deployment of strategic cruise missiles since
    1934

Description: Annapolis, Maryland : Naval Institute Press, [2020] | Includes
    bibliographical references and index.

Identifiers: LCCN 2019055286 | ISBN 9781682473894 (hardback)

Subjects: LCSH: Cruise missiles—United States—History.

Classification: LCC UG1312.C7 P65 2020 | DDC 359.8/2519—dc23

LC record available at https://lccn.loc.gov/2019055286

♾ Print editions meet the requirements of ANSI/NISO z39.48–1992 (Permanence of Paper).

Printed in the United States of America.

28 27 26 25 24 23 22 21 20   9 8 7 6 5 4 3 2 1

First printing

With appreciation of the love and support of
Jane O'Connell | Beverly Polmar

Contents

Contents

Perspective

Cruise missiles—also referred to as "guided missiles"—are widely employed tactical and strategic weapons, capable of striking ground or ship targets with conventional or nuclear warheads. The sea-based cruise missile in the U.S. and Soviet arsenals initially had a land-attack role: to deliver nuclear warheads against targets in the enemy homeland. Subsequently, both navies as well as other some other fleets have developed tactical anti-ship and anti-submarine cruise missiles. Beginning in the 1970s, with advances in cruise missile technology, the U.S. and Soviet fleets again deployed not only tactical missiles but strategic cruise missiles for strikes against an enemy homeland.

The term "strategic" entails a weapon developed primarily to strike an enemy's homeland. The targets for such weapons could be an enemy's military-industrial installations or population centers. Of course, the two types of targets often are in proximity to one another or even the same.

Much of this book addresses the U.S. Navy's Regulus missile program—the world's first submarine weapon for attacking an enemy homeland with a nuclear warhead—and the Soviet Navy's similar cruise missile efforts. Prior to Regulus, a few of the world's submarines had deck guns for assaulting coastal targets; indeed, the British built a class of "submarine monitors" with large-caliber guns for that purpose.

After the Regulus, more advanced cruise missiles and ballistic missiles were sent to sea in submarines to attack an enemy's cities and military installations. Certain of these U.S. and Soviet/Russian land-launched, nuclear-armed cruise missiles also are examined in the context of their competitiveness with sea-based missiles for roles and resources. Also, at times, briefly, the services considered the technology of other services' missiles for their own use.

The term "cruise missile" refers to an unmanned, expendable, aerodynamic vehicle, usually propelled by an air-breathing (jet) engine and carrying a conventional or nuclear warhead. Cruise missiles can be easily distinguished from ballistic missiles by their "wings," which provide aerodynamic lift. Some cruise missiles, such as the Soviet Styx and the French Exocet, are propelled by rockets rather than air-breathing engines.

Cruise missiles may use remote human guidance in the terminal phase of flight or be totally autonomous. The cruise missile is an attack weapon, normally not a reconnaissance or surveillance vehicle. However, the U.S. Navy's Tactical Tomahawk (Block IV) has the capability to send battle damage video images of areas overflown prior to its own impact.

The world's first operational strategic cruise missile was developed during World War II: the V-1, a German Air Force (Luftwaffe) initiative to compete with German Army (Wehrmacht) developmental V-2 ballistic missile for the role of long-range bombardment of England. The designation letter *V* stood for *Vergeltungswaffen*, "retaliation weapon."

Late in the war the United States obtained copies of the V-1 cruise missile, reverse-engineered it, named the "new" weapon the Jet Bomb 2 (JB-2), and began its production for use by the U.S. Army and Navy in attacks against Japan. The war ended before the missiles could be used in combat. Similarly, the German V-2 became the basis for ballistic missile development in the United States and in the Soviet Union. The German V-1 thus became the progenitor of the first generation of land-attack cruise missiles in both the United States and the Soviet Union.

The U.S. Navy version of the JB-2—named Loon—went to sea on board submarines for tests and trials in 1947. Its role was land bombardment with a conventional, high-explosive warhead. The anti-ship role also was considered for the JB-2. This Navy effort led to the development of the Regulus land-attack cruise missile, which carried a nuclear, later a thermonuclear, warhead.

While this book in large part centers on the development and deployment of the U.S. Navy's Regulus cruise missile, it also compares that weapon with the contemporary land-based cruise missiles developed by the U.S. Air Force—the Matador, Mace, and Snark—and with the contemporary Soviet sea-based strategic cruise missiles. The Regulus and Air Force cruise missiles carried nuclear warheads for strategic attacks on Soviet, Soviet-bloc European, and Chinese targets. Similarly, Soviet sea-based cruise missiles armed with nuclear warheads initially were developed to strike targets in the United States and presumably, after the early 1960s disagreements between the Soviet Union and China, targets in the latter country. Subsequently, most Soviet cruise missile programs had as their primary targets U.S. Navy aircraft carriers, which at that time operated nuclear-armed strike aircraft that presented a major threat to the Soviet homeland.

The Regulus was the U.S. Navy's operational strategic cruise missile of the late 1950s and early 1960s. It was the nation's first submarine-launched "strategic deterrent" weapon; it was also placed on aircraft carriers and cruisers. The improved Regulus II missile, with higher speed and almost double the range of the initial Regulus, was developed and made ready for production. Also in that period, more advanced U.S. sea-based strategic cruise missiles were in development: the Rigel, a ramjet-propelled, supersonic cruise missile; and the Triton, a ramjet-powered, Mach 2.5-plus cruise missile with inertial guidance and terrain-following capability. However, the U.S. Navy's rapid and successful development of the Polaris Submarine-Launched Ballistic Missile (SLBM), as well as budgetary constraints, caused the cancellation of Regulus II as well as the follow-on Rigel and Triton. Submarines armed with the Regulus I missile continued on "deterrent" patrols in the North Pacific until mid-1964, when they were replaced by Polaris missile submarines.

With the retirement of Regulus in 1964, strategic cruise missile development in the U.S. Navy experienced doldrums. In the 1970s development of land-attack cruise missiles resumed with the Tomahawk, initially designed as a "theater" weapon with a nuclear warhead. Significantly, the Tomahawk was designed from the outset to be launched from standard, 21-inch (533-mm) submarine torpedo tubes. That criterion was demanded by Admiral Elmo R. Zumwalt, the Chief of Naval Operations.

While the Tomahawk was developed specifically for naval use from surface ships and submarines, subsequently a land-launched version named Gryphon was developed as a theater nuclear weapon and operated by the U.S. Air Force. Deployment of this missile began in European NATO nations as a counter to Soviet deployment of theater nuclear weapons in Eastern Europe. (The Tomahawk also was suitable for aircraft launch, although neither the U.S. Air Force nor Navy adopted that concept.)

Subsequent Tomahawk variants with conventional warheads were developed for the land-attack and anti-ship missile roles, launched from surface ships as well as submarines. Sea-based Tomahawk missiles with conventional warheads were employed extensively and very effectively in the Gulf War (1991) and in several subsequent conflicts and crises.

The Soviet Navy's cruise missile programs, like those of the United States, initially were strategic, land-attack weapons. These programs evolved into primarily anti-ship weapons. However, whereas the United States discarded land-attack cruise missiles in favor of SLBMs until the development of the Tomahawk, the Soviets apparently retained a potential land-attack capability in their specialized cruise missile submarines. Later Russian missile development provided torpedo-tube-launched land-attack weapons, which beginning in 2015 were employed against targets in Syria from surface ships as well as submarines.

As this book went to press both the United States and post-Soviet Russia are continuing the development of advanced cruise missiles for the land-attack roles and constructing specialized, cruise missile–armed submarines.

★   ★   ★

The authors of this book owe a considerable debt to the seminal work of David K. Stumpf, PhD—*Regulus: The Forgotten Weapon* (1996). He dug deeply into the Regulus cruise missile program and interviewed many of the personnel involved for their firsthand accounts of how the program was brought to reality and of the weapon's operations. He fully supported the authors of this project.

The authors also are in debt for assistance in the writing of this book to intelligence analyst Ray Robinson, submarine technologist K. J. Moore, and historian Dr. David A. Rosenberg. The authors also benefited from earlier discussions with Rear Admiral Thomas A. Brooks, Director of Naval Intelligence; Academician Sergei Kovalev, the dean of Soviet missile submarine designers; Academician A. V. Kutineikov, head of the Malachite design bureau; Rear Admiral Walter Locke, head of the U.S. Navy's Tomahawk missile program; Viktor Semyonov, of the Rubin design bureau; Vice Admiral Levering

Smith, head of the Polaris project; Academician I. D. Spassky, head of the Rubin design bureau; and Rear Admiral Wayne E. Meyer, head of the U.S. Navy's Aegis air/missile defense program.

Also, several members of the Naval Institute Press staff helped to bring this project to fruition, in particular Janis Jorgensen, Glenn Griffith, Caitlin Bean, and Naval Institute Press director Richard Russell. Finally, the authors are indebted to Pelham Boyer for his excellent copyediting.

One of the authors of this book had a comprehensive tour of the iconic, nuclear-propelled Regulus submarine *Halibut* and the smaller, diesel-electric submarine *Growler*. He was able to learn much about the Regulus program from the crew of the *Halibut* and from his longtime mentors, two preeminent U.S. submarine officers of that period—Vice Admiral F. J. "Fritz" Harlfinger and Captain Dominic A. Paolucci. He also had the privilege of many lengthy discussions on missile-armed submarines with numerous Soviet/Russian submarine officers and submarine designers, both in the Soviet Union/Russia and in the United States.

The second author served in the Regulus missile submarine *Barbero* (SSG 317), was the nuclear warhead officer of a Guided Missile Unit, and commanded a non-missile submarine and a submarine division. He also held several significant shore assignments related to submarines and undersea warfare.

Norman Polmar
John O'Connell

Abbreviations *and* Terms

AAF — Army Air Forces (U.S.)

ABL — Armored Box Launcher

ACM — Advanced Cruise Missile

AFB — Air Force Base

AGM — Air-to-Ground Missile

AHPNAS — Advanced High-Performance Nuclear Attack Submarine

ALCM — Air-Launched Cruise Missile

ASCC — Air Standardization Coordination Committee

ASCM — Anti-Ship Cruise Missile

ASW — Anti-Submarine Warfare

ATRAN — Automatic Terrain Recognition And Navigation

Baro — Barometric switch used from 1958 to trigger the detonation of the nuclear warhead in a Regulus cruise missile (The Baro replaced the targeting radar used to determine detonation altitude of the warhead above the target.)

Blue Bird — Tactical version of Regulus I armed with a nuclear or thermonuclear warhead

BuAer — Bureau of Aeronautics (U.S. Navy)

BuOrd — Bureau of Ordnance (U.S. Navy)

BuShips — Bureau of Ships (U.S. Navy)

Buzz Bomb — British slang for German V-1 cruise missile

CEP — Circular Error Probable (the radius of a circle in which one-half of the impacts are predicted to occur)

CNA — Center for Naval Analyses (U.S.)

CNO — Chief of Naval Operations

ComSubLant — Commander, Submarine Force Atlantic Fleet (U.S.)

ComSubPac — Commander, Submarine Force Pacific Fleet (U.S.)

DARPA — Defense Advanced Research Projects Agency (U.S.)

DoD — Department of Defense (U.S.)

Doodle Bug — British slang for German V-1 cruise missile

Drone — pilotless aircraft

DSMAC — Digital Scene Matching Area Correlator

xiv Abbreviations and Terms

"Dump"	radar command to the Regulus missile to nose over into a terminal dive on its target	MT	megaton (millions of tons of high explosive)
ECCM	Electronic Counter-Countermeasures	NAAS	Naval Auxiliary Air Station
ECM	Electronic Countermeasures (active or passive)	NATO	North Atlantic Treaty Organization
ELINT	Electronic Intelligence	NavAir	Naval Air Systems Command (U.S.)
ESM	Electronic Surveillance Measures (passive)	NSM	Naval Strike Missile
FBM	Fleet Ballistic Missile	ONR	Office of Naval Research (U.S.)
FTM	Fleet Training Missile	OpNav	Office of the Chief of Naval Operations (U.S.)
FTV	Flight Test Vehicle	OpTevFor	Operational Test and Evaluation Force
GLCM	Ground-Launched Cruise Missile	OST	Operational Suitability Test (test to destruction of a nuclear weapons system, with no nuclear material involved)
GMU	Guided Missile Unit (U.S. Navy)		
GPS	Global Positioning System		
GRAU	Glavnoye Raketno-Artilleriyskoye Upravleniye (Main Missile and Artillery Directorate, Soviet/Russian)	P/A	pilotless aircraft
		PUFFS	Passive Underwater Fire Control Feasibility System (AN/BQG-4)
HE	high explosive	RAF	Royal Air Force (British)
ICBM	Intercontinental Ballistic Missile	RAM	Regulus Assault Missile
		Red Bird	training version of Regulus missile
INF	Intermediate-range Nuclear Forces	RIN	Regulus Inertial Navigation
IOC	Initial Operational Capability	RORSAT	Radar Ocean Reconnaissance Satellite
IRBM	Intermediate-Range Ballistic Missile	RPV	Remotely Piloted Vehicle
JATO	Jet Assisted Take-Off (rocket)	SAC	Strategic Air Command (U.S.)
JCS	Joint Chiefs of Staff (U.S.)	SALT	Strategic Arms Limitation Treaty
JMEWS	Joint Multi-Effects Warhead System	SCM	Strategic Cruise Missile
KT	kiloton (thousands of tons of high explosive)	SDV	Swimmer Delivery Vehicle

SEAL	Sea-Air-Land (Navy special operations team)	STAWS	Submarine Tactical Anti-ship Weapon System
SINS	Ships Inertial Navigation System	TASM	Tomahawk Anti-Ship Missile
SIOP	Single Integrated Operational Plan (U.S. plan for the use of nuclear weapons)	TEL	Transporter Erector Launcher (vehicle)
		TERCOM	Terrain Contour Matching
SLAM	(1) Standoff Land-Attack Missile	TLAM	Tomahawk Land-Attack Missile
	(2) Submarine-Launched Assault Missile	TLAM(N)	Tomahawk Land-Attack Missile (Nuclear)
	(3) Supersonic Low-Altitude Missile	TM	Tactical Missile
		Trounce	Radar guidance for control of Regulus missiles.
SLAMEX	Submarine-Launched Assault Missile Exercise		
SLBM	Submarine-Launched Ballistic Missile	UAV	Unmanned Aerial Vehicle
		UDT	Underwater Demolition Team
SLCM	(1) Sea-Launched Cruise Missile		
	(2) Submarine-Launched Cruise Missile	V-1	German cruise missile
		V-2	German ballistic missile
		VDL	Video Data Link
SM	Strategic Missile	VLF	Very-Low Frequency
SNA	Soviet Naval Aviation	VLS	Vertical-Launch System
STAM	Submarine Tactical Missile	VPM	Virginia Payload Module
STAR	Steam-Assisted Regulus (launcher)	VU	utility squadron (U.S. Navy)

U.S. Navy Ship Designations

APS	transport submarine		DER	radar picket escort
AS	seaplane tender		DL	frigate
ASSP	transport submarine		DLG	guided missile frigate
AV	seaplane tender		LCS	littoral combat ship
AVM	missile test ship		LPSS	transport submarine
BB	battleship		LST	tank landing ship
CA	heavy cruiser		SM	submarine minelayer
CB	large cruiser★		SS	submarine
CG	guided missile cruiser		SSA	cargo submarine
CGN	guided missile cruiser (nuclear propelled)		SSB	ballistic missile submarine
			SSBN	ballistic missile submarine (nuclear propelled)
CV	aircraft carrier			
CVA	(1) attack aircraft carrier		SSG	guided missile submarine
	(2) heavy aircraft carrier★★		SSGN	guided missile submarine (nuclear propelled)
CVB	large aircraft carrier			
CVE	escort aircraft carrier		SSN	submarine (nuclear propelled)
DD	destroyer		SSP	transport submarine
DDG	guided missile destroyer		SSX	experimental submarine★★★

★ Unofficially known as "battle cruiser."

★★ Used only for the canceled *United States* (CVA 58).

★★★ In the U.S. Navy this designation applied only to the midget submarine *X-1* (SSX 1).

U.S. Cruise Missile Designations

After World War II the U.S. Navy developed a designation system for guided missiles, with SSM (followed by a sequential number) indicating "surface-to-surface missile." A joint Army-Navy system was established on 14 May 1947, again with SSM indicating surface-to-surface missile, plus service identification and numeral, Army projects assigned odd numbers and Navy projects even numbers.

In 1962 the Department of Defense established a joint designation system for all U.S. military aircraft and missiles, a system that remains in use.

U.S. Navy Surface-to-Surface Cruise Missiles

Missile	Manufacturer	Pre-1947 Navy Designation	Post-1947 Navy Designation	1962 DoD Designation	Target Drone Designation
JB-2	Willys–Overland	KGW-1	KGW-1	none	
Loon	Willys–Overland	Earlier KGW-1, later LTV-N-2	KUW-1, LTV-N-2, SSM-N-1	none	
Triton		SSM-N-2	none	none	none
Rigel	Grumman	XSSM-N-6	XSSM-N-6	none	none
Regulus I	Chance Vought	none	SSM-N-8	RGM-6	KDU-1/ BQM-6C
Regulus II	Chance Vought	none	SSM-N-9	RGM-15	KD2U-1
Tomahawk	General Dynamics	none	none	BGM/ RGM/ UGM-109	none

U.S. Army Air Forces/U.S. Air Force Surface-to-Surface Cruise Missiles⋆

Missile	Manufacturer	Pre-1947 USAAF Designation	Post-1947 USAF Designation	Post-1955 USAF Designation	1962 DoD Designation
JB-2	Willys–Overland	JB-2	JB-2	none	none
Matador	Martin	SSM–A-1	B-61	TM-61	MGM-1
Snark	Northrop	XM775A	B-62 SSM–A-3	SM-62	none
Navaho	North American	none	XSSM–A-2	XSM-64	none
Mace	Martin	none	TM-76	TM-76	CGM/ MGM-13
Gryphon	General Dynamics	none	none	none	BGM-109G

⋆TM = Tactical Missile; SM = Strategic Missile

1st letter B = multiple launch environments; M = mobile ground vehicle launch;
R = surface ship launch; U = underwater (submarine) launch

2nd letter G = surface attack

3rd letter M = missile

Soviet/Russian Missile Designations

Soviet/Russian cruise missiles were assigned U.S.-NATO designations in two series: (1) an alpha-numeric indication of the missile's role and numerical sequence (i.e., of being identified); and (2) a NATO reporting name that indicated the missile's purpose. The alpha-numeric designations were assigned by the Air Standardization Coordination Committee (ASCC).*

The alpha-numeric designation for all submarine missiles is SS-N-( ), the SS indicating surface-to-surface (both surface and sub-surface launched) and the N indicating a naval missile. The letter X immediately after the N was used to indicate a missile in the development or test stage.

The NATO reporting names for all SS-N-( ) series missiles begin with the letter S, names such as Shaddock, Serb, and Sark. Not all missiles have code names assigned. There is ambiguity in official records in some cases as to which missiles or variants have been assigned given code names.

Each Soviet/Russian submarine missile type has a designation assigned by the Glavnoye Raketno-Artilleriyskoye Upravleniye (GRAU), the Main Missile and Artillery Directorate (essentially dating back to 1862) of the Ministry of Defense. The term "rocket" (for missile) was added in 1960. GRAU designations are not known for all missiles.

*The name of this committee was changed in 2005 to the Air and Space Interoperability Council (ASIC). For the background of ASCC see Thomas-Durell Young, *Supporting Future U.S. Alliance Strategy: The Anglo-Saxon, or "ABCA" Clue* (Carlisle Barracks, Pa.: U.S. Army War College, 1990), available at: http://www. dtic .mil/dtic/tr/fulltext/u2/a223332.pdf.

Bombardment from the Sea

AS EARLY AS WORLD WAR I (1914–1918) submarines were constructed for bombarding enemy lands. In 1916 the Royal Navy began the construction of large, diesel-electric submarines that would be uniquely armed with 12-inch/40-caliber (305-mm) naval guns to bombard shore targets as well as to engage enemy ships. Of the four large M-class submarines originally authorized, three were built, the *M-1*, *M-2*, and *M-3*; the fourth was broken up for scrap before her completion. These underwater giants were armed with four bow torpedo tubes in addition to the 12-inch gun and a single 3-inch anti-aircraft gun.

As the submarine *M-1*—originally designated *K-18*—was being built, the British Admiralty became concerned that spies would reveal the project to the Germans, who would then construct similar big-gun submarines for use against Britain. Journalist Don Everitt wrote:

> This aspect of the M boat project weighed heavily on the minds of the Sea Lords. It no longer seemed so important "to keep abreast of what appeared to be an expected development," one of the justifications used at the planning stage. Before long all work on the *K18* alias *M1,* was stopped. Tarpaulins were draped over her. The plans were hidden. Someone had decided that the Germans had not thought of the idea, and it was better to deny the boat to the Navy than to let the enemy have a sight of her.[1]

Thus only the *M-1* was completed only shortly before World War I ended in November 1918, and she saw no action. The *M-2* and *M-3* were completed in 1919.

The submarines *M-1* and *M-2* were 295 feet, 9 inches in length, and each had four 18- inch (457-mm) diameter torpedo tubes; *M-3* was slightly longer, 305 feet, 9 inches, to

The *M-1* was one of three British submarine monitors armed with 12-inch/40-caliber (305-mm) guns, the first submarines designed with a primary role of land attack. Their guns were the largest ever mounted in undersea craft. None of the three submarines of this class saw action in World War I. *Imperial War Museum*

accommodate larger, 21-inch (533-mm), torpedo tubes. Their design displacement was 1,594 tons surface/1,946 tons submerged. The 12-inch guns were spare weapons that had been manufactured for the *Formidable*-class battleships.[2] The submarine mounting allowed the guns to elevate to 20 degrees, depress five degrees, and train 15 degrees in either direction from centerline. The gun was aimed and fired by the periscope officer while the submarine was submerged with part of the barrel protruding above the water, using a bead sight on the end of the gun that was aligned on the target using the periscope. The submarine had to surface entirely to reload the gun, a procedure that took three minutes after surfacing. The range of the 12-inch guns was listed as some 15,000 yards; 40 rounds of ammunition were carried within the submarine.

The *M-1* was lost with all 69 men on board in a collision with a Swedish collier in the English Channel in November 1925. The large guns were removed from the *M-2* and *M-3* as a consequence of the Washington Naval Treaty of 1922; the *M-2* then was converted to a seaplane carrier in 1925, with a hangar installed in place of the gun turret. Thus modified the *M-2* operated a small, folding-wing, Parnall Peto floatplane that was catapulted off a track and, after coming down at sea, was recovered and hoisted back on board by a crane atop the hangar. She, too, was lost with all 60 men on board in January 1932, to hangar flooding.

In 1927 *M-3* was converted to a minelayer, with stowage for 100 mines on a conveyer belt that ran along her upper deck. They were discharged through a door in her stern. She was scrapped in 1932 upon completion of the minelaying trials.

A senior British naval officer, Vice Admiral Sir James Jungius, discussing the previous *steam-propelled* K–class submarines and the giant M-boats, wrote of their designers that "they were imaginative folk who dreamed them up, but the engineering wasn't as good as the imagination."[3]

After World War I the British built one more "big gun" submarine, the *X-1,* completed in 1925. Her design was based on German "cruiser" submarines. She was armed with four 5.2-inch (132-mm) guns in twin gunhouses as well as six bow torpedo tubes. The *X-1* was to have been a commerce raider.

The submarine was a failure. Two of her four diesel engines were taken from surrendered German U-boats and caused continuous problems, while her three-minute minimum diving time was considered a major liability. The Admiralty quietly cancelled plans for the *X-2*. The *X-1* was taken out of service in 1933 following damage in a shipyard accident; she was scrapped three years later, without publicity.[4] For many years the British kept details of the *X-1* and her failings under the stamp "Most Secret."

Other navies also experimented with submarines carrying large-caliber guns, but none were intended primarily for land bombardment. The French submarine *Surcouf*, completed in 1934, was armed with two 8-inch (203-mm) guns for use against merchant ships. Among her other unusual features were a special compartment to house prisoners taken from enemy merchant ships and provisions for a small floatplane to search for

The problem-plagued, short-lived British submarine *X-1* seen at Malta. She has a built-up deck casing with twin 5.2-inch gun mounts forward and aft of the conning tower. The plan for an *X-2*, possibly improved and with all-British engines, was quietly abandoned. *U.S. Naval Institute Photo Archive*

targets. After the British M-class "boats," she carried the largest guns ever mounted in a submarine.

During the 1930s the U.S. Navy built three V-class submarines armed with two 6-inch / 53-caliber (152-mm) guns: the *Argonaut* (SM 1, later APS 1), *Narwhal* (SS 167), and *Nautilus* (SS 168).[5] There was no intention of employing the guns for shore bombardment; rather, the 6-inch guns—the largest ever fitted in U.S. submarines—were for use against enemy merchant ships. During the U.S. Marine commando raid on Japanese-held Makin Island in August 1942, in which the Marines were landed on the South Pacific island by two submarines, the *Nautilus* used her 6-inch guns to fire on targets ashore.

The standard gun armament for most of the world's submarines in the 1920s and 1930s was a single 3-inch (76-mm) or 4-inch (102-mm) gun, useful for sinking an unarmed merchant ship or fishing craft, thus conserving expensive torpedoes, of which only limited numbers could in any case be carried in submarines. During World War II most U.S. fleet submarines carried one or two 5-inch (127-mm) deck guns plus lighter anti-aircraft guns and machine guns. On a few occasions the weapons were used to fire on coastal targets.

The world's largest non-nuclear submarines ever constructed were the Japanese *I-400* Special Submarines (*Sen-Toku,* or "Sto"), of which three units were completed in 1944–1945. These submarines were intended to carry three of the relatively large Aichi M6A1 Seiran attack floatplanes. They mounted only one 5.5-inch (140-mm)

The short-lived French "submarine cruiser" *Surcouf* mounted the second largest guns ever carried by a submarine—two 8-inch (203-mm) weapons in a single turret forward of her conning tower. She was completed in 1934 and was sunk in the Caribbean in a collision with a merchant ship in February 1942, with the loss of all 130 men on board. *U.S. Navy*

The *Argonaut* was one of three U.S. submarines constructed in the late 1920s armed with two 6-inch/53-caliber (152-mm) deck guns—the largest guns ever fitted in U.S. submarines. In this view there is a torpedo and torpedo loading crane under the forward 6-inch gun. The *Argonaut* was built as a minelayer and originally was "named" the *V-4*. *U.S. Navy*

Sailors read mail in front of a 6-inch gun on the submarine *Argonaut* in 1942. Built as a minelaying submarine (SM 1), the *Argonaut* later was classified as a transport submarine (APS 1). She never carried her "lineal" number, SS 166. *U.S. Navy*

deck gun in addition to ten 25-mm anti-aircraft guns. None of these submarines saw combat in the war.

There were two efforts during World War II to launch short-range, unguided shore bombardment rockets from surfaced submarines. Germany was the first nation to attempt to undertake an actual project to launch projectiles from a submarine: During May–June 1942, underwater U-boat firings of short-range rockets were carried out by the German missile test facility at Peenemünde on the Baltic Sea. These tests were conducted from the submarine *U-511,* to whose deck six rocket-launching rails had been welded. Waterproof cables had been run from the rockets to a firing switch inside the submarine. The only modification to the rockets was waterproofing them by sealing their exhaust nozzles with candle wax.

The firing tests, from a depth of some 25 feet, were entirely successful. A reported 24 rockets were launched from the U-boat and additional rounds fired from a submerged launch frame. The slow movement of the submerged submarine through the water had no effect on the accuracy of the rockets. The 275-pound projectiles had a range of five miles. The only problem encountered was an electrical ground that caused two rockets to fire simultaneously. Nevertheless, this concept was not developed into an operational weapons capability.[6]

Near the end of World War II in the Pacific, a U.S. submarine conducted impromptu bombardments of Japanese coastal facilities using unguided 5-inch-diameter rockets. In July 1945, the USS *Barb* (SS 220), commanded by Medal of Honor–winner Eugene Fluckey, attacked the towns of Shikuka, Shiritori, and Kashiho on Hokkaido, the northernmost of the Japanese main islands.

Fluckey obtained a 12-round rocket launcher, which he had bolted to the submarine's deck forward of the conning tower, and 72 rockets. Their range was short, around 5,000 yards, and the damage inflicted was effectively negligible. As for their accuracy, it was estimated that in a salvo of 12 rockets about one-half would fall within a circle of about 100 to 150 yards' radius. Fluckey's efforts were not part of any official Navy or submarine force program but reflected individual initiative on the part of an aggressive submarine commander who was finding fewer and fewer targets at sea for his torpedoes.

A "formal" U.S. Navy program for shore bombardment from the sea would have to await the development of the cruise missile in Germany, and it would employ cruise missiles instead of short-range, unguided rockets or naval guns. The German efforts to rearm began in secret shortly after the end of World War I in response to the Treaty of Versailles. That accord, imposed in 1919 by the victorious Allies, forbade Germany from possessing submarines, tanks, military aircraft, chemical weapons, or long-range artillery.[7] German artillery officers who had fought in the war read the treaty carefully and noted that it did not mention the word "rocket."

Primitive battlefield rockets had been used in European warfare as early as the 1700s—the American national anthem tells of the "rockets' red glare" during the British naval bombardment of Fort McHenry in Baltimore Harbor in 1814.[8] The rockets of the 1700s and 1800s were inaccurate, short-range weapons, and by the start of the 1900s they had generally been replaced by the much more accurate rifled field artillery. Thus, in the 1920s German artillerymen were able, by turning their attention to rocketry, to evade the restrictions on long-range artillery. Their efforts would lead to the development of the A-4 ballistic missile, better known as the V-2: *Vergeltungswaffe 2*, or Retaliation Weapon 2.[9]

A rearmed Germany initiated World War II in September 1939, smashing into Poland and then, in 1940, into the Low Countries and France. After the surrender of France in June 1940, the German Air Force undertook an intensive bombing of Britain to force surrender negotiations, or failing that, to support an invasion across the 20-mile-wide English Channel. The German Air Force (Luftwaffe), however, was trained and organized specifically for the close air support of the German Army. It had performed in outstanding fashion in the skies over Poland, Belgium, Holland, and France in 1939–1940. Its Ju 87 Stuka dive-bombers supported the German Army's newly developed *Blitzkrieg* (lightning war) tactics of fast-moving armored forces *(panzers),* while Me 109 fighters controlled the skies over the battlefields.

However, the German Air Force was not up to the task of subduing the British. The Battle of Britain during the summer and fall of 1940 saw Britain's integrated, radar-based air defense system, with its outstanding Hurricane and Spitfire interceptors, defeat the Luftwaffe's best efforts to gain air supremacy.[10] Without air supremacy no cross-channel invasion of the British Isles was possible. Although Germany controlled most of Western Europe, Great Britain therefore lay out of reach, except for air attacks and naval operations against British shipping. The failure of the German Air Force to destroy the Royal Air Force's Fighter Command, in favor of a night terror bombing campaign against London and other cities, however, served to open up the field of long-range attack to the German Army, which had a long-range ballistic missile under development.

The German Army could not achieve super-long-range guns, but it would have long-range rockets.[11] By the fall of France in June 1940, the Army's rocket development had led to design of the A-4. The A-4, as its designator implies, was the fourth in a series of experimental, liquid-fuel ballistic missiles developed by German Army artillery officers and scientists in work that had begun in the early 1930s.[12]

The first successful flight of the A-4 (later V-2) missile occurred on 3 October 1942, at Peenemünde. *Reichsmarschall* Hermann Göring, the head of the Luftwaffe, had boasted that "if it flies it belongs to me." But the A-4 missile was firmly in Army hands, whose senior officers could argue convincingly that in reality it was an extension of long-range artillery. The concern of the Air Force's leadership was that the German Army might be able to bombard the British into seeking surrender, which the Luftwaffe had earlier failed to do.

Technicians from the German missile test facility at Peenemünde and sailors install rocket-launching rails on the submarine *U-511*, commanded by *Korvettenkapitan* Fritz Steinhoff. His brother, Ernest Steinhoff, was a brilliant engineer at Peenemünde, and together they conceived the idea of launching rockets from a submerged submarine. *Imperial War Museum*

Cruise Missile Progenitor

The implicit Army competition with Luftwaffe bombardment of Britain spurred the latter into development of a long-range cruise missile. The German Air Force's seminal V-1 cruise missile stemmed from research begun in 1928 by German engineer Paul Schmidt. He had been interested in providing vertical lift to a conventional airframe and in April 1931, had been granted a patent on a pulse-jet engine. Schmidt's device was similar in principle to an automobile engine, which has valves that open and shut rapidly to admit an explosive mixture into a combustion chamber and then exhaust it. In Schmidt's pulse-jet engine, flapper valves at the front of the engine chamber opened and shut rapidly to admit "pulses" of air that, combined with a fuel mixture, was ignited by a sparkplug. The exhaust was an open tube.

Schmidt was able to obtain funding for his experiments from the Research Division of the Ministry of Communications of the democratic Weimar Republic (1919–1933). Later the financial support continued under the German Aviation Ministry. His was the first jet engine project to garner the German government's support.[13]

In 1934 Schmidt, in collaboration with Dr. G. Madelung, submitted to the Aviation Ministry a proposal for a "flying bomb." The design included a pulse-jet engine in the after fuselage, guidance components, and a warhead mounted forward. But the Aviation Ministry rejected it as "technically dubious and uninteresting from a tactical viewpoint."

The following year things began to look brighter for the two inventors. Schmidt gained sponsorship from several respected figures, among them Professor Adolf Busemann, one of the first proponent of swept-back wings; Dr. Walter Dornberger, the leading figure in the Army's ballistic missile work; and Dr. Wernher von Braun, who later would lead development of the A-4 (V-2) missile and, much later, the American space rocket program. The Aviation Ministry took a new interest in Schmidt's flying bomb idea and granted development money.

In 1938, the first successful auto-ignition of the pulse-jet took place. In 1941 the SR 500 pulse-jet was tested successfully. By 1942 this pulse-jet engine was able to deliver 1,650 pounds of static thrust.[14] For comparison, British officer and jet-engine inventor Frank Whittle's W-2B turbojet engine, used in the Gloster Meteor jet fighter, developed a static thrust of 1,000 pounds.[15] (The Me 262, Germany's first operational jet fighter, was to make its initial flight in July 1942, propelled by two Jumo 004A turbojet engines, each providing 1,852 pounds of thrust. The Me 262 first flew on 18 April 1941, with piston engines; the first flight with turbojet engines was on 18 July 1942. The Me 262 became operational in April 1944.)

In 1939, following the Aviation Ministry decision to develop turbojet engines, its technical branch asked Argus Motoren Gesellschaft of Berlin, a manufacturer of small aero engines and superchargers, to develop a pulse-jet. In November 1939, work began at the firm under Dr. Fritz Gosslau, who was unaware of Schmidt's work in the same field. His group developed and tested a model pulse-jet engine that same month. In February 1940, connection finally was made with Schmidt, and discussions about the theory and mechanics of pulse-jet engines took place. Schmidt's flapper valve was superior to the Argus-developed flow valve, and it was substituted in the Argus engine. Later the engine was officially designated the Argus-Schmidt engine; basically, it was the Argus firm that developed the V-1 pulse-jet engine.[16]

In January 1941, the Argus engine was tested on an automobile, limited to 60 miles per hour by the available roads. The engine first flew in April 1941, mounted under a Gotha Go 145 biplane; in a later test an Me 109 fighter flew with the Argus engine mounted under its fuselage. Other trials included the Do 217 and Me 110 aircraft with the pulse-jet mounted above their fuselages, and Ju 88s and He 111s with the engines suspended from wing bomb racks. During summer 1941 tests a modified Gotha Go 242 cargo glider became the first aircraft to be powered solely by a pulse-jet engine.

The definitive Argus As 109-014 engine was fueled by a 140-gallon tank. The fuel, a low-octane gasoline, was pushed by compressed air into the engine, where it mixed with air and was detonated by a single Bosch sparkplug mounted in the chamber. The sparkplug was used for the first ignition; thereafter the heat of the combustion chamber ignited the fuel-air mixture. There were 42 ignitions (fuel-air detonations) per second.

In March 1942, Robert Lusser of Fieseler Aircraft Works mentioned his interest in a flying bomb to an engineer of the Aviation Ministry. On 10 June 1942, an Aviation Ministry scientific committee under the direction of Field Marshal Erhard Milch met to discuss the flying bomb project. Dr. Gosslau showed the group a sketch of the device. Nine days later the Aviation Ministry approved production of flying bombs—cruise missiles.

On 19 June, the Ministry placed an order for a flying bomb as Project P-35. The Fieseler Company was to build the airframe, thus an *Fi* designation, Fi 103, was assigned. Argus supplied the pulse-jet engine; the Siemens Company provided the Askania autopilot in the weapon's guidance section; and the Walters Company handled design of the takeoff ramp and catapult arrangements. The Fieseler Works at Kassel was responsible for overall coordination and assembly of the weapon.

The new weapon was given the German name *Kirshkern* (Cherry Stone) early in the development process. For deception purposes the missile was called a *flak ziel gerat,* or anti-aircraft target.

The first airframe launch took place from Luftwaffe test facilities at Peenemünde from under the fuselage of an Fw 200 Condor bomber aircraft in early 1942. During aircraft-carry flight tests the pulse-jet's rhythmic explosions damaged the metal skins of test aircraft. To reduce such damage to an actual missile, the engine was mounted above the missile's tailfin, clear of the airframe. By May 1943, most of V-1s teething problems had been resolved, and in June 1943, the Wachtel Training and Test Command was established to work out the operational use of the missile.[17]

The V-1 would carry a high-explosive warhead of 1,850 pounds some 160 miles. It was designed to fly at altitudes from 980 to 8,000 feet. The missile was capable of delivering a variety of poison gases as well as incendiary devices.[18] However, only the high-explosive warhead was actually used in combat. The flight direction of the V-1 was controlled by a gyroscope and a magnetic compass, and a small propeller was used as a "range counter." When the number of propeller revolutions reached a preset value, the missile engine shut off and the missile tipped over into a dive toward the ground. The warhead exploded on contact.

The weapon was designed to be launched from a catapult 82 feet long, enough distance to generate the air flow to the pulse-jet engine needed to sustain flight. It also could be—and was—launched from carrier aircraft. On 24 December 1942, the first launch of a powered missile took place from a land rail at Peenemünde.

By July 1943, an anti-aircraft *(flak)* regiment had been established for launching V-1s. There were 12 launch batteries—each with six launch ramps—and a maintenance and supply battery, altogether some 4,000 men in the regiment. The Luftwaffe provided separate units to handle V-1 site defense, communications, and supply functions.[19]

As the Luftwaffe pushed development and testing of the V-1 missile, British intelligence discerned some indications of the weapon's existence. Alerted by the

The German V-1 Flying Bomb was the world's first cruise missile developed to attack an enemy's homeland. While almost all V-1s were land-launched, some were launched from aircraft, and in the post-war period American copies were launched from surfaced submarines. *Imperial War Museum*

mysterious so-called Oslo Report, British intelligence was on the lookout for signs of new German weapon development. Ferdinand Mayer, a German mathematician and physicist, had visited Oslo, Norway, in early November 1939. Alarmed by Hitler's policies, he had typed a report on German military developments and delivered it covertly to the British embassy in Oslo. Rapidly forwarded to British intelligence in London, it was the first clue to Germany's startling missile advances.

From time to time further information filtered back to England about German missile development. Aerial reconnaissance photographs of the area around Peenemünde finally revealed two separate weapons, one an airplane-like device, the V-1, and the other a freestanding, large rocket, that would become the V-2. The first launching of the German Army V-2 ballistic missile at Peenemünde took place on 3 October 1942, almost three months before the first Luftwaffe V-1 cruise missile flight.

As more intelligence was obtained, plans were made to attack the facilities at Peenemünde. In August 1943, in Operation Hydra, the Royal Air Force Bomber Command undertook a massive bombing strike. The attack was specifically intended to kill German scientists and technicians involved in the missile programs. It was partially successful, albeit at a high cost, with 40 bombers out of the 596 taking part shot down and others severely damaged. More than 700 people at Peenemünde, including scientists, were killed. The death toll also included hundreds of European slave laborers.

Because of the attack, V-1 cruise missile production, worked by thousands of slave laborers, was moved, first to Brusterort, a Navy base northwest of Königsberg, and later to the underground tunnels of Mittlewerke. This latter facility was at Kohnstein, a hill just outside the town of Nordhausen.

A V-1 cruise missile falls on London; St. Paul's Cathedral is in the foreground. London and, subsequently, the port of Antwerp in Belgium were the primary targets for the 22,400 V-1 missiles that were launched by the Germans. *U.S. Air Force*

The Luftwaffe favored open-field sites for launch of the V-1, but Hitler, impressed by the concrete submarine pens constructed for the Navy in France, favored heavily reinforced sites. Göring negotiated a compromise, with some fixed sites and some open field. Two hundred fifty-two concrete V-1 launch sites were incorporated in the "Atlantic Wall," the system of fortifications designed to block an Allied invasion of the French coast. Each of the launch sites had a rail launcher, powered by a gas generator, similar to an aircraft carrier's catapult arrangement; the rail hurled the V-1 missile into the air at a speed high enough for the pulse-jet engine to sustain flight.

Some of the launch ramps were aligned on London, others on British ports on the English Channel.[20] The V-1's range, originally 160 miles, was extended to 250 miles by increasing fuel capacity, reducing the size of the warhead, and substituting lighter, wooden wings for the earlier metal wings.[21]

The Cruise Missile Campaign
On 16 May 1944, Field Marshal Wilhelm Keitel, the German Army commander, issued a directive based upon an order from Hitler: "Long range bombardment of England will begin in the middle of June."[22] *Eisbar* (Polar Bear) was the code word for opening

attacks on London with V-1 flying bombs; it was issued on 13 June 1944, one week after the Normandy landings. The aim point for the V-1s was the Tower Bridge in central London.[23] On that first day ten V-1s were launched: four crashed immediately after leaving their launch ramps, and two failed to cross the Channel; three others exploded near London; and the tenth detonated near Gravesend.[24] Casualties and damage were minor.

The V-1 missile had several limitations. In daylight it could be seen, and it could be detected by radar by day or night. It could be shot down by anti-aircraft gunfire or by Allied fighters. Another problem was its inaccuracy. The CEP of a V-1 missile in August 1944 was about 11 miles at an average range of 150 miles.[25] The Fieseler Company had claimed that one-half of the production missiles would have a CEP of 3.7 miles.

The V-1 warhead contained 1,850 pounds of high explosive (amatol), enough to destroy a large building with a direct hit and kill or maim scores of people in the immediate vicinity. Thus, given its limited accuracy the V-1 cruise missile was a pure "terror weapon." The V-1 campaign was specifically intended by Hitler as retaliation (as its name implied) for the RAF bombing of German cities.

Despite the failure of the V-1 as a "strategic" weapon to force British capitulation, the campaign continued. By 16 June 1944, some 40 catapult launchers were operational. A massive V-1 attack began that night, and by noon on the 16th 244 missiles had been launched. Forty-five of the missiles crashed shortly after launch, but the others proceeded toward England.

In 80 days more than 100 "buzz bombs" a day were launched at British targets, with 316 missiles on one day in August. On 7 July 1944, the first operational air-launch of a V-1 took place, from an He 111 bomber and aimed at Southampton. Some 1,200 of the missiles were air-launched from He 111H twin-engine bombers. During the campaign V-1s wrecked or damaged more than one million buildings, killed 6,184 people, and seriously injured almost 18,000. The Dutch port of Antwerp, important for supplying the Allied armies fighting in Europe, also was a principal target for V-1s.

A total of 22,400 V-1 missiles were launched against Allied targets during the war.[26] They took a heavy toll of civilians in England and newly liberated Europe (France, Belgium, and Holland), but were ineffective militarily, not even slowing the Allied ground and air operations that ended in the total defeat of Nazi Germany in early May 1945.

In technical terms also, the V-1 was not a perfect weapon: 8,564 of the missiles (about 43 percent) launched against England or Antwerp failed or were destroyed by defending fighters or anti-aircraft fire. On 17 June a V-1 took an unintended 180-degree turn in flight and crashed on top of a specially prepared "Führer Bunker" in France where Hitler was conferring with his generals about the recent Allied invasion of Normandy.[27] The missile exploded, but due to the strength of the bunker inflicted no injuries on the assembled officials.[28]

Countering Cruise Missiles

The V-1s generally flew at altitudes of 2,000 to 3,000 feet on steady courses. Most were launched at night, to avoid interception by Allied fighters. Although V-1s were, as noted above, vulnerable to interceptors and anti-aircraft guns, they were not quite easy targets. The missiles crossed the Channel at altitudes too low to be detected by radar at great distances. As V-1s burned fuel their speed increased, and by the time they reached the "fighter areas" they were flying at more than 400 miles per hour. In response, the British established staggered air defense zones using anti-aircraft guns, barrage balloons, and interceptor aircraft for defense in depth.

RAF Tempest fighters scored 636 V-1s shot down, the most of any Allied aircraft type. Other fighters that tried to down V-1s were Spitfires, Mustangs with boosted engines, Mosquitoes, and Gloster Meteors, the last Britain's first jet-propelled fighter.

The altitude band in which the V-1s flew was too high for light anti-aircraft guns (20-mm and 40-mm) and too low for the heavier British 3.7-inch guns, which had problems traversing fast enough to track them.[29] The U.S. Army contributed SCR-584 gun-laying radars and proximity-fused anti-aircraft ammunition, the latter five times as effective as ordinary, time-fused ammunition.[30] Barrage-balloon cables snagged and downed some V-1s, but the Luftwaffe rapidly installed cable-cutting blades on the missile's wings to counter that defense. British intelligence did its best to deny the Germans exact knowledge of actual V-1 and V-2 missile accuracy, but in this case the Luftwaffe had to have gained information about losses to barrage-balloon cables to have modified the V-1's wings.

In 1944, before the Battle of the Bulge, Otto Skorzeny, a talented German special operations officer, discussed with Heinrich Himmler, leader of the Waffen-SS, the military arm of the Nazi Party, the possibility of employing modified, long-range V-1 missiles against New York. Himmler appeared to be fascinated with the idea, thinking that it would prove a morale-breaker. He was so enthusiastic that Skorzeny and several others present had to point out the many technical problems to be solved. The idea quickly petered out.[31]

Another short-lived proposal was for a piloted variant of the V-1, to be flown by volunteers in an effort to compensate for the poor accuracy of the missile. The pilot was to parachute from the V-1 after pointing the missile at its target—a dubious procedure.

The concept of a piloted V-1, reportedly, was proposed directly to Hitler by German aviatrix and national hero Hanna Reitsch. She is said to have recommended that the pilots fly the missile into their targets, "kamikaze style." Hitler, while not enthusiastic about the proposal, did approve producing a few V-1s with cockpits and, for trials, a rigid landing gear.

One test flight is said to have been made. Most sources cite Reitsch as having made that flight. But Willy Fiedler, test director of the V-1 program, was more likely the only person to ever "fly" a V-1.[32]

★   ★   ★

In his book *The Rocket and the Reich*, aviation historian Michael Neufeld argued that the V-1 was inaccurate and employed "too early" to have any significant effect on the war. In his opinion, the V-1s were crude area-bombardment missiles and not very cost-effective, considering their inaccuracy and relatively small warhead.[33] In *Impact*, written several years after Neufeld's book, Timothy King and Benjamin Kutta draw a somewhat different conclusion: that the V-1 and V-2 weapons did in fact have significant overall impacts upon Allied plans and operations and caused a massive expenditure of scarce resources to deal with them.

It would take the post-war development of nuclear warheads to provide early cruise and ballistic missiles sufficient explosive force to offset their rather large CEPs and turn them into massively destructive weapons. Later, inertial navigation, Global Positioning System (GPS), and terrain-matching radar would turn cruise missiles into precision weapons, highly effective even with high-explosive warheads.

Table 1-1. German Attacks on the London Area

1940–1941★ every night (Sept.–Oct. 1940)	~200 German bombers per night	40,553 killed
June–Sept. 1944	2,419 V-1 missiles	6,184 killed 17,981 injured
Sept. 1944–Feb. 1945	1,190 V-2 missiles	2,754 killed 6,523 injured

★ German aircraft bombed London for 57 consecutive nights beginning 7 September 1940; the Blitz against London lasted eight months. One in six Londoners was bombed out of his/her home at least once.

Loon Goes to Sea

GERMAN V-1 CRUISE MISSILES were first launched against targets in England in mid-June 1944. Parts salvaged from unexploded V-1 crashes in England were recovered and hurriedly air-shipped to the United States. On 12 July 1944, some 2,500 pounds of V-1 parts were flown to the Wright-Patterson Air Base in Ohio. They were carefully examined, and a reverse-engineered copy of the V-1 was produced in only 17 days. It was dubbed Jet Bomb 2 (JB-2).[1]

The U.S. Army almost immediately ordered 1,000 JB-2s for combat use.[2] Early plans indicated that some 75,000 would be required for the campaign against Japan. The Navy took delivery of 351 missiles from the Army order; both services planned to use conventional-warhead missiles against Japan. The production contracts were let to Republic Aviation (later sub-contracted to Willys-Overland) for the JB-2 airframe; to Ford for the pulse-jet engine; to Jack and Heintz for controls; to Alloy Products for pressure vessels; to Monsanto for rocket boosters; and to Northrop for launch sleds. The initial contract, issued to Republic on 2 August 1944, from the Army Air Forces Materiel Command was for 1,000 flying bombs; later the orders were increased to 50,000!

JB-2 trials were conducted at California's Muroc Dry Lake.[3] About 50 unsuccessful launches took place before, on 12 October 1944, the JB-2 flew as intended. The first operational version of JB-2 was delivered to the AAF in January 1945.[4]

On 14 January 1945, General Henry Arnold, the head of the Army Air Forces, directed that 75,000 JB-2s be produced. On the following day an AA-1 priority was assigned to the program, the same priority as given to the B-29 Superfortress long-range bomber. However, AAF officers in Europe were more guarded in their enthusiasm. As early as July 1944, General Carl Spaatz, commander of U.S. Strategic Air Forces in the European Theater, had stated that there was no need for pilotless aircraft in his theater except in the case of bad weather when piloted aircraft were grounded.[5]

In late January 1945 the AAF determined that the JB-2 program would cost $1.5 billion to produce the missiles and would require one-quarter of the European Theater's merchant shipping to send them to Europe; accordingly, the War Department ruled against continued mass production of the JB-2. All production was terminated in September 1945, with 1,385 missiles having been delivered.

In February 1945, accuracies of 500 yards at 50 miles and 1,000 yards at 100 miles were predicted for air-launched JB-2s. During tests that spring a pair of JB-2s was suspended under the wings of a B-17 Flying Fortress and released at an altitude of 5,000 feet. Planned drops from B-29 Superfortress and B-24 Liberator bombers were cancelled, but B-17 trials continued. Of ten attempts at Wendover Air Base in Utah, only four were successful. Far from the predicted accuracies for air-launched missiles, the actual results obtained were six miles at 80 miles (14 test flights) and 12 miles at 127 miles (20 test flights).[6]

Navy Cruise Missiles

In November 1944, Admiral E. J. King, the Chief of Naval Operations, expressed interest in the flying bomb program for use against land targets and potentially against enemy ships, possibly for launching from escort or "jeep" aircraft carriers.[7] The Navy's Bureau of Aeronautics (BuAer) obtained 57 JB-2s from the AAF and contracted with Republic Aviation to produce another 100 missiles. The Navy named its JB-2 cruise missile Loon on 16 April 1945. Proposed launch platforms included tank landing ships (LSTs), the PB4Y-1 Liberator aircraft (the Navy's version of the B-24 Liberator), and ground launch ramps. Plans called for employing the weapon in day and night attacks at ranges to 100 miles against land and sea targets.

A May 1945 Navy study indicated that the initial operational date for the Loon would be August–September 1946. At the time the United States was planning for the invasion of the Japanese home islands in November 1945; the war was expected to end no earlier than the spring of 1946. When instead the war suddenly ended in August 1945, following the atomic bombing of Hiroshima and Nagasaki, the Navy, like the Army and Army Air Forces, began the task of demobilization of the massive forces that had been built up during the war. The Navy also began to look at restructuring for what the future might bring, including close consideration of new technologies. The Loon guided missile fit into the category of new weapons to be carefully explored.

On 11 September 1945—a little more than a week after Japan's formal surrender— Vice Admiral Charles Lockwood, the commander of submarines in the Pacific, ordered, "Investigate the possibility of a long range 'buzz bomb' to be launched from torpedo tubes when submerged."[8] In late 1945 the Navy established Project Derby to train Navy personnel to assemble, launch, and guide such a missile. The Navy Loon was substantially improved over the original V-1 missile: radio controls, a radar beacon

for guidance by shipboard or airborne radars, and a wing-blow-off system to improve terminal accuracy.

The first launch of a Loon took place on 7 January 1946: the engine quit immediately after launch, and the missile crashed about one mile offshore from Point Mugu, California. The Navy, like the AAF, and as the Germans had, was finding that early cruise missiles were temperamental machines that had to be treated delicately if they were to perform properly.

On 5 March 1946, the Navy Department authorized the modification of two World War II–built fleet submarines into missile-launching boats:[9] The USS *Carbonero* (SS 337) and USS *Cusk* (SS 348), both based at San Diego. The USS *Norton Sound* (AV 11, later AVM 1), a modified seaplane tender, also was included in the project.[10] At about this time an *Essex* (CV 9)–class aircraft carrier and the unfinished battle cruiser *Hawaii* (CB 3) also were considered as prospective missile launching platforms, but those proposals soon were dropped.

The USS *Cusk* (SSG 348) with a Loon missile ready for launch; note the missile hangar fitted aft of the conning tower. The *Cusk*, shown in November 1948, was one of scores of World War II–built "fleet boats" that were converted to a variety of specialized roles. As an SSG she retained her original conning tower structure. *U.S. Navy*

The USS *Norton Sound* (AV 11) conducts a Loon cruise missile launch on 12 October 1949. The seaplane tender—later redesignated AVM 1—was an important platform in the Navy's development of guided missiles, guns, radars, and fire control systems. *U.S. Navy*

The Navy project was placed under BuAer, since it involved an "aircraft," albeit unmanned.[11] The Loon was 27 feet long, had an 18-foot wingspan, and weighed 5,020 pounds when fully fueled and ready for launch. The fuel tank held 180 gallons of either high- or low-octane gasoline. Missile stabilization was provided by three air-driven position and rate gyros. An aneroid unit and a magnetic compass controlled altitude and heading though the gyro. A launch rail, employing a slotted-tube gunpowder catapult, was used to get the missile up to minimum flying speed (220 mph), beyond which the pulse-jet engine could maintain flight. The Loon's maximum range was only 120 nautical miles; its cruise speed was 371 miles per hour within an altitude band of 2,000 to 6,000 feet.

Although a close copy, the Navy's Loon was not identical to the German V-1. The Loon was tracked by radar, and its flight was controlled by radio signals. There were four radio commands:[12]

- "Check one"—which altered the missile's course to the right (one degree each signal).
- "Check two"—which altered the missile's course to the left (one degree for each signal).
- "Check three"—which activated the missile's beacon transponder so that, if desired, control could be passed to another submarine (closer to the target).

- "Check four"—the "dump" signal, which cut fuel to the missile and sent it diving onto the target.

The launch procedure was described by Captain John H. Bothwell, who as a junior officer served in the *Carbonero*:[13]

> The captain's first launch command would be to "jet air." On a small launch control panel, mounted above the radar console, a button would initiate the flow of air from the boat's 3,000 [pounds-per-square-inch] system that provided the necessary air flow. For a pulse-jet to function either the bird has to go through the air or the air has to go through the bird. The command "metering air" followed immediately. This pressurized the fuel tank, forcing fuel through the spray nozzles and into the combustion chamber. "Engine Start" fired the spark plug, and the missile came to life with a thundering roar heard—and felt—throughout the boat. The "rumble" was deafening and always seemed to take us by surprise. The engine quickly came to full speed, and the command "launch" brought rocket motor ignition, hurling the sled and missile skyward. After 2.2 seconds the JATO [rocket] units would burn out and the launch sled would fall into the sea astern, but the Flight of the Loon had begun.

On 12 February 1947, the modified submarine *Cusk,* operating out of Port Hueneme near Point Mugu, where Loon handling facilities were set up, launched a Loon cruise missile off Point Mugu. The *Carbonero* also launched a Loon and acted as an at-sea guidance and control platform for the tests.

The USS *Carbonero* (SS 337) preparing for a Loon cruise missile test flight off Point Mugu, California, about 1949. The *Carbonero* was not designated as an SSG although the submarine continued missile launch and control work into the 1950s. Note the absence of a missile hangar. *U.S. Navy*

The *Carbonero* launches a Loon missile off of Point Mugu in June 1949. The booster rocket used to launch the Loon from a short ramp still is attached beneath the missile. These early Loon operations provided useful experience for the Navy men who would operate the Navy's guided missile submarines. *U.S. Navy*

There were numerous problems with the early missile firings, both from launch rails ashore at Point Mugu and at sea. Dr. Wilhelm Fiedler, a German former V–1 scientist, helped Navy personnel understand and solve the difficulties. One early problem was that the missile tended to pitch up sharply after leaving the launch rails. Rocket booster alignment was the problem. With no pilot on board to correct attitude, the missile could easily be lost to this phenomenon.

During a memorable Loon exercise on 7 July 1948, the missile's fuel tank exploded on the after deck of the *Cusk* when the booster rockets fired. The *Cusk* was "buttoned up," all hatches secured with all crewmen inside. Her commanding officer, Commander Fred Clarke, immediately submerged the boat to extinguish the fire on deck. When the smoke cleared, anxious observers on nearby ships were horrified to see . . . *nothing!* The onlookers, aghast, feared that the *Cusk* had been destroyed in the explosion, until the submarine slowly surfaced, with no apparent damage except for scorch marks on her after deck.

In August 1947, based on successful test results, the Navy directed that submarine launchings of Loons continue through 1949 to develop terminal guidance procedures and tactical concepts for the use of the Regulus missile, which was under development.

In September 1947, the *Cusk* entered the Mare Island Naval Shipyard for the installation of a small hangar aft of her sail to allow her to store a Loon while submerged.

A Loon missile exploded during a launch countdown on board the *Cusk* on 7 July 1948, while the submarine was operating off Point Mugu, California. There were no casualties in the accident as the submarine was "buttoned up" for the missile launch and suffered only minor damage. *U.S. Navy*

Although the *Carbonero* also launched Loon missiles, she had no hangar installed. The hangar justified redesignating the *Cusk* as the Navy's first missile submarine—SSG 348—on 20 January 1948.

In May 1948, the *Cusk* launched and successfully guided a Loon missile for 46 miles, "splashing" it within 100 yards of the target, Begg Rock, near Navy-owned San Nicolas Island, California.[14] On 26 January 1949, a Loon was successfully launched from the test ship *Norton Sound*.

One year later, in May 1949, the Office of the Chief of Naval Operations directed the Commander, Submarine Force Pacific Fleet to determine the operational capabilities of the Loon missile. Accordingly, Project Pounce evaluated its launching equipment, tracking and guidance capabilities from shore and from submarines, missile maintenance, and launch procedures. Some six months later Operation Miki was staged in Hawaiian waters. The submarine tender USS *Sperry* (AS 12) carried four Loon missiles from San Diego to Pearl Harbor for transfer to the *Cusk* and the *Carbonero*, which had sortied from Port Hueneme to Hawaii under simulated wartime conditions.[15] The First Fleet, some 70 ships, was strung out over 50 nautical miles on a northeast heading from Oahu.

The *Cusk* and the *Carbonero*, about two miles apart in the channel between the islands of Oahu and Molokai, each launched a Loon missile to serve as targets for the First Fleet's anti-aircraft guns and for interceptor aircraft.[16] The *Cusk* missile launched properly, but then splashed about 25 miles downrange because of engine failure. The *Carbonero* then launched a Loon. It flew well and was untouched by anti-aircraft fire from the assembled warships. After the ships had their tries, Navy fighter aircraft were sent after the Loon, which was flying at 300 miles per hour at 10,000 feet. They too failed to down the missile, which finally ran out of fuel and crashed into the sea.

The Commander, Submarine Division 51, Commander John S. McCain Jr., submitted a lengthy report about Loon missile tests, including the Operation Miki phase.[17] He noted an 83 percent launch rate success, 90 percent guidance success, 100 percent success in tracking the missiles with radar, and a successful "forward deployment" in Operation Miki. Nevertheless, he opined that the Loon was not really a viable tactical weapon. It would serve to assist research and development for a future cruise missile program.

The two modified submarines continued to launch Loons, providing considerable experience for submariners as well as missile technicians and engineers. One *Carbonero* launch to remember occurred just after a petty officer had painted—in bright red—the Soviet hammer-and-sickle symbol and "Molotov's Cocktail" on the side of the missile as it was about to be fired. It turned out to be one of the few missiles of which control was lost in flight. The errant missile headed landward and, with fuel exhausted, crashed into the sea off Santa Monica. A local fisherman found the wreckage and "excitedly reported it to the Coast Guard who arrived on the scene without delay, obviously not wanting to be left out of World War III."[18]

Almost from the start of the program there were discussions at various Navy levels of how to "weaponize" the Loon. But the 61 missiles launched by the two submarines in 1948–1949 demonstrated only a 40 percent chance of hitting within a mile of the target, 70 percent within five miles (from a distance of 60 miles). Also, once the submarine was on the surface it could take 30 minutes or more to extract the missile from the hangar, place it on the launch rail, and prepare it for launching. Also, after launching the weapon the submarine had to remain at periscope depth to provide radar guidance.

In March 1950, the *Cusk* launched a Loon missile and, after guiding it for one-half of the 50-mile flight, turned it over to a shore facility on San Nicolas Island. The missile impacted about 360 yards from its target, Begg Rock. This exercise marked the first successful missile guidance transfer operation. In May 1950, the *Cusk* guided a Loon missile for a distance of 105 nautical miles.

That same month the Office of the Chief of Naval Operations directed the establishment of Project Trounce within Project Derby. Trounce was to prepare submarine personnel for operational evaluation of the new Regulus cruise missile. The Trounce project also would evaluate the new guidance concept of employing paired-pulse radar signals to send commands to the missile instead of the radio commands used with the Loon. The older arrangement was thought to be too vulnerable to Electronic Countermeasures (ECM) that could cause the loss of guidance during a missile attack.[19]

Neither the Loon nor Regulus missile saw action during the Korean War, which began on 30 June 1950 with the North Korean invasion of South Korea. However, unmanned F6F-5K Hellcat aircraft were used in that conflict as explosive assault drones. Six modified Hellcats, each carrying a one-ton bomb, were flown off the aircraft carrier *Boxer* (CV 21) and were radio-controlled by AD-4Q Skyraider aircraft that guided them to their targets—a North Korean bridge and tunnel. These attacks, the first flown on 28 August 1952, inflicted minor damage on the targets.[20]

Loon Terminated

In March 1950, the Navy terminated the Loon missile program to make way for the Regulus. The Loon program had been important in introducing the submarine-launched cruise missile into the fleet and in training naval personnel who would go into the Regulus program.

Could the Loon have become a combat weapon? With the Regulus missile not expected to become operational until 1954, a nuclear-armed Loon could have provided the Navy a limited nuclear missile capability for the land-attack role. The possibility was based upon the Bureau of Ordnance's proposed development of a 1,750-pound, air-burst nuclear bomb. It was a complicated proposal and eventually came to naught.[21] Also, a project initiated at Los Alamos in 1951—and cancelled in 1952—would have developed a B10 nuclear warhead (12 to 15 kilotons) for the Loon missile.[22] Still, a war reserve of 25 Loon missiles was established and funding was provided for some improvements to the missile.

On 4 May 1951, the *Cusk* and the *Carbonero* took part in Operation Rex, a simulated Loon missile attack on the port of San Diego. The "loyal" U.S. Navy opposition included one escort carrier, three destroyers, five destroyer escorts, and all the available anti-submarine aircraft in southern California. None of them detected either the *Cusk* or the *Carbonero*. The *Cusk* surfaced and simulated launching a Loon missile, which was itself simulated by a manned P-80 Shooting Star aircraft that flew the flight path from launch point to target as radar-directed by the two submarines. After the "launch" the *Cusk* submerged, having been on the surface for 18 minutes, and then radar-guided the "missile" from periscope depth for the next 55 minutes. The *Carbonero* then took over and completed the guidance to target. Given that the Loon was limited to a 2,100-pound, high-explosive warhead, the effect in wartime might have been embarrassing to the defenders, but it would not have been very damaging.

Similar Submarine-Launched Assault Missile Exercises (SLAMEXes) were conducted along the Atlantic and Pacific coasts of the United States during the late 1950s and early 1960s. They usually included U.S. diesel-electric submarines simulating Soviet cruise missile boats. A large number of those simulated Soviet submarines were able to reach their assigned positions undetected and simulate launching missiles despite strong air and surface ship anti-submarine forces.[23]

In June 1951, Phase 1 of the Trounce radar guidance was ready for testing; Phase 2, to include Electronic Counter-Countermeasures (ECCM), was scheduled to be tested in mid-1952. However, Phase 1 results were so satisfactory that Phase 2 ECCM testing was reduced. A particular problem, however, involved time delay in transmitting guidance signals to the missile. The vacuum-tube technology of the era was barely able to deal with that problem.

The standard submarine air search radar, the SV-1, had an antenna that was only marginally effective for missile guidance in the normal 360-degree rotating mode. It subsequently was modified to allow a 10-to-20-degree sector scan centered on the axis of the intended missile track. Radar signal sources had to be carefully calibrated so that two submarines could guide the same missile in sequence.[24] The missile's transponder beacon, necessary to avoid having to rely only on "skin tracking" of the missile, could be detected only in the middle seven to eight degrees of the sector scan. This placed great importance on training radar operators and meant that radar missile guidance was more of an "art form" than a routine evolution dictated by science.

On 28 June 1951, the *Cusk* launched a Loon missile with Trounce guidance. The Launch and initial guidance were satisfactory, but an engine failure led to a "splash" about 15 nautical miles downrange. Twenty-two days later Point Mugu launched another Loon from shore and successfully Trounce-guided it from the beach; guidance then was taken over by the *Cusk* and then by the *Carbonero*. By 1952, all Loon missile flights were being executed with Trounce radar guidance.

The ECM tests at the end of Phase 1 had established that the Trounce radar guidance had low susceptibility to countermeasures. Phase 2 called for modifications to the SV-1 radar, now relabeled SV-5. Polar coordinates (bearing and range) were used to establish an intended missile flight path from launch reference point to the target. Navigational offsets of the submarine's position with respect to the launch reference point were inserted into the CP-98 computer to update the data. Flight tests began in late December 1952.

The Navy replaced Project Pounce—Loon missile evaluation—with Project SLAM (Submarine-Launched Assault Missile) on 10 September 1952, in preparation for Regulus. SLAM would involve continued launching and guidance of Loon missiles to maintain personnel proficiency and test operational readiness.

Sea-Based Nuclear Strike

The Navy's cruise/guided missile development became part of a broad effort by the Navy to acquire a nuclear-strike capability. The Army Air Forces—which became the U.S. Air Force on 18 September 1947—sought absolute control of the nation's nuclear strike mission. Within the U.S. Navy a controversy ensued over what should be the sea service's role—if anything—in the delivery of nuclear weapons. As early as 22 July 1946, Assistant Secretary of the Navy for Air John L. Sullivan, as acting Navy secretary, wrote to President Harry S. Truman arguing that the mobility and flexibility of aircraft carriers suited them for the mission of launching nuclear-armed strike aircraft. Sullivan concluded: "I strongly urge that you authorize the Navy to make preparations for possible delivery of atomic bombs in an emergency in order that the capabilities of the Carrier Task Forces may be utilized to the maximum advantage for national defense."

At the time the Navy had limited access to atomic bomb information, although both of the B-29 Superfortress bombers that dropped atomic bombs on Japan had had naval officers on board as their nuclear weapon officers. No naval aircraft at the time was capable of carrying an atomic bomb. Beginning in early 1948 several P2V Neptune patrol bombers—which had a nominal range of some 4,500 miles and held the world's long-distance, unrefueled flight record from 1946 to 1952—were employed in takeoff trials from the large *Midway* (CVB 41)–class aircraft carriers. (On 29 September 1949, a P2V took off from *Midway* with then–Secretary of Defense Louis Johnson in the copilot's seat.)

Twelve of the twin-piston-engine Neptunes were modified to the P2V-3C configuration to carry the Mark 8 atomic bomb and to take off from the three *Midway*-class carriers. Takeoffs were made with the aid of rocket canisters (JATO "bottles").[25] However, the aircraft could not land on board. They were loaded on the carriers at pierside by cranes; after a nuclear strike mission, they were to land at friendly airfields or come down at sea, where, it was hoped, surface ships or submarines would rescue the crews. Although landing a P2V-3C on a carrier—with arresting hook—was proposed and regularly practiced on specially marked runways ashore, no actual carrier landings were attempted.

The first overseas operation of P2V-3C aircraft occurred in February 1951, when three Neptunes and six of the new carrier-capable AJ-1 Savage aircraft—designed specifically to carry an atomic bomb—were deployed to Port Lyautey (now Kenitra) in French Morocco. The AJ-1s operated from *Midway*-class carriers in the Mediterranean; the Neptunes operated from shore bases, ready to be loaded on carriers in the event of war or—more likely—to fly strikes against the Soviet Union from NATO land bases.

The dozen P2V-3C Neptunes were operational as nuclear strike aircraft until early 1952. They were succeeded by a series of long-range, carrier-based nuclear strike aircraft: the AJ-1 Savage, A3D Skywarrior, and A3J Vigilante. Many other smaller, carrier-based aircraft also could carry nuclear weapons; the two most notable—both were procured in very large numbers—were the piston-engine AD Skyraider and the diminutive, turbojet A4D Skyhawk.[26]

The Navy's attack aircraft carriers, like the Regulus missile submarines, were to be withdrawn from the strategic strike role in the mid-1960s because of the success of the Polaris Submarine-Launched Ballistic Missile (SLBM) program. However, whereas the Regulus program would be completely dismantled, aircraft carriers would retain a nuclear strike capability into the late 1980s, although removed from the "strategic" role. (That meant they no longer kept nuclear-armed aircraft on alert on their decks with pilots already briefed on targets within their range in the Soviet Union and China.) Interestingly, even in the post–Cold War era, some Russian naval leaders and government officials were still to consider carriers to have a potential nuclear strike capability.

The Regulus Missile

DURING THE FALL OF 1945 the Navy's Bureau of Aeronautics had sizeable amounts of money available for aircraft research and development. It also was looking to the future and potential roles for "unmanned aircraft," including their use as surface-to-surface missiles.

A BuAer study group under the direction of Commander Grayson Merrill reviewed existing American, British, and German guided missile technology to help direct future research. In December 1945, the group issued a 60-page report addressing requirements for pilotless aircraft in the fleet. As a result of that effort, 18 study contracts for unmanned aircraft (including missiles) were issued to 12 aircraft manufacturers, as BuAer expanded these efforts to missiles rather than only unmanned aircraft.

One of these firms was Chance Vought, a very successful aircraft manufacturer with the F4U "bent-wing" Corsair fighter in production. The F4U was one of the best fighter aircraft of World War II. Flown initially by the Marines from land bases in the South Pacific and later by the Navy and Marine aviators from aircraft carriers, it shot down large numbers of Japanese aircraft with very few losses. The Corsair was in production longer than any other U.S. piston-engine combat aircraft—from 1938 to 1952—in several variants: the F4U and AU were, produced by Chance Vought; the FG, by Goodyear; and the F3A, by Brewster. The Corsair also was flown extensively in combat by the U.S. Navy and Marine Corps during the Korean War and by the French forces in Indochina in the 1950s. Britain's Fleet Air Arm and several other countries flew the Corsair as well.

In 1945, Chance Vought had three advanced aircraft in various stages of development: the F5U "Flying Pancake," the F6U Pirate turbojet fighter, and the F7U Cutlass turbojet fighter. The F6U was the U.S. Navy's first production jet fighter, while the F5U and F7U incorporated radical design concepts. BuAer solicited Chance Vought to submit proposals for several pilotless aircraft—or "P/As," another term then used for guided missiles. Ranges from 25 to 300 nautical miles were considered; in June 1946, BuAer issued Chance Vought a contract for a short-range pilotless aircraft.

In the same period, BuAer decided to focus on an interim, subsonic P/A that could be carried and launched by fleet submarines. Because development of the preferred ramjet technology would take a substantial amount of time, the decision was made instead to use proven turbojet propulsion technology for the P/A.[1]

The decision by BuAer to proceed with the development of a subsonic cruise missile probably had a link to the Navy's desire to join the Air Force—established as a separate service in September 1947—as soon as possible in the nuclear weapons delivery role. The Loon was too small to carry a contemporary nuclear warhead, but a larger subsonic cruise missile with a range of hundreds of miles could be nuclear armed and would give the Navy a role in nuclear strike.

On 21 May 1947, Chance Vought submitted an interim proposal for a subsonic, nuclear-armed cruise missile. In June the firm submitted the complete proposal for the missile. To reduce program costs for development and training, the package included a Flight Test Vehicle (FTV), as similar as possible to the tactical strike missile; fitted with retractable landing gear and a parachute brake, it could be recovered and reused. Chance Vought also proposed doubling the design's safety factor in order to eliminate structural testing for the missile, further reducing development costs. BuAer officials agreed to all of the firm's proposals.[2]

BuAer undertook a great deal of coordination with the submarine community in the development of the missile. During 1947 there were two Submarine Officer Conferences in Washington, D.C., to discuss topics of interest to the submarine community and to get general agreement on future efforts.[3] The topic of cruise missiles was prominent in these meetings.

On 4 August 1947, Chance Vought's chief engineer and program engineer met with representatives from the Office of the Chief of Naval Operations (OpNav), the Bureau of Ships (BuShips), Bureau of Aeronautics (BuAer), the Office of Naval Research (ONR), and West Coast submarine officers.[4] The submarine officers were those involved with the Loon testing then in progress and thus brought to the table the most recent operational experience with that program.

These discussions included the virtues of surface-launch versus submerged-launch approaches. It was accepted by the submarine officers present that surface launch of the missile would eliminate costly development work and speed up reaching an operational capability. No one expressed concern about being surfaced within a few score of miles of an enemy coast. The weakness of the Japanese anti-submarine efforts during World War II most likely had an impact on post-war U.S. submarine officer thinking. If the Japanese Navy ASW been more effective and as a result the kill rate of U.S. submarines had been higher, the views of American officers might have reflected more caution with respect to surfacing to launch missiles.[5]

BuAer and Chance Vought decided to use the already proven and highly reliable Allison J33 turbojet engine for the new missile. It was in large-scale use in the Air Force

P-80 Shooting Star fighter aircraft. Although this engine would limit the missile to subsonic speeds, the choice of a proven and in-production power plant eliminated the time and cost of developing a new engine.[6]

On 20 September 1948, BuAer authorized a contract for the production of 30 Flight Test Vehicles, a quantity later for budgetary reasons reduced to ten.[7] The FTV was to differ as little as possible from the tactical missile. There were three versions of the Regulus missile: (1) the FTV, later dubbed the Fleet Training Missile (FTM), which had a tricycle landing gear and a drag parachute for recovery; (2) the tactical missile, which substituted additional fuel and a nuclear warhead for the landing gear and drag parachute; and (3) the target drone version (designated KDU-1), similar to the FTV but with additional fuel and telemetry equipment to measure interceptor missile miss distances.

Wind tunnel tests with small-scale P/A models were used to confirm the validity of the missile's form. The original design provided both upper and lower vertical rudders, the vertical rudder to balance buffeting as the missile transitioned from subsonic horizontal flight to a supersonic terminal dive on its target. The wind tunnel tests did in fact verify the design concepts, but after two FTV flights the missile's lower rudder was discarded as unnecessary, making the stowage and the launching procedure on board a submarine easier.

The Regulus missile was launched from a short rail-launcher from land or a surface ship; the launcher also could be fitted to a submarine's deck. The missile used two rocket boosters that accelerated it to flying speed and then fell away. The Regulus missile had a unique symmetrical, "zero lift" wing—that is, the distance between front and rear were the same on the upper and lower surfaces. On a standard aircraft wing, the distance measured from front to rear along the upper surface is longer, generating, as air passes over it, relatively low pressure above the upper wing surface and thereby producing lift. For the Regulus missile, designed to enter a vertical power dive to a point above the target, an ordinary wing configuration would be a problem: the missile would tend to "walk" off the target in the direction perpendicular to the upper wing surface. In horizontal flight the missile flew at about a seven degree up-angle, which helped to generate lift. The Regulus missile design began before there was a nuclear warhead available for it, and Chance Vought apparently approached the task as they would have for a conventional warhead, where the miss distance was critical. With a nuclear warhead a miss of several hundred feet would be only of slight technical interest.

Early in 1949 the Navy and Air Force were in competition for guided missile funding. The Air Force Matador cruise missile was similar to the Regulus, using both the J33 jet engine and rocket-boosted launch from ramps. However, the Regulus had a training version that was recoverable by design; Matador did not. The ability to fly a training missile repeatedly provided a larger number of "miss distance" collection opportunities for the Regulus and therefore a higher level of confidence in accuracy than was possible for the other weapon, as well as lower overall program costs.

Two solid-fuel rocket boosters enabled the Regulus missile to achieve flight speed from a stationary launcher. The Regulus was the Navy's first strategic missile, being forward deployed on conventional and nuclear-propelled submarines as well as on surface ships. *U.S. Navy*

Still, in recognition of the missiles' similarities, on 10 May 1949, the Department of Defense's Research and Development Board directed the combining of the Matador and Regulus programs under overall Navy direction. Navy and Air Force officials discussed the directive and agreed that the Matador test program should continue as planned, while the Navy would examine the adaptability of Matador for submarine operations. The Navy decided that Matador was not easily adaptable to submarine hangar storage and launch, since it used a single, large booster rocket fitted underneath the missile body vice the two small booster rockets fitted along the sides of the Regulus. Matador was to be cancelled, but the Korean War led to the program's reinstatement as an Air Force weapon.

Producing Regulus

Chance Vought began the production of five Regulus Flight Test Vehicles on 20 May 1949, for delivery between June and December 1950. The first FTV radio controlled landing was set for 30 June 1950. At this time Chance Vought also was involved in the conversion of two Navy P-80 Shooting Star fighters to airborne radio control platforms for the test vehicles, one redesignated TV-1 (one seat), the other TV-2D (two seats).[8]

A Regulus training missile lets down for landing under the control of a TV-2 Shooting Star chase plane. One pilot in the TV-2 flies the aircraft while the second pilot controls the missile. The training missile had no brakes, but employed a drag parachute to slow and stop after touchdown. *U.S. Navy*

In June 1949, Rear Admiral Daniel Gallery, Assistant Chief of Naval Operations for Guided Missiles, requested that OpNav's Atomic Energy Division begin development of a nuclear warhead for the Regulus missile. In mid-September the Military Liaison Committee, the Defense Department's link to the weapon development components of the national-level Atomic Energy Commission, recommended four types of cruise missile to carry nuclear warheads, one of them Regulus.[9]

In the early 1950s several advances in nuclear warheads decreased their weight and size and made carriage by smaller aircraft feasible. Whereas in 1945 the Little Boy (dropped on Hiroshima) and Fat Man (Nagasaki) bombs weighed 9,700 and 10,213 pounds, respectively, the Mark 5 bomb developed in the early 1950s was in the 3,000-pound range. It also had a greatly increased yield—some 40 to 50 kilotons compared to about 15 kilotons for World War II bombs. The Mark 5 yield varied with the size of the nuclear capsule that was inserted into the weapon "pit." The W5 missile warhead, based on the Mark 5 bomb, ranged in weight from 2,405 to 2,650 pounds and thus could be used in the Regulus and Matador cruise missiles.

The flight testing of Regulus was divided into two phases. In Phase A, Chance Vought was responsible for planning and conducting the tests, the Navy for range and base facilities; in Phase B, the Navy conducted the tests with Chance Vought support. Both phases served to train Navy personnel in the handling of the missile.

On 12 February 1950, the first group of Chance Vought personnel that had been preparing to work with the Regulus missile arrived at Edwards Air Force Base, California (formerly Muroc Field). The wide-open spaces at Edwards provided ample room to verify the flight characteristics of the new missile; later launches would be conducted from Navy facilities at Point Mugu, or offshore on an airstrip on San Nicolas Island.

After extensive tests that moved the FTV around on the ground (on its wheels) under the control of a chase plane overhead, the missile was ready for flight. The first Regulus FTV flew on 12 November 1950. It took off after a takeoff roll controlled by a chase plane. Shortly after takeoff FTV-1 failed to respond to pitch orders, began to bank, and crashed near the runway. Telemetry data and photographic records allowed reconstruction of the flight, and careful investigation of the debris enabled Chance Vought engineers to determine the cause of the loss of control. Following extensive reliability testing of various components, Chance Vought was ready to resume flight testing.

The FTV-2 took off and flew successfully on 29 March 1951. When it landed, the drag parachute bloomed but then collapsed; however, there was no damage to the missile thanks to the dry lake bed over which it rolled out. This was the first of 13 successful missile flight tests during an eight-month period. In November 1951, a test Regulus missile outran an Air Force F-86E Sabre in flight tests.[10]

On 3 November 1952, an FTV simulating a tactical Regulus missile was launched from test ship *Norton Sound* off the coast of California and landed at San Nicolas Island. It was the first shipboard launch of the Regulus. The FTV concept involved radio control to the target by accompanying aircraft; aircraft carriers would use the airborne control concept with tactical missiles, while submarines and cruisers would guide their Regulus missiles with Trounce radar.

On 16 December 1952, the aircraft carrier *Princeton* (CVA 37), operating off Point Mugu, launched an FTV, simulating a tactical missile, with an F2H-2P Banshee control aircraft.[11] The missile was flown to the Begg Rock target, where radio control was handed off to other aircraft, and the missile was successfully landed on San Nicolas Island.[12] Chance Vought personnel, assisted by a Navy team from Guided Missile Training Unit 5, conducted the launch. Meanwhile, on 1 July 1952, a Guided Missile School had been established at the Fleet Air Defense Training Center at Dam Neck, Virginia, to train officers and enlisted personnel in operating and maintaining the Regulus missile.

On 1 January 1953, Project Derby, which had been supporting the Loon missile program, was disestablished, and at the same time Guided Missile Unit (GMU) 50 was established under the aegis of Submarine Squadron 5 at San Diego. Later that year GMU-50 was augmented with Navy personnel from Guided Missile Training Unit 5 who had been undergoing Regulus training at Edwards and Point Mugu.[13]

Also, on 15 September 1953, Guided Missile Group (GMG) 1 was established at San Diego to provide support detachments to aircraft carriers and cruisers that would carry the Regulus missile. A similar unit, GMG-2, was established at about the same time to support Regulus operations in the Atlantic Fleet.

Table 3-1. Navy Guided Missile Units

Unit	Established	Disestablished/ Merged/Redesignated	Notes
GMTU-5	March 1951	June 1954; merged with GMU-50	Established to begin Regulus training
GMU-50	January 1953	March 1957; redesignated GMU-90 and moved to Pearl Harbor	Established for Loon training; in June 1953, additionally took on Regulus training
GMU-51	October 1955	June 1959	Established to support the *Barbero* in the Atlantic; equipment and personnel transferred to GMU-10 in June 1959
GMU-90	March 1957	Redesignated GMU-10 in July 1959	
GMU-10	July 1959	June 1966	

The Navy was ready to begin operations of its first cruise missile that could deliver a nuclear warhead—the Regulus I. The first Regulus submarines, the USS *Tunny* (SSG 282) in the Pacific and the USS *Barbero* (SSG 317), in the Atlantic, both began launching Regulus cruise missiles to flesh out the operational concept for nuclear strike against land targets. That concept included specially equipped guidance submarines, both diesel-electric and nuclear-propelled with specially trained crews. The process began with a cruise missile launch from the SSG several hundred miles from the target. The launching submarine guided the weapon along its intended flight path about one-half the distance to the target. The guidance submarine, on station closer to the target, would take over and control the missile to its dump point. The missile would dive to a preset altitude above the target where its radar altimeter would cause the warhead to detonate. "Contact crystals" would ensure detonation just above the ground if the radar fusing failed.

The Regulus missile system underwent few changes after 1956. The missile itself, with the exception of a wing-fold modification to fit the hangars of later submarines, was unchanged. Warhead fusing was modified in 1958 to substitute barometric switches for

The USS *Tunny* (SSG 282) on the surface in 1953. She has a streamlined conning tower but was not one of the GUPPY conversions for enhanced underwater performance. The hangars on the *Tunny* and *Barbero* (SSG 317) could each hold two Regulus I missiles. *U.S. Navy*

A Regulus I missile is lowered onto the *Tunny*. The twin rocket boosters are attached; note that the wings are folded for stowage in the hangar. The missile's projecting "slippers" that fit into the submarine launch rails are clearly visible. The *Tunny*'s hangar door is partially open. *U.S. Navy*

radar sensing of detonation altitude. A significant change took place that same year when the W5 nuclear warhead was replaced by the W27 thermonuclear warhead, increasing the nuclear yield from the kiloton range to 1.9 megatons.

At various times the Regulus cruise missile was considered for roles other than that of strategic bombardment. These included:[14]

- Reusable reconnaissance (equipped with a TV camera)
- Chemical and biological agent dispensing
- Long-range nuclear air defense
- Ground support for Marine Corps operations

None of these roles was ever pursued.

At one point the Regulus cruise missile was considered for procurement by both the U.S. Army and Marine Corps. The new U.S. Air Force blocked those Army efforts while frequency incompatibility with Marine radar equipment ended that initiative. The idea of using a nuclear warhead for "close support" later seemed ludicrous, but at the time there was a great downward proliferation of nuclear weapons in the U.S. armed forces (as well as in the Soviet military establishment). In the U.S. Army it reached the battalion level with the Davy Crockett, a 0.25-kiloton weapon fired by a recoilless rifle.

The Regulus Submarines

THE USS *TUNNY* WAS RECOMMISSIONED as a Regulus guided missile submarine (SSG 282) at the Mare Island Naval Shipyard on 6 March 1953. She had been constructed during World War II as a *Gato* (SS 212)–class fleet submarine. The term "fleet submarine" referred to several similar classes of U.S. submarines designed prior to World War II to scout for and to support the battle fleet. That goal proved to be a chimera as fleet speeds increased during the 1930s. The fleet submarine was propelled on the surface by four diesel engines and when submerged by two electric motors; the diesels charged the batteries that powered the electric motors. On the surface these submarines could make about 20 knots and submerged some nine knots.

During her conversion to a missile submarine the *Tunny* had a hangar installed aft of her conning tower that was capable of accommodating two Regulus missiles in a rotating "cage," a hydraulically raised launch rail on deck aft of the hangar, and a missile control center fitted aft of the control room, where the guidance computer was located.[1] To reduce costs, Chance Vought had been directed to design Regulus so that two missiles could be carried in a hangar the size of that fitted to the USS *Perch* (SSP 313) during her conversion to a troop transport submarine several years earlier. Additional lead ballast was provided in the *Tunny* to offset the buoyancy of the missile hangar.

One of the *Tunny*'s four diesel engines was removed to provide space to install hydraulic equipment for the missile launcher. Her four after torpedo tubes were removed, and the after torpedo room became an additional berthing compartment for the crew and missile technicians. She was the first submarine conversion for the Regulus program.[2] On 15 July 1953, the *Tunny* launched a Regulus fleet training missile off Point Mugu; under the control of a chase plane it was successfully recovered at San Nicolas Island.

The USS *Barbero* was the Navy's second Regulus missile submarine. Also a fleet submarine built during World War II but of the later *Balao* (SS 285) class, in 1948 the *Barbero* had been converted at the Mare Island Naval Shipyard to a cargo-carrying submarine (redesignated SSA 317). Her stern torpedo tubes and two (of four) diesel engines had been removed. The submarine's berthing and mess spaces had been relocated, and space had been provided for carrying cargo within the pressure hull. She was fitted with 36-inch access hatches for loading and off-loading cargo. Also, two of her diesel fuel tanks were modified to carry gasoline.[3]

The *Barbero* had been one of a trio of conversions intended to evaluate the potential role of submarines in amphibious operations, including raids, building on the submarine-launched assault on Japanese-held Makin Island in 1942. The two other fleet boats involved were the *Perch* and *Sealion* (SS 315), which were converted to transport submarines (SSPs); these each could carry up to 100 troops, with their landing rafts and other gear in deck hangars. As the complementary cargo submarine (SSA) the *Barbero* participated in several amphibious exercises from October 1948, through March 1950, after which she was again placed in reserve in June 1950.

On 1 February 1955, the *Barbero* began her second conversion—to a Regulus missile-launching submarine. During conversion to an SSG she acquired a large hangar for two missiles, identical to that on the *Tunny*; a retractable missile launching ramp aft of the hangar; and missile guidance equipment. Two of her diesel engines having already

The *Barbero* on the surface preparing for an exercise Regulus launch circa 1960. The Regulus had to be extracted from the hangar, placed on the launcher, wings spread, and other preparations made on deck prior to launch. This was in contrast to the similar Soviet Shaddock missiles, which were launched directly from canisters/hangars. *U.S. Navy*

Crewmen on the *Barbero* prepare a Regulus training missile for a "Missile Mail" flight. The missile's wings still are folded as it sits on the submarine's launch rails. The "Missile Mail" effort garnered publicity for the Navy in the early missile age. *U.S. Navy*

been deleted, the *Barbero* had only one (the after) engine room; the empty forward room now given over to hydraulics for the hangar and launch ramp. She also had the BPQ-1 Trounce missile guidance radar fitted, the production version of the experimental PX-1 radar installed on the *Tunny*. The early guidance radars in the *Tunny* and the *Barbero* were later replaced with the BPQ-2. (The later USS *Grayback*, *Growler*, and *Halibut* all were fitted with the BPQ-2. The P-1X and BPQ-1 computers used polar coordinates—bearing and range—while the BPQ-2 computer used *X* and *Y* coordinates and allowed a missile tracking team to run training problems simulating a missile launch and tracking evolution.)

The *Barbero* was recommissioned as SSG 317 on 28 October 1955. After her missile conversion she initially operated off the West Coast. In March 1956, she transferred to the Atlantic Fleet and began Regulus training out of Norfolk, supported by GMU-51 at Yorktown, Virginia. Three Atlantic Fleet diesel-electric submarines were fitted with radar guidance equipment to assist the *Barbero*.

In June 1959, the *Barbero* participated in a "Missile Mail" public relations stunt involving the U.S. Post Office Department. A branch post office was "established" on board the *Barbero* and some 3,000 postal covers were postmarked "USS *Barbero* 8 June 1959, 9:30 a.m.," and loaded into a training missile. The Regulus was launched at sea about 100 miles off the Florida coast. Under the control of a chase plane the missile was successfully landed at Mayport, Florida, 22 minutes later. There the mail was taken off and entered into the U.S. postal system ashore.

In late 1958, the Navy decided to consolidate all Regulus operations in the Pacific. The *Barbero* and the guidance-radar equipped submarine *Medregal* (SS 480) were transferred to the Pacific, arriving at Pearl Harbor in August 1959.

"New" Regulus Submarines

The USS *Grayback* (SSG 574), the third Regulus missile submarine, had originally been ordered as a diesel-electric attack submarine. She was redesigned after construction began at the Mare Island Naval Shipyard. She was commissioned on 7 March 1958. Her sponsor—who christened the submarine at launching—was Mrs. John A. Moore, the widow of the commanding officer of the first USS *Grayback* (SS 208) when she was lost in action in World War II.

The *Grayback* had twin missile hangars forward, faired into her bow. Each hangar was designed to stow one of the later and larger Regulus II or two Regulus I missiles. For launching the missiles were moved from the hangars onto a complicated launch mechanism between the hangars and the streamlined sail structure. The launcher could shift to line up with either hangar and then rotate and elevate to fire. (Initially many of the launcher switches were located in "pressure-proof" modules outside the pressure hull; when the submarine was submerged leaks caused constant problems, and the system had to be redesigned and simplified.)

The USS *Growler* (SSG 577), the fourth Regulus submarine, was built at the Portsmouth Naval Shipyard in Kittery, Maine, being commissioned on 30 March 1958. Her sponsor also was a submarine commanding officer's widow, Mrs. Thomas B. Oakley, the wife of the last captain of the USS *Growler* (SS 215), lost on her eleventh war patrol during World War II. The *Growler*—while considered to be a sister ship of the *Grayback*—was designed from the outset as a missile submarine and had slightly different dimensions: the *Grayback* was 334 feet long, while the *Growler* was 317 feet, 7 inches,

The *Grayback* (SSG 574)—the U.S. Navy's first purpose-built missile submarine—enters San Diego with a Regulus I missile prominently displayed on her launcher. The twin Regulus hangars were faired into the submarine's forward hull. *U.S. Navy*

and the *Grayback* had a 30-foot beam as against *Growler'*s 27 feet, 2 inches. In general, however, their designs and missile arrangements were similar.

After completing her working-up period, the *Growler* went to the Caribbean for her first Regulus missile launch operations, which were supported by GMU-51. She returned to Portsmouth for post-shakedown repairs and then sailed for the Pacific via the Panama Canal, arriving at Pearl Harbor in September 1959.

★　　★　　★

Shortly after her arrival at Pearl Harbor the *Growler'*s first commanding officer was relieved by Lieutenant Commander Robert Crawford. On the very day he took command, 14 June 1960, just after the ceremony, a serious accident occurred involving the nuclear attack submarine *Sargo* (SSN 584), also moored at the submarine base at Pearl Harbor. While the *Sargo* was loading liquid oxygen from a tanker truck at pierside, a hose broke and an oxygen-fed fire engulfed her after torpedo room.[4] The fire could only be extinguished by submerging the *Sargo'*s stern, leaving the after torpedo room hatch open and thus flooding the compartment. The damage was considerable and one sailor was killed.

The *Sargo* had been scheduled to get under way the following day with the king of Thailand on board. The *Growler* was selected to fill in and take the royalty to sea. Her new commanding officer was summoned to the Submarine Flotilla 5 offices that evening to get

A view of the USS *Growler* (SSG 577) from the starboard quarter. Each of her two forward hangars could accommodate two Regulus I missiles; the *Grayback* and *Growler* were designed to carry two of the later and larger Regulus II missiles. *U.S. Navy*

a quick briefing on the protocol involved. When Crawford, a very large and deep-voiced man, began to get excited and loud about the whole affair, the flag lieutenant, Lieutenant Charles Diesel, remarked, "Captain, they sure gave you command of the right submarine." Crawford wheeled on Diesel and asked sharply, "What do you mean by that?" Diesel answered, "Well, she is USS *Growler*, and you are sure doing a lot of growling."

Crawford laughed.

The *Growler* got under way the following day with the king of Thailand on board. The royal visit and cruise went very well.

Adding Nuclear Propulsion

The USS *Halibut* (SSGN 587) was the fifth Regulus submarine; she differed from her predecessors in having nuclear propulsion. The *Halibut* initially was to have been a diesel-electric missile submarine, but her design was changed to nuclear propulsion in January 1956, and she was laid down two months later. She was built at Mare Island, the second nuclear-propelled submarine to be constructed there. Her sponsor at her launching in 1959 was the wife of Representative Chester "Chet" Holifield of California, a strong supporter of Admiral H. G. Rickover, the director of (and driving force behind) naval nuclear propulsion.[5]

The *Halibut* was commissioned on 4 January 1960. Unlike the new *Grayback* and *Growler*, with their twin hangars in their bows, the *Halibut* had a single large hangar that

The USS *Halibut* (SSGN 587)—the U.S. Navy's only nuclear-propelled submarine constructed specifically for the guided missile role. The large protuberance on the bow is her hangar door; the hangar could house five Regulus I or four Regulus II missiles. *U.S. Navy*

could accommodate four Regulus II missiles or five of the smaller Regulus I weapons. The Navy's Special Projects Office, then developing the Polaris missile system, decided to test and evaluate the Ships Inertial Navigation System (SINS) on the *Halibut*, planned for Polaris submarines.[6] Thus she was the Regulus submarine best equipped for precise navigation. (Subsequently the *Grayback* and *Growler* also were fitted with SINS.)

The *Halibut*, however, was actually the world's *second* nuclear-propelled submarine with a missile armament. The first was the USS *George Washington* (SSBN 598), a ballistic missile submarine that had been commissioned five days before the *Halibut*. (The first Soviet nuclear-propelled cruise missile submarine, the *K-45* of the Project 659/Echo I design, was placed in commission on 28 June 1960.)

The *Halibut* was intended only as a transitional SSGN design. A larger and more-capable Regulus missile submarine was on the drawing boards: the *Permit* (SSGN 594), approximately 350 feet long with a slightly smaller displacement than the *Halibut*'s. The *Permit* SSGN was to carry four Regulus II missiles. Admiral Arleigh A. Burke, the Chief of Naval Operations, had in January 1958 put forward his vision for the fleet in the 1970s that included a force of 12 nuclear-propelled cruise missile submarines armed with weapons having a range of 1,000 miles or greater. Navy planning at that time called

An artist's sketch of planned *Permit* (SSGN 594)–class submarines, each intended to carry four 1,200-nautical-mile Regulus II cruise missiles. Unlike the *Halibut,* which had a single hangar for missiles, the *Permit* design provided four individual hangars for the Regulus II. Eleven SSGNs of this class were proposed—not one was built. *U.S. Navy*

for the first three *Permit* submarines to be funded in fiscal year 1958 (SSGN 594–596), a fourth ship in fiscal 1959, and seven more units to be built subsequently, for a class total of 11 submarines. This would be in addition to a force of 40 or more nuclear submarines armed with Polaris (ballistic) missiles.[7] (The new *Grayback* and *Growler* diesel-electric missile submarines were not addressed in the Burke document.)

Thus, there were to be 12—or at least 14, including the new diesel boats—submarines armed with Regulus II strategic cruise missiles.

5

Regulus in Surface Ships

ALTHOUGH REGULUS WAS DESIGNED as a submarine-launched strategic cruise missile, a 1952 decision by the Navy to evaluate the Regulus Assault Missile (RAM) concept opened the program to deployment on board surface ships—aircraft carriers and cruisers. With respect to Regulus on carriers, naval aviators were not enthused; they already had manned aircraft to deliver nuclear bombs and operating "unmanned aircraft" from carriers could cause flight deck handling and "traffic" problems.

Cruiser sailors were more receptive. Regulus missiles could provide cruisers with a long-range strategic attack capability, giving them a reach far beyond the range of their 8-inch guns and enormous explosive power. At that time cruisers were employed primarily for anti-aircraft defense of aircraft carriers and gunfire support for operations ashore.

Carrier Operations

The RAM concept envisioned the launch of Regulus missiles from carriers and their guidance to the target by carrier-based control aircraft. The first shipboard launch of a Regulus had occurred on 3 November 1952, from the missile test ship *Norton Sound*, and on 16 December 1952, the first Regulus launch from a carrier occurred (see page 32). The carrier *Princeton* (CVA 37), operating off the California coast, had launched an FTV simulating a tactical Regulus missile, with an F2H-2P Banshee serving as the control aircraft.[1]

These shipboard trials were conducted with the "desert launcher," a frame device that was elevated for firing the missile and fitted with wheels for movement on board ship or on land. On the *Princeton* the launcher, which had to be positioned near electrical outlets, blocked one of the ship's two flight-deck catapults. Still, the carrier launch and airfield recovery were successful, and demonstrated the feasibility of the RAM shipboard concept.

44

The aircraft carrier *Princeton* (CVA 37) launching a Regulus I missile during a 1952 training evolution. The concept of launching guided missiles from carriers was not popular with naval aviators, who considered the Regulus to be encroaching on carrier-based attack aircraft missions. *U.S. Navy*

Subsequently, four *Essex* (CVA 9)–class carriers were fitted to launch Regulus missiles, with additional ships planned for the modification. In the fall of 1953, aviation Utility Squadron 3 (VU-3) at North Island, San Diego, which already had handled F6F Hellcat target drone operations for Pacific Fleet anti-aircraft training, took on the responsibility of providing RAM detachments with chase planes on board carriers to launch and control Regulus missiles. Because of the heavy aircraft traffic at the North Island naval air station, the unit soon moved to Brown Field, an auxiliary naval air station southwest of San Diego.[2] The squadron flew swept-wing F9F-6P Cougar aircraft as chase planes.

By mid-June 1954, the Bureau of Aeronautics was expressing concern over the RAM concept and its impact on carrier flight operations. Not only would Regulus launches impact the tempo of carriers' operations and flight deck movements, but the carriers were to supply guidance aircraft for both their own Regulus strike missiles and those launched from nearby cruisers. However, Rear Admiral John Sides, head of the Guided Missile Branch in the Office of the Chief of Naval Operations, supported the RAM concept, and its development proceeded.

During 1954–1955 four Regulus launches took place from the carrier *Hancock* (CVA 19). On 16 October 1954, just prior to a Regulus launch, the *Hancock* made a high-speed turn that almost sent the ponderous desert launcher, with a fueled missile, over the side. In response to the resulting concerns of the carrier community, Chance Vought developed the Steam-Assisted Regulus (STAR) launcher, which served as checkout and handling dolly and could easily be attached to a carrier's steam catapults to launch the

The carrier *Hancock* (CVA 19) launches a Regulus missile using the expendable launching cart that was accelerated to initial flight speed on the ships' port catapult. After launch the cart fell into the sea ahead of the carrier and was lost. *U.S. Navy*

missile. The STAR itself was expendable and would be lost overboard during the launch. Two *Hancock* launches, on 19 and 20 October, proved the viability of the STAR.

Another milestone was achieved on 15 March 1955, when the *Hancock* conducted a successful and unique Regulus operation: the only aircraft carrier–launched and submarine-guided missile flight of the entire program. Following the missile launch from the carrier the submarines *Cusk* and *Carbonero* guided the missile in succession, using their Trounce radars. The event opened new possibilities for Regulus strikes from surface ships. The carrier RAM detachments' F9F-6P Cougars had a range of approximately 250 nautical miles, while that of the Regulus missile itself was 500 nautical miles. The employment of guidance submarines could take full advantage of the missile's capabilities. However, this additional range potential was never used in Regulus test flights during carrier or cruiser deployments in the Western Pacific.

★   ★   ★

On 5 August 1955, the *Hancock* sailed from San Diego for a Western Pacific deployment with the Seventh Fleet. On board the carrier were four Regulus missiles with

W5 nuclear warheads. On 8 August, in Hawaiian waters, the carrier conducted an Operational Suitability Test (OST) with one of the missiles that had high explosives but no nuclear components in its warhead. Chase planes sent the missile up to 35,000 feet for the cruise phase, brought it down to 100 feet for the approach to the target, and then zoomed it up to 1,500 feet for the final approach and dive on Ka'ula Rock, a barren islet and prominent rock located 150 miles west of Honolulu and about 20 southwest of Kauai.

Two more OST launchers took place in the Western Pacific during the *Hancock's* deployment, using as a target Okino Daito Shima, a rock jutting prominently above the sea several hundred miles southeast of Okinawa. After a pass over the target the tactical missile—without its nuclear component—was itself used as an aerial target by carrier-based F9F-8 Cougar fighters. The control pilot had to slow the missile so that the fighters could intercept it, an indication of the missile's potential wartime effectiveness. No additional aircraft carrier deployments with Regulus missiles took place in the Pacific Fleet. In the Atlantic, the carrier USS *Randolph* (CVA 15) deployed to the Mediterranean with three Regulus missiles. The USS *Lexington* (CVA 16), also a Pacific Fleet ship, launched one Regulus training missile.

A total of eight aircraft carriers participated in Regulus test launches or fleet deployments:

CVA 14 *Ticonderoga*	CVA 37 *Princeton*
CVA 15 *Randolph*	CVA 38 *Shangri-La*
CVA 16 *Lexington*	CVA 42 *Franklin D. Roosevelt*
CVA 19 *Hancock*	CVA 60 *Saratoga*

The *Lexington's* launch would to mark the end of carrier-based Regulus operations. As noted, carrier aviators were not pleased with the space Regulus I missiles took up on the hangar and flight decks or with how they interrupted air operations. Further, the diminutive Douglas A4D (later A-4) Skyhawk, which became operational in 1956, could carry a variety of conventional weapons as well as nuclear bombs, could deliver them with more accuracy than the missile, had speed comparable to the Regulus I, and was a smaller target. Also, later models of the Skyhawk had a night attack capability.[3]

Interesting Proposals

Nevertheless, the concept of launching Regulus and other cruise missiles from surface ships still was being advocated by some naval officers and influential civilians. For example, George Fielding Eliot, at the time dean of American military correspondents, in 1958 published a small volume entitled *Victory Without War: 1958–1961*. The book, issued by the semi-official U.S. Naval Institute, advocated the procurement of massive numbers of Regulus II missiles, whose range, he wrote, could be extended to 2,000 miles and that could be launched from aircraft carriers:[4]

Let us imagine 20 of these missiles grouped on a *Forrestal*-class carrier, ready to be fired from her four steam catapults—five missiles to each catapult. Each group of five missiles is programmed for a different target. The rate of fire can be as fast as one missile from each catapult every two minutes. . . .

The logistics of the Regulus system is not complicated. We can, during 1958, take three older carriers from the reserve fleet (the *Boxer, Franklin,* and *Bunker Hill*) and fit them as missile transports. These ships have the speed, fuel capacity, and sea-keeping qualities to accompany task forces in all weather conditions. Each missile transport could provide stowage for as many as 400 Regulus II missiles. Each [carrier] could operate from her flight deck a number of helicopters which could be used to deliver the missiles to the [attack] carriers as the tactical situation might require.

But the era of carrier-launched Regulus missiles had ended.

Cruiser Operations

Cruisers initially were envisioned as missile-launching ships with only a short-range guidance capability. Control aircraft from nearby aircraft carriers would then control the missiles to carry out the RAM missions. Four heavy cruisers of the *Baltimore* (CA 68) class were chosen for modification to carry and launch Regulus missiles: The USS *Helena* (CA 75), *Toledo* (CA 133), and *Los Angeles* (CA 135) in the Pacific Fleet and the *Macon* (CA 132) in the Atlantic Fleet. The ships each had a main battery of nine 8-inch guns with a maximum range of approximately 15 nautical miles; the effective range was somewhat less.

The *Los Angeles* was the first cruiser to undergo the Regulus modification, carried out at the Mare Island Naval Shipyard in 1954. Her floatplane hangar under her fantail was fitted to stow three Regulus I missiles, and a short rail launcher was installed on the weather deck above.[5] The *Los Angeles* conducted her first Regulus launch on 28 October 1954, with aircraft from Utility Squadron 3 controlling the missile in a pass over San Nicolas Island. The missile was successfully landed on that island and recovered. Later that year the *Los Angeles* launched two more missiles; one was lost shortly after booster separation, the other was recovered ashore.

In January 1955, the first Trounce-radar guided flight from the *Los Angeles* took place. Subsequently the *Los Angeles* successfully controlled two Regulus missiles launched from Point Mugu. In February the *Los Angeles* deployed to the Seventh Fleet in the Western Pacific carrying three Regulus I missiles with nuclear warheads in the first cruiser–Regulus missile deployment. Passing through Hawaiian waters en route to the "WestPac," the *Los Angeles* conducted an OST missile launch.

Upon return from her Western Pacific cruise in August 1955, the *Los Angeles* acquired an improved launcher, a modified version of the launcher installed in *Tunny*. In October she participated in tests of the cruiser Trounce system and on 18 and 19 October successfully launched four Regulus missiles. A week later the cruiser guided a Regulus

The heavy cruiser *Los Angeles* (CA 135) launches a Regulus missile during a demonstration in August 1957. These ships mounted a main battery of nine 8-inch/55-caliber (203-mm) guns. The carrier *Ticonderoga* (CVA 14) is in the background. *U.S. Navy*

missile throughout a 56-minute flight out to 210 nautical miles, the longest duration Trounce guidance flight thus far. (That missile had been launched from Point Mugu.[6]) On 21 March 1956, the *Los Angeles* executed the first of 11 successful Regulus missile launches for an Operational Test and Evaluation Force (OpTevFor) test program. On 5 June the *Los Angeles* conducted an OST launch in Hawaiian waters and then continued on to another Western Pacific deployment. She fired a second OST missile on 18 August at a target off Okinawa. The cruiser also participated in a resupply evolution involving the delivery of a replacement Regulus missile and nuclear warhead to the ship by an Air Force C-124 Globemaster cargo plane at an airfield in the Western Pacific.

During the years from 1955 to 1961, the *Los Angeles* deployed six times to the Western Pacific, each time carrying three Regulus missiles with nuclear warheads. One of these deployments was in an emergency situation—the Quemoy-Matsu Island crisis in August 1958. Her last Regulus missile launch was conducted 28 February 1961. Over a six-year period the cruiser launched 43 missiles, losing only two training missiles. The *Los Angeles* was decommissioned in November 1963.

In June 1955, the *Helena* became the second heavy cruiser modified to carry Regulus missiles. Her first missile launch, conducted on 17 August of that year, was a failure; the missile crashed shortly after launch. Two days later she launched a training missile that was successfully recovered. In January 1956, the *Helena* deployed to Seventh Fleet carrying three missiles with nuclear warheads in her hangar and a fourth missile on her fantail, protected by a tarpaulin, apparently sans nuclear warhead. On 17 June 1956, in the Western Pacific, the *Helena* conducted a missile launch that was widely publicized in by international news media. She initially guided the missile herself and then turned it over to a control aircraft from the carrier *Lexington* that delivered it to the target, Okino Daito Shima off Okinawa. The *Helena* returned from the Western Pacific in October 1957. The following month she launched a missile and guided it for 112 nautical miles, then turned it over to the submarine *Cusk,* which guided it for another 70 nautical miles and then passed it to the *Carbonero* for another 90 nautical miles to the target at San Nicolas Island, where the missile was recovered—a flight of just over 270 nautical miles.

In August 1958, after refresher training that included five Regulus missile launches, the *Helena* departed for another Western Pacific deployment with missiles. The final "WestPac" deployment of a cruiser armed with Regulus was, again, the *Helena,* from January through June 1960. In March 1961, the *Helena* made her final Regulus launch. During her time as a Regulus-armed ship she launched 32 missiles: five failed at launch, two were lost in flight, and 25 were successes. The *Helena* was decommissioned in June 1963.

The *Toledo* was the third Pacific Fleet cruiser modified to carry Regulus missiles. On 16 May 1956, she launched her first missile, in one of eight successful launches in a row. Their average range was 230 nautical miles. The *Toledo* made four Seventh Fleet deployments with Regulus missiles. In May 1958, she fired a missile off Okinawa while taking part in the cruiser evaluation of the BPQ-2 guidance radar. On 17 April 1959, she conducted her final missile launch. During her career as a Regulus-armed ship the *Toledo* launched 21 missiles, losing only one. She was decommissioned in May 1960.

The *Macon* was the only heavy cruiser in the Atlantic Fleet to carry the Regulus missile. She was modified from January to March 1956 at the Philadelphia Naval Shipyard. A missile detachment from Guided Missile Group 2 joined the *Macon,* and on 18 May her first launch took place, off the Virginia Capes. Over eight days the *Macon* successfully launched six missiles.

The Suez Canal crisis of 1956 was unfolding in the Middle East at the time. In July the *Macon* sailed for the eastern Mediterranean Sea and assisted with the evacuation of American citizens from the troubled area. In November, after operations with the Sixth Fleet in the Mediterranean she returned to Norfolk.

In early 1957, during Operation Springboard, an annual major Atlantic Fleet exercise, the *Macon* operated off the southern coast of Cuba with submarines. On 14 March she launched two missiles with "series guidance" by the submarines *Barbero* and *Torsk* (SS 423). The target was at a distance of some 220 nautical miles, off Leeward Point near Guantanamo Bay. The *Macon* deployed in Operation Strikeback in the

North Atlantic in September 1957, carrying Regulus missiles with nuclear warheads. The exercise lasted nine days, ranging from Norway's North Cape to the western Mediterranean Sea. The cruiser simulated several Regulus launches against Soviet-bloc targets in Eastern Europe.

The *Macon*'s last Regulus launch took place 29 September 1958, part of a test of the air defense radar system for the northeastern United States. The cruiser launched the missile about 90 nautical miles off Boston and guided it for 100 nautical miles to the naval air station at New Brunswick, Maine, where it was recovered. During her period as a Regulus ship the *Macon* made 20 launches—all successful. The cruiser was decommissioned in March 1961.

Beyond these heavy cruisers, the Navy planned to install the improved Regulus II cruise missile on several "new" cruisers. These were three World War II–era heavy cruisers that had been totally rebuilt into air-defense missile ships as the *Albany* (CG 10) class (with additional conversions planned), and the one-of-a-kind, nuclear-propelled missile cruiser *Long Beach* (CGN 9). The missile ship conversions were completed in the early 1960s, and the *Long Beach* was commissioned on 9 September 1961, becoming the world's first nuclear-propelled surface warship.[7] The cancellation of the Regulus II left these ships with only anti-air and anti-submarine weapons.[8] (There was, briefly, consideration given to installing the Polaris ballistic missile in the *Long Beach*.)

Supporting the Fleet

Guided Missile Unit 52 was established at North Island in June 1953 to provide Regulus missiles to Pacific Fleet aircraft carriers and cruisers. After a year of training the unit moved to the less congested Brown Field. There training with drone aircraft controlled by VU-3's RAM detachment took place. Several months later GMU-52 returned to North Island, where its missiles and nuclear warheads were located. On 20 August 1954, a GMU-52 missile was launched by the *Norton Sound,* in the first of a number of Regulus launches from that missile test ship.

GMU-52 had an unusual experience involving an Army guided missile team. The soldiers were assigned on temporary duty to GMU-52 to keep the Army current in the guided missile field. Army team members launched two Regulus missiles from the Marine Corps air station at Mojave, California, and participated in 11 other Regulus missile launches. In September 1955, GMU-52 was disestablished, its personnel assigned to Guided Missile Group 1 at North Island.

In the Atlantic area, Guided Missile Unit 53 was established in mid-1954 at the naval air station on Chincoteague Island, Virginia. Its personnel had trained at Edwards Air Force Base and at Point Mugu, from where in October 1954, they had moved to the East Coast, with a Utility Squadron 4 RAM detachment, to support Regulus carrier and cruiser operations in the Atlantic Fleet.

GMU-53's first Regulus missile launch came on 24 March 1955. The missile made a 28-minute flight and was recovered. There followed 18 additional successful flights, training missile crews for Atlantic Fleet carriers and cruisers. All of these launches were of Regulus KDU-1 drones, which acted as targets for the USS *Mississippi* (AG 128) as part of the Terrier surface-to-air missile program.[9] These target operations usually ended with a missile recovery at Chincoteague.

On 26 September 1955, GMU-53 was disestablished and combined with a VU-4's missile detachment to form Guided Missile Group 2. The group thereafter supported Regulus drone flights as well as training for aircraft carrier and cruiser operations.[10]

Training for War

BY 1960 THERE WERE FOUR DIESEL-ELECTRIC SUBMARINES (SSG) and one nuclear-propelled submarine (SSGN) operational with the Regulus land-attack missile. Although deployed with Regulus I cruise missiles, the later submarines were configured to later carry the more-capable Regulus II missile. The five Regulus-armed submarines were:

The *Halibut* (SSGN 587) fires a Regulus Operational Suitability Test (OST) missile in the Western Pacific. Regulus I missiles were regularly test-launched, resulting in a highly reliable weapon. Steaming nearby is the carrier *Lexington* (CVA 16). *U.S. Navy*

Submarine	Completed as SSG/SSGN	Regulus I Missiles	Regulus II Missiles
SSG 282 *Tunny*	1953	2	—
SSG 317 *Barbero*	1955	2	—
SSG 574 *Grayback*	1958	4	2
SSG 577 *Growler*	1958	4	2
SSGN 587 *Halibut*	1960	5	4

How and where these submarines operated within specific geographic areas was decided by a flotilla commander.[1] He and his staff assigned operating areas and dealt with operational liaison with other "type" commanders, such as the fleet's surface and air commanders. The flotilla commander was responsible for "water space" management—ensuring that two or more U.S. submarines were not assigned to the same operating area or, if they were, that they were kept separated by "horizontal" or "vertical" boundaries.

Above the squadron and flotilla commanders was the Commander, Submarine Force, one in the Atlantic Fleet, one in the Pacific Fleet. That officer—a rear or vice admiral—was responsible to their respective fleet commander for all aspects of submarine training, administration, readiness, and operations. During the 1959–1964 period of the Regulus deterrent patrols, the launching and guidance-only submarines were each assigned to one of two divisions within Submarine Squadron 1 at Pearl Harbor:

Division 11: The *Barbero*, *Tunny*, and *Halibut* (launching and guidance); *Cusk* (guidance only)

Division 12: The *Grayback* and *Growler* (launching and guidance); *Carbonero* and *Medregal* (guidance only)

Local training operations were controlled by the flotilla commander, but the submarine force commander might directly control the submarines when appropriate, especially outside local operating areas.[2] With respect to Regulus nuclear deterrent patrols, the patrol operation orders were issued by Commander, Submarine Force Pacific, who exercised direct operational control of the Regulus boats. Material support for those submarines was provided by the submarine base at Pearl Harbor; major work was undertaken at the adjacent Pearl Harbor Naval Shipyard.

Regulus training missile launches from submarines took place in the Hawaiian operating areas from the late 1950s through 1964. The missile-launching submarine was scheduled for exercise missile launches by the division commander, who directly supervised training. The guided missile unit prepared a fleet training missile—a Red Bird—and delivered it at pierside, where a base crane was used to hoist it on board.

The submarine's launch position was always within sight of land, to enable determination of exact navigational position by visual bearings. The flight path was pre-calculated from a reference point near the launch location to the target, and that data was input into the radar guidance computer.

The guidance team in the submarine had two components: the personnel manning the radar guidance computer, and those who kept a secondary manual plot of the missile, using radar data. The manual track was a fallback in case of failure of the guidance computer. A submarine navigation team calculated the craft's position every several minutes and input the changing offsets from the reference point into the computer. The guidance computer took those offsets and transmitted "left" or "right" steering signals to the missile to keep it on the flight path. Wind effects too might require "steers."

The training missile's target was Ka'ula Rock. Radar on the island of Kauai tracked the missile as it approached the target and recorded its exact position when the dump signal was transmitted by the guidance submarine. By that method was determined the miss distance of each missile. In wartime the missile would dive on the target and reach supersonic speed before detonating its nuclear warhead at a predetermined altitude. In peacetime the training missile continued over the target, and the chase planes assumed radio control to land it at Bonham airfield, the auxiliary landing strip on Kauai.

Chase planes were key components of these training launches. They flew from the Barbers Point naval air station on the western side of Oahu, extensively coordinating with the missile launching submarine, Utility Squadron 3 (which provided the planes), and the submarine flotilla staff, which scheduled missile test flights. These aircraft would fly to the launch area, establish communications with the launching submarine, and when the missile was ready to launch, dive towards the submarine and give the "fire" signal to the submarine's missile officer. Because the Regulus missile had a high subsonic speed and chase planes were usually no longer first-line aircraft, a premature missile launch might leave the planes in a tail chase and unable to keep up with the missile.

When the missile left the submarine's launching ramp it climbed to a preset cruise altitude. The chase plane pilots tested their radio controls to ensure the missile was responding, then turned control back over to the submarine, which radar-guided the missile to target. Once the dump signal was given, the chase planes took control and attempted to fly the missile to a safe landing at Bonham airfield on Kauai. If successfully landed, the missile would be shipped by barge to Oahu and taken to the GMU facility, where it was refurbished for another training flight.

Several submarines, both diesel-electric and nuclear-propelled, were fitted for missile guidance; each was fitted with Trounce guidance radar and computers. In the Atlantic Fleet the conventional submarines *Medregal* (SS 480), *Runner* (SS 476), *Torsk* (SS 423), and *Argonaut* (SS 475) were designated as "guidance submarines."[3] In the Pacific Fleet five nuclear attack submarines had guidance equipment installed: the *Swordfish* (SSN 579), *Sargo* (SSN 583), *Sea Dragon* (SSN 584), *Sculpin* (SSN 590), and *Snook* (SSN 592).

The wartime concept of operations called for the missile submarine to launch more than 150 nautical miles from the target and to initiate radar guidance. The guidance submarine would be waiting submerged closer to the target and would take over for the final leg of the missile's flight. This arrangement made the launching submarine less vulnerable to coastal enemy anti-submarine forces while surfaced. The guidance submarine would be operating at periscope depth with the Trounce radar mast raised. Communications between the two submarines were by single-sideband radio and were limited to very brief, coded signals.

However, the deterrent patrols carried out by Regulus submarines from 1959 through 1964 involved only missile launching boats, which would guide their own missiles to the targets.

Setting the Standard

In early February 1959, the SSG *Grayback* arrived in Pearl Harbor and began preparations for her first Regulus training missile launch in the Hawaiian area. One of the key elements in a successful launch was the alignment of each rocket booster through the center of gravity of the fully fueled missile. Each submarine's missile launching system had an alignment jig, a relatively delicate optical device to perform this vital function before a launch.

On this occasion, before the system alignment was conducted, several of the *Grayback*'s officers brought their rocket booster alignment jig to the GMU-10 facility to be checked against the alignment standard that was maintained by the missile unit. They set up their jig at the GMU and then departed, one of them remarking casually that the alignment reference standard was "out of whack."

The *Grayback* got under way and went to sea for the launch. The countdown proceeded smoothly, the "fire" signal was given by the chase plane pilots, and the missile officer on the *Grayback* pressed the "fire" button. The missile left the launcher and promptly corkscrewed into the sea. The *Grayback* came back to port with a somewhat crestfallen crew.

The GMU's officer-in-charge set up an informal inquiry to determine what had gone wrong. The investigators asked the *Grayback*'s officers to describe in detail the short flight path that the missile had followed before it hit the water. The investigators concluded that the "flight" of the missile clearly indicated that the booster rockets had been misaligned. They then calculated the degree of misalignment necessary to cause the reported behavior of the missile. Someone now recalled the offhand comment about the GMU alignment standard being in error; the investigators asked the officer who had said that to estimate by how much. What he described was precisely the reverse of the misalignment that the investigators had calculated after the flight.

The investigators asked to be shown where the *Grayback*'s own alignment jig was stowed. The officer took them to the submarine's starboard Regulus hangar and showed them the jig's mounting bracket—on the inside of the starboard hangar door, a massive, hinged device weighing several tons. Whenever the door was shut, massive vibrations occurred, and they were being transmitted directly to the mounting bracket and thus to the alignment jig. Problem solved!

No one on the *Grayback* had recognized the potential for misalignment, and her officers had casually dismissed the clear evidence of it when they checked their jig. If the problem had not been discovered at the time and a launch order had later been received on deterrent patrol, the *Grayback* might have suffered successive missile launch failures at a crucial time.

Most Regulus submarine training missile launches were routine, as described above. The radio transmissions conducted during each evolution were closely monitored at the GMU. Some, however, were particularly memorable.

One was a training missile launch by the *Tunny* off Kaena Point, the northwestern point of the island of Oahu. The launch took place on schedule, but the Regulus did not respond to the chase plane's radio control transmissions and started flying erratically over Oahu. The *Tunny* herself was unable to control the missile with radar signals. At one point the missile's uncontrolled excursions sent it over downtown Waikiki at an altitude of about 10,000 feet. Although there was no warhead, the training missile weighed about 10,000 pounds and carried 300 gallons of highly flammable JP-4 fuel. A vision of disaster that would ensue if it crashed into tourist-crowded downtown Waikiki was in the minds of the GMU-10 listeners and others connected with the exercise. Finally the missile spun out and crashed harmlessly into a ravine in the hills outside Camp H. M. Smith, headquarters of the U.S. Pacific Command.

GMU-10 sent an expedition into the rugged terrain north of Camp Smith to retrieve the missile's secret Trounce radar guidance equipment. The team found the missile after two days of searching, buried up to its tailpipe. After removing the guidance device (the secret components of which were buried too deeply to be of concern) the search party left the wreckage for the amazement of future aviation archeologists.

★   ★   ★

Regulus training operations were "easy"; the boats returned to the Pearl Harbor submarine base after each "shoot." Nonetheless, and beyond the training of the SSG/SSGN crews, these operations were vital for exposing problems in a weapons system that though relatively crude and in many respects unique was the harbinger of an effective, survivable, sea-based, nuclear deterrence system.

Deployments and Patrols

IN FEBRUARY 1955, the heavy cruiser *Los Angeles* sailed for the Western Pacific for deployment with the Seventh Fleet. She carried four Regulus cruise missiles with W5 nuclear warheads, providing the fleet with a nuclear weapons delivery capability in addition to that already available by nuclear strike aircraft on board the fleet's aircraft carriers.

In August that same year the carrier *Hancock* deployed to the Seventh Fleet with four Regulus Attack Missiles with W5 nuclear warheads in addition to her nuclear strike aircraft. After 1955 the cruisers *Helena* and *Toledo* as well as the *Los Angeles* provided a nuclear RAM capability in the Pacific Fleet, and the *Macon* provided the same in the Atlantic Fleet. In 1956, the year of the Suez Crisis, the carrier *Randolph* deployed to the Sixth Fleet in the Mediterranean with Regulus missiles. In that period the submarines *Tunny* and *Barbero* carried submarine-launched Regulus missiles in the Pacific and Atlantic Fleets, respectively.

During the Lebanon Crisis of 1958, both *Tunny* in the Pacific and *Barbero* in the Atlantic deployed to forward launch stations in readiness to conduct nuclear strikes against targets in the Soviet Union. Although at that time submarines were a minor factor in the aggregate of the U.S. Navy's sea-based nuclear weapons strike capability, they had the advantage of far greater concealment than was possible for the forward-deployed aircraft carriers and cruisers with nuclear weapons.

★ ★ ★

Subsequently, all five Regulus-armed submarines were based in the Pacific, and beginning in 1959 they began a series of continuous deterrent patrols in the northwest Pacific off of the Kamchatka Peninsula. On that Siberian geographic feature were several Soviet air bases and—most important—the Petropavlovsk submarine base complex.

The heavy cruiser *Toledo* (CA 133) launches a Regulus missile. Several heavy cruisers deployed to the Western Pacific with Regulus I missiles, providing the ships with a nuclear strike/land-attack capability. U.S. heavy cruisers also served as gunfire support ships in the Vietnam War. *U.S. Navy*

Regulus submarines were assigned from two to five targets in the Petropavlovsk region, depending upon the number of missiles carried.[1]

Regulus nuclear warheads detonating over Soviet airfields and the submarine complex would have blown a hole in the Soviet air defense network that would facilitate the passage of Strategic Air Command bombers to their targets in the Soviet Far East. Also, submarine-launched missiles would have destroyed any missile submarines at the base, while preventing submarines from rearming and refueling there in a protracted conflict. The Soviet submarines based at Petropavlovsk had direct access to the Pacific Ocean, unlike those based farther south at Vladivostok, which had to transit narrow straits into the Pacific.

Deploying Regulus Submarines

While on station off the Siberian coast the Regulus missile–carrying submarines were constrained by detonation "windows"—the time periods within which their warheads had to be detonated. These windows were necessary to integrate all planned nuclear attacks on Soviet targets and to avoid interference of nuclear detonations with attacks by U.S. manned strategic bombers.

These Regulus submarine patrols continued, back to back, until May 1964.

The first of the regularly scheduled Pacific deterrent patrols was made by *Tunny*, the oldest of the SSGs, during October–December 1959. The patrol lasted 55 days and was one of the shortest nuclear deterrent patrols by a U.S. submarine. Although non-missile-carrying guidance submarines had operated with the launching submarines in the development of the RAM concept, none operated with the deployed SSG/SSGNs.

Beginning in mid-1961, in an effort to keep at least four Regulus I missiles continuously on station in the western Pacific, the *Barbero* and *Tunny* began deploying together; the *Grayback* and *Growler* each deployed separately with four missiles; and the nuclear-propelled *Halibut* carried five missiles. From mid-1958, each Regulus I was fitted with the W27 nuclear warhead in place of the W5. The W27 had a rated explosive force of 1.9 megatons—more than 100 times the explosive power of the approximately 15-kiloton weapons used in the atomic bomb attacks on Hiroshima and Nagasaki. Thus, four Regulus missiles could place a total of 7.6 megatons of explosive power over Soviet targets. By comparison, a contemporary carrier-based AD Skyraider could carry one of eight available nuclear bombs with yields varying from eight kilotons to one megaton.[2] The large, 35-ton A3D Skywarrior could carry two nuclear bombs from a selection of nine types, their yields each ranging from one kiloton up to 3.8 megatons.[3]

The Regulus deterrent patrols were a serious and sobering business, particularly for those individuals who had knowledge of the targets and the missile yields. In a rather bitter attempt at humor, during their early patrols the *Barbero's* crew posted the course and distance from patrol areas to Tahiti in the conning tower. If the boat fired a Regulus missile with a nuclear warhead there probably was not much point in returning to Pearl Harbor, which by the time she arrived would probably be radioactive slag—better to sail to Tahiti and see if the native maidens there would welcome visiting sailors.

★   ★   ★

The squadrons of nuclear-propelled Polaris ballistic missile submarines that succeeded the Regulus SSG/SSGNs enjoyed almost unlimited funding, presidential-level support, and considerable publicity.[4] Significant milestones were widely announced. When the pioneer *George Washington* (SSBN 598) sailed from Charleston in November 1960, to undertake the first Polaris deterrent patrol, the Blue crew commanding officer, Commander James B. Osborne, was publicly presented at dockside with the Legion of Merit and the ship with the Navy Unit Citation.

The *George Washington* and her 40 sister ships were brand new submarines, with unlimited nuclear power for propulsion and "hotel" services (i.e., lights, refrigeration, heating). Each wardroom even included a Navy doctor to take care of medical emergencies on board and a supply officer to supervise the stowage and issuing of spare parts and the running of the crew's mess. Both assignments were a first in the U.S. submarine service. Contemporary diesel-electric and nuclear attack submarines as well as the Regulus boats had to make do with an enlisted hospital corpsman, and the supply and commissary/mess officer was frequently "George"—the most junior line officer in a non–Polaris submarine. Upon completion of the first planned, 60-day Polaris patrol Commander Osborn would turn his submarine over to the alternate, or Gold, crew, while his Blue crew would have some 60 days ashore for rest, leave, and training before again going to sea.

On the day in November 1960 that the *George Washington* sailed on the first Polaris strategic deterrent patrol, the 16-year-old *Barbero* was on station off Kamchatka. Like the other SSG/SSGNs, the *Barbero* had only one crew: the SSG/SSGN sailors would joke that they belonged to the "Black and Blue crews," since they had no respite, as did the "Blue and Gold" sailors of the Polaris SSBNs. The Regulus crews were fascinated to read in the newspapers that the *George Washington* had sailed. Their own situations were quite different. There were no press releases about *Barbero*'s departure. Only family and friends watched as the twice-converted World War II–built diesel-electric submarine departed for a five-month saga. The *Barbero*'s first deterrent patrol lasted 69 days. The *Barbero* sailed northward from Pearl Harbor on the surface, except for dives to avoid detection by ships or aircraft when her ESM (Electronic Surveillance Measures) gave warning of them.

The average SSG/SSGN deterrent missile patrol was 69 days long; the longest was 102 days by the nuclear-propelled *Halibut,* and for the diesel-electric submarines 83 days, the *Tunny* having that dubious honor.

Most Pacific Fleet submarines getting ready for a "special operation" would load food and other provisions for 60 days.[5] The *Barbero* normally loaded for 90 days, lest the delay of a relief submarine keep her on station longer than planned. These "extra" provisions presented a stowage problem, as most compartments in the boat already had a layer of food cases underfoot. The *Barbero*'s solution was to place cases of canned goods in the missile hangar, in and around the two Regulus missiles.

Regulus submarine had typed "bills" in each compartment outlining valve and equipment settings for emergencies and appropriate actions to be taken. In the *Barbero* there also was a "Strip Hangar" bill, dedicated to removing food cases rapidly from the hangar and redistributing them about the submarine to clear the hangar for action if a launch order was received. The food in the hangar was consumed first, and after about two weeks under way the hangar was restored to its normal state of "non-food" readiness.

As an SSG approached her assigned deterrent patrol area she spent less time on the surface and more time submerged. To remain undetected visually she would run submerged during the daylight hours at snorkel depth, using her diesel engines for propulsion, and surface after dark. After the SSG entered the assigned patrol area she remained submerged at all times and each night came up to periscope depth to snorkel, charging the batteries that powered her submerged transit during daylight hours.

Each SSG/SSGN maintained a 24-hour listening watch on Very-Low Frequency (VLF) radio channels to ensure the receipt of missile launch orders or any indication of a change in defense condition (readiness). During the *Barbero*'s first two patrols, in 1960–1961, the listening requirement meant she had to be at periscope depth at all times. Prior to her third patrol a floating-wire antenna was installed that permitted the submarine to spend daylight hours as deep as 200 feet, with constant VLF reception available through the floating wire. Often she would hover to conserve battery power, resting on a thermal layer at depth. The other diesel-electric submarines had similar limitations and used similar work-arounds,. However, the *Halibut,* with nuclear power, did not need to snorkel and recharge her batteries.

It was most certainly intentional—*and correct*—that the Regulus deterrent patrols were not publicized. Commander, Submarine Force Pacific's operational orders instructed the SSG/SSGNs to patrol outside the 12-mile Soviet territorial limit. Neither ComSubPac nor higher authority wanted an inadvertent intrusion into Soviet waters. In practice, to reduce the possibility of detection by Soviet forces, the submarines actually remained considerably farther offshore, their exact patrol positions still classified. They would have approached closer only if necessary to strike certain targets if an order to fire Regulus missiles was sent.

On some of her patrols the *Tunny* was an exception to the normal forward operations practice of the diesel-powered SSGs to be submerged from the time they entered assigned patrol areas until their departure. One of her commanding officers decided that rather than snorkeling after dark to charge batteries, he would bring the boat up to the surface, trimmed down by the bow to put her BQR-2B passive sonar as deep as possible to detect surface contacts. Her ESM gear was expected to provide warning of any approaching Soviet radar-equipped surface ship or aircraft. Thus semi-submerged, she would lie to or proceed at slow speed complete her battery charge. The practice appeared to work in the desolate, isolated northwest Pacific.

During one of her early patrols the *Barbero* experimented with two somewhat novel practices. The first exchanged day for night, and the second provided "leave" on board for watch officers under way. Because the submarine snorkeled each night and her diesel engines running made her relatively noisy, the commanding officer decided to have daytime routine carried out during the period of darkness, when the noise produced while snorkeling would cover any noisemaking activities by the crew. Her sailors would then have relatively quiet "daytime hours." A drastic change in mealtimes was required: breakfast began at 1800, lunch was served at midnight, and supper began at 0800. Except for the conning watch officer and the watch quartermaster, who looked through the periscope during their watches, the crew quickly adjusted, having no way to look outside of the hull to ascertain the "real time." For a watch officer or quartermaster in the conning tower it was disconcerting to see sunrise through the periscope and then, after being relieved, go below to eat *supper.*

The "on board leave" routine originated in the fact that there were seven watch officers on the *Barbero* available to fill the two positions of conning officer (in the conning tower) and diving officer (in the control room). Someone had the bright idea to leave the rotation at one in three, as usual, and allow the "spare" officer to take a week "off" to tend to his routine departmental or division duties and—to some extent—just relax. During the week off the spare officer had no watch responsibilities but was on call to handle message decryption, which normally devolved upon one of the watch officers who had just been relieved and was trying to sleep. It seemed to work well. Each watch officer got his week off during the two-month patrol.[6]

On her first deterrent patrol the *Barbero* suffered a serious garbage ejector problem. All garbage on board the SSG/SSGNs was stowed in weighted mesh bags and disposed of daily through a garbage ejection tube to keep Soviet ships from retrieving floating garbage that could provide a clue to SSG/SSGN patrol areas. Early during her patrol, in late 1960, several *Barbero* crew members used unauthorized procedures to equalize pressure inside the garbage ejector with sea pressure when below periscope depth; the outer door of the garbage ejector blew open and jammed. That forced the *Barbero* for the remainder of her patrol to submerge no deeper than 100 feet, for fear of flooding the submarine through the ejection tube. She completed the patrol in that condition and had to go into dry dock at her next upkeep to repair the casualty. Strange happenings occurred to the Regulus submarines.[7]

Polaris submarines, fitted with inertial navigation, were able to launch missiles accurately while remaining submerged in the deep ocean. Unlike them, the two oldest Regulus submarines had to move in close to the Soviet coastline, where their preselected missile launch points were located. These points were just offshore. The intended flight path of the missile was a straight line from the launch reference point to the target. If ordered to "launch," the SSG would check her position with visual bearings on headlands on the Kamchatka coast through a periscope, surface, run a missile out on deck, and launch. Surface launch took about ten minutes, during which time the submarine was especially vulnerable to detection and attack.

Once the missile was away, the SSG/SSGN would submerge to periscope depth and guide the missile to its dump point using radar. During the missile's flight the navigation team would input actual submarine position offsets from the reference point into the missile guidance computer to adjust continually for the physical offset of the radar antenna from the reference point as the submarine moved.[8]

Again, unlike Polaris missile submarines, which following a deterrent patrol turned the boat and its repair list over to the alternate Blue or Gold crew, the one-crew Regulus submarines went to an upkeep port and their crews stayed on board—supervising maintenance work being performed by the support activity and doing themselves repairs that were within their capabilities. There was no downtime for the crews, although in 1961 the Pacific submarine command succeeded in increasing the SSG/SSGN personnel allowances enough so that a few of the crew could be left ashore during one patrol as a respite.

After the upkeep period the Regulus crewmen provisioned the boat and set out for another patrol. The usual cycle was two patrols and transits of about 65 to 70 days each, with a one-month upkeep period between the patrols.

About this time the Commander, Submarine Force Pacific became concerned that commanding officers of submarines based at Pearl Harbor were not showing a new Polaris recruiting film to their crews: there was an urgent need for volunteers for that duty. The film, entitled *Man and the FBM* (Fleet Ballistic Missile), was professionally made and interesting to watch. It was an excellent recruiting film.

ComSubPac directed that each submarine commanding officer in Pearl Harbor certify in writing that the film had been shown on board and that all of his crew members had seen it. The *Barbero* was deep into her maintenance and turn-around when her officers and enlisted men went on board a berthing barge in the shipyard, where the film was dutifully shown. The reaction of the crew was fascinating but would not have been understood by the Submarine Force commander had he been present: the sailors literally fell off their benches in wild laughter as they watched. The contrast between the shiny new Polaris submarines with their advanced equipment, berthing spaces, and unlimited electric power and the old, worn-out *Barbero* was ludicrous. The *Barbero* sailors felt like snotty-nosed street urchins with their faces pressed against the window glass of an ice cream parlor, watching the rich kids eat chocolate sundaes and knowing that they would never have any.

The *Barbero*'s officers and crew also now learned that rather than in place of the one-in-five rotation then in effect in the SSG/SSGN force, ComSubPac had decided to deploy *Barbero* and *Tunny* as a two-boat team (as discussed above) so that there would be at least four Regulus missiles on station at all times. When the *Barbero* personnel learned how soon they would be sailing for another two-patrol cycle the officers withheld that information from their wives lest they pack up their children, leave Oahu, and go home to their mothers in disgust.

The *Barbero* finished her three-month upkeep and repair period on a Saturday morning and moved from the Pearl Harbor shipyard to the adjacent submarine base, using her battery-electric motors for propulsion. Because of the tight schedule, no sea trials were conducted as was usually done after yard periods. On Sunday the *Barbero*'s duty officer and duty section were heavily engaged in air-testing each compartment to ensure watertight integrity. Early in the evening the final air-tight test was successfully completed, and it was time to start a battery charge so that the submarine would be ready to get underway on Monday morning for at-sea training.

The enlisted electrician in charge in the maneuvering room lined up one of the submarine's diesel engines to charge batteries and then started to put the second engine on charge as well. Immediately the air was filled with sparks. The duty officer and the electrician discussed the symptoms: the only explanation could be that a generator had been improperly installed during the shipyard work, sending current in the wrong direction. They carefully put one engine-generator on line and checked propeller shaft rotation. It turned the way it was supposed to—so far so good. Then they put the other engine-generator on line and checked shaft rotation. *It turned the wrong way.* That generator's electrical output had been reversed.

The *Barbero* had only two main diesel engines and needed both fully operational to go to sea. Both generators had received extensive shipyard attention during the yard period. By 0800 on Monday the shipyard technicians had rewired the generator, a battery charge had been completed, and the *Barbero* was under way.[9]

Weather versus Regulus Submarines

Submarine operations in the North Pacific off the Kamchatka Peninsula, particularly during typhoon season or the winter, were very hard on men and machinery. Early in the summer–fall typhoon season the storms originate in the South Pacific and follow a generally westerly course, tending to cross the Philippines and travel westward to Indochina or southern China. As the season progresses, their tracks move toward the northwest. They cross Taiwan or Okinawa and go on into northern China or the Korean Peninsula. Toward the end of the season they curve east of the main Japanese islands and then just east of the Kamchatka Peninsula—directly through the Regulus SSG/SSGN patrol areas. Of the five SSG/SSGNs, only the nuclear-propelled *Halibut* was free of the nightly necessity to come up to periscope depth (about 60 feet measured from the keel) to snorkel to recharge batteries for the next day's submerged operations.

Snorkeling during a typhoon is an "activity" that few submariners have experienced, and those who have greatly regret that they had to. Sailors on the submarine's diving planes had to be rotated every 15 minutes because of the physical work and psychological strain of keeping the boat steady, while their supervising diving officers had to be relieved every hour.

When snorkeling the SSG routine was to choose a course that would blow the snorkel exhaust smoke away from the snorkel intake mast, lest those odorless, carbon-monoxide fumes be pulled into the boat, slowly poisoning the crew. Snorkeling directly into or away from the seas usually resulted in a "dumbbell" effect, the submarine's bow thrust up and down. The course normally selected during snorkeling is in the troughs of successive waves, preferably at right angles to their direction. Rolling up to 20 degrees to each side was not unusual at snorkel depth. Depth control, too, was a constant problem. A snorkel's head valve shuts when seawater washes over the intake mast. When that happens the diesel engines—charging the batteries—draw a vacuum. U.S. submarine diesel engines had vacuum cutouts that automatically shut the engines down at a certain point to avoid asphyxiating the crew.

When the snorkel mast again rises above the waves the head valve opens, the vacuum breaks, and the situation quickly returns to "normal." If a sailor had a cold and went to sleep during a snorkel cycle he would usually wake up with his head feeling like someone had been beating it with a ball-peen hammer all night.

Heavy weather in the North Pacific was commonplace. On one occasion in 1960 the *Barbero,* on the surface south of Adak, Alaska, in the western Aleutian Islands en route to her first Regulus deterrent patrol, was hit by a freak wave. The sea stove in her port bridge bulwark several feet and sent green water over her raised periscope. (The officer of the deck had obtained permission several hours earlier to come below, along with the lookouts, because of the weather and was using the raised periscope for lookout.) Suddenly, the *Barbero rolled more than 70 degrees.* Both of the submarine's gyroscopes tumbled. All hands grabbed at something to hold onto and tried to keep their footing. Men in the forward torpedo room were thrown out of their bunks; several had to be sent to the naval hospital in Adak when the *Barbero* pulled in to refuel several days later.

In early 1962 the *Barbero* came back to Pearl Harbor at the conclusion of her fourth Regulus patrol with no superstructure aft of the conning tower and all of the topside piping exposed. The missing superstructure had been ripped off by heavy seas during winter snorkeling off the Kamchatka Peninsula. Other Regulus submarines returned from patrols in the North Pacific with large pieces missing from their superstructures.

★   ★   ★

Water temperature was another factor during the winter months. The salt in seawater keeps it from freezing at 32 degrees Fahrenheit. Injection temperatures—that is, seawater temperature measured at the submarine's hull entry point—off the Kamchatka Peninsula during December and January were often 27 or 28 degrees. In older submarines—like the *Tunny* and *Barbero*—the torpedo rooms were single hulled, while the several other compartments between the two had adjacent ballast or fuel tanks, which provided some insulation. Ice formed on the inside of the single-hull torpedo rooms during extremely cold weather. Cold weather sleeping bags were issued to crew members who berthed in those compartments, which were, to be polite, uncomfortable. All of the officers and sailors in those submarines were issued wool trousers and shirts, and heavy sweaters.

In the *Barbero*, Lieutenant Eugene Lindsey, the missile officer, and Lieutenant John O'Connell, the missile guidance officer, lived in a two-man stateroom on the starboard side of the after battery compartment, just aft of the commanding officer's stateroom. Lindsey used "missile tape" to seal off the small ventilation ducts in their stateroom to eliminate the flow of cold air. O'Connell contributed an old tee-shirt to stuff in the main ventilation duct that supplied air to their stateroom. The result was that the extremely cold air flowing through the starboard ventilation ducts in the after battery compartment was directed into the commanding officer's stateroom!

The *Barbero*'s commanding officer at that time, Lieutenant Commander Robert Blount, sometimes came into the wardroom wearing heavy clothing, including a jacket and gloves, to get a cup of hot coffee. He would say to Lindsey or O'Connell, "Man, it's bitter cold in my stateroom. How is your stateroom?" They always would answer, "Yes sir, Captain, ours is really cold." Blount never realized that the pair were at the heart of his problem.[10]

Laundry was another issue in the diesel-electric missile submarines. Unlike the Polaris submarines, equipped with washers, dryers, and sets of special-fabric uniforms that could be rotated frequently, the older Regulus boats had no laundry facilities. The usual routine was to wear a set of clothing, including underwear, for a week, then take a brief bath in a fold-down wash basin, and put on fresh underclothes for the next week. Everyone on board smelled equally bad, thus there was no problem.

The *Barbero* had serious freshwater problems during her first Regulus patrol. A distiller drive belt failed, and the spare drive belts turned out to be too long. One of the engineers managed to build a "Rube Goldberg" rig that increased the distance between the motor shaft and the distiller shaft so the oversize belts could be used. But there was another problem: the stills could make freshwater only at a very limited rate, and the cells of the *Barbero*'s old batteries needed to be topped off with distilled water every other day. The routine was to distill seawater into freshwater and then distill that freshwater to obtain water of sufficient purity for use in the battery cells.

The top priority for freshwater in the *Barbero* was keeping the submarine's aging batteries in good condition. The next priority was the cleanliness of food handlers—the cooks and stewards. The crew, except for food handlers, came last. The boat's showers were closed for 33 days. Mid-patrol "shower day" was celebrated by all hands with a standard "Navy shower"—wet oneself briefly, shut off the water, soap up, then rinse off. The next shower for all hands, including the commanding officer, would be the night before entering port after another 30 days or so.

Two things made long, arduous Regulus submarine patrols bearable: good food and a good stock of movies.

Preparing to Launch

Navigating from Pearl Harbor to the patrol area and back was done primarily by traditional celestial navigation: early morning star sights leading to a 0800 position report to the commanding officer; morning sun line; noon position based on observation of local apparent noon; afternoon sun line; and evening star sights to determine the 2000 position. Because the four diesel-powered SSGs transited mostly on the surface, their navigators took their sights using marine sextants. The nuclear-propelled *Halibut* could conduct her transits submerged, relying on her inertial navigation system. She could update her position with observations through a periscope sextant. All of the Regulus submarines had Loran (originally denoting Long-Range Navigation) sets, a hyperbolic radio navigation system.

Even at long ranges, visual bearings could be taken on the mountain peaks of the Kamchatka Peninsula; range could be roughly determined by measuring the angle of elevation, knowing the height of the peak from the available charts. During an early patrol, one submarine's watch officers plotted through the periscope a particularly beautiful, symmetrical, cone-shaped, snow-covered peak on the peninsula. When the sonarmen reported low frequency noise from the general direction of the peak, the visual and acoustic bearings were carefully plotted. Eventually the watch officers concluded that the peak was the top of an inactive volcano and the sonarmen were hearing the magma shifts deep beneath. Thereafter, when visibility was limited, sonar could provide bearings to the distinctive noise, giving the watch team a line of bearing that was dependable.

Each of the SSG/SSGNs had a dead reckoning analyzer-indicator set that, given an accurate starting position and inputs from the speed log and a gyrocompass, roughly calculated the submarine's current position. This was read in latitude and longitude from a pair of dials. Visual or celestial observation-based fixes were updated the analyzer-indicator set. En route to and from patrol and while on station the dials were kept covered, so that only the quartermasters of the watch and watch officers could read the submarine's location. That information was considered top secret. The remainder of the crew was briefed that they were on a dangerous and important mission, carrying nuclear-armed missiles, and operating close to the Soviet Union. But crewmen were not given specific information about the patrol area, nor were they briefed on the targets for their missiles.

The Regulus submarines did not use their radars while in the patrol area lest a Soviet electronic intercept post detect the transmission and send air or surface forces to investigate. Neither did they use active sonar, for the same reason. Fathometer readings were taken sparingly, if at all; the submarines normally operated in very deep water.

If the order had come to launch missiles against Soviet targets, the *Tunny* and *Barbero* would have had to move in close to the Soviet coastline to obtain accurate navigation fixes. The *Grayback, Growler,* and *Halibut,* all equipped with SINS, would probably also move in close for an accurate fix, but they could then move well offshore, while their BPQ-2 guidance computer was updated by SINS.

During the *Grayback*'s final deterrent patrol, in 1964, she experienced severe difficulty maintaining depth. Her stern planes seemed to have little effect. Conning officers swore at the diving officers, who in turn swore at the planesmen, who could only swear at the planes themselves. Upon completion of the patrol the *Grayback* pulled into the port of Naha, Okinawa. When she backed down while coming alongside the pier, a serious casualty occurred: the starboard stern diving plane fell onto the starboard propeller, knocking it off the shaft. The submarine finally got alongside, lines were secured, and divers were summoned to investigate the damage.

The divers found that the submarine's port stern plane was missing. Apparently it had fallen off much earlier, presumably in the North Pacific, after which the actions of the stern planesmen had no effect. The *Grayback* had unknowingly been for many weeks submerged with only her bow planes operational. When the backing "bell" was ordered at Naha the loose starboard stern plane rotated into the propeller, which carried away. After some work during at Naha and a repair period at the Subic Bay shipyard in the Philippines, the *Grayback* returned to Pearl Harbor. Her future career as a Regulus missile submarine was in serious jeopardy.

However, there also was another and far more positive event in the *Grayback*'s career as a Regulus missile submarine: on 16 September 1958, the *Grayback* launched the only Regulus II missile to be fired from a submarine in the southern California operating area. (The Regulus II program was cancelled later that year; see chapter 9.)

★   ★   ★

There also were medical incidents during Regulus patrols, probably the most significant involving the *Tunny*. In two cases the submarine's commanding officer was directly affected. The first took place during the *Tunny*'s third deterrent patrol, when Commander Morris Christensen, her commanding officer, fell ill. He was diagnosed with appendicitis by the boat's hospital corpsman. Lieutenant Commander Peter Fullinwider, the executive officer, wanted to end the patrol and head for the hospital at Adak. The commanding officer refused to leave the patrol station.

The hospital corpsman dosed him with large amounts of penicillin, packed him in ice, and confined him to his bunk on intravenous feeding for about five days. Only the corpsman, the executive officer, and the senior petty officer—the chief of the boat—were aware of the situation, in itself remarkable in the close quarters of a submarine at sea. The other officers and crewmen were told that the commanding officer was busy studying for admission to the nuclear power program. After five or six days Commander Christensen responded to the treatment and was able to resume his normal duties. When the *Tunny* returned to Pearl Harbor a large contingent of medical officers was there to greet the boat, which greatly confused the commanding officer's wife until her husband explained the situation. Christensen's infected appendix was removed a short time later.

In Pearl Harbor between patrols the Regulus submarines were involved in crew training in torpedo and missile firing, as well as the upkeep and maintenance of the submarine. The supply officer on the *Tunny* learned that Polaris submarines were authorized to stamp their material requisitions with "POLARIS ACTION" in large letters, which was in keeping with the high priority afforded by the Navy to Polaris matters. The stamp obligated supply facility personnel to give urgent priority to the Polaris submarine requisitions.

The *Tunny*'s supply officer thought about the supply priority situation, went to the nearest office supply store, and had a "REGULUS ACTION" rubber stamp made for use with his requests to the supply activities. Thereafter the *Tunny* requisitions seemed to be handled with special urgency at the supply depot in Pearl Harbor—they were filled in record time. All was well until the commanding officer of the supply depot paid an angry visit to the headquarters of Submarine Force Pacific at Pearl Harbor to demand to know who had authorized the *Tunny*'s stamp. A "cease and desist" order was quickly forthcoming. The other Regulus submarine officers heard about it and wondered why they had not thought of the idea themselves.

The 40th and final Regulus deterrent patrol was made by the *Halibut*, the newest of the five SSG/SSGNs and the only one with nuclear propulsion. The *Halibut* returned to Pearl Harbor on 14 July 1964, marking the end of the Regulus deterrent patrols— and no one was happier than the crews of the Regulus submarines. In 1962 it was estimated that Regulus submarines spent 47 percent of their time in transit or deployed and another 25 percent at sea in local operations and training.[11]

Table 7-1. Regulus Submarine Patrols

Submarine	Patrols	Period	Avg. Length	Longest Patrol
SSG 282 *Tunny*	9	Oct. 1959–Apr. 1964	64.7 days	83 days
SSG 317 *Barbero*	8	Sep. 1960–Mar. 1964	68.1 days	81 days
SSG 574 *Grayback*	9	Sep. 1959–Nov. 1963	65.8 days	81 days
SSG 577 *Growler*	8	Mar. 1960–Dec. 1963	69.1 days	80 days (twice)
SSGN 587 *Halibut*	7	Feb. 1961–July 1964	75 days	102 days

A detailed list of Regulus submarine patrols is found in David K. Stumpf, *Regulus: The Forgotten Weapon* (Paducah, KY: Turner, 1996), 181.

Regulus Aftermath

REGULUS SUBMARINE DETERRENT PATROLS ended in July 1964—with a whimper. No publicity revealing the arduous Regulus patrols nor their significance ensued. During the next few years the five missile submarines were sunk as a target (*Barbero*), decommissioned and placed in reserve (*Grayback* and *Growler*), and remained in service, being converted for other roles (*Tunny* and *Halibut*). The two submarines remaining in commission no longer needed their missile or nuclear weapons personnel, and those men left for other Navy assignments. The other ratings, such as enginemen, electrician's mates, quartermasters, and torpedomen, remained with their submarines.

In May 1964, the *Grayback* and *Growler* sailed in company from Pearl Harbor to the Mare Island Naval Shipyard for decommissioning and layup in reserve. Both suffered mechanical breakdowns off Diamond Head, Hawaii. After on-board repairs they got under way again and reached the California shipyard.

The *Barbero* was the first Regulus submarine to die. She was sunk as a torpedo target off Oahu on 7 October 1964. The planned sinking with a Mark 37 warshot torpedo from the USS *Greenfish* (SS 351) nearly turned into a debacle. The torpedo struck the *Barbero*'s stern and exploded but did not sink her. The target remained on the surface. As sunset approached it appeared that she was likely to become a menace to navigation, wallowing around southwest of Oahu in the open sea without any lights to mark her as "not under command." Finally, a P-2 Neptune patrol aircraft from the Barbers Point naval air station sank her with depth charges.

Transport Submarines

Her near-sister *Tunny* continued missile launch operations in Hawaiian waters. On 6 June 1964, she fired her 100th Regulus missile, the last one to be launched from a submarine, as a target for destroyer anti-aircraft guns. It was a remarkable record for a 22-year-old submarine and for the Regulus program.

The *Tunny* then underwent a conversion at the Puget Sound Naval Shipyard into a troop transport submarine (APSS 282), being in the yard from January to July 1966. She then was sent to the Subic Bay naval base in the Philippines to take over the forward-deployed transport submarine duties from the *Perch* (APSS 313), which was to be retired from service and scrapped. These transport submarines carried Marine raiding parties and underwater demolition teams on clandestine missions.

Since 1948 the *Perch* and *Sealion* (APSS 315) had operated as troop transport submarines, in the Pacific and Atlantic, respectively. The "retired" *Perch* was homeported at San Diego until December 1959, then moved to Mare Island and placed in reserve. Recommissioned in November 1961, she conducted training on the West Coast until March 1963, when she was forward deployed to the Philippines. The *Sealion* operated in the Atlantic until June 1960, when she was decommissioned. Reactivated a year later, she resumed training operations with Marines and Navy special forces until again placed in reserve in February 1970.

At the Puget Sound yard, workmen removed the *Tunny*'s missile launcher from her after deck, stripped out her Regulus missile handling and guidance equipment, and installed bunks for troop berthing in the hangar. There already was access to the hangar through a hatch in the *Tunny*'s pressure hull, and ventilation was now supplied to the structure. The *Tunny* had rubber boat stowage lockers installed under her superdeck, along with air-inflation manifolds, similar to those in the *Perch*. Like the *Perch*, the *Tunny* could now carrying Marine teams for rubber boat assaults on targets ashore, as well as Navy special forces for incursions into enemy waters. In February 1967, the *Tunny* shifted home port to Subic Bay and took over submarine transport duties from the *Perch*. The former SSG subsequently carried out covert operations in Vietnamese waters during the Vietnam conflict.

During one Navy SEAL special operation a humorous incident took place—at least it seemed that way to the *Tunny*'s crew.[1] Two SEALs got "locked into" the forward torpedo room escape trunk from the sea. Unknown to the SEALs, they were accompanied by a large and very poisonous sea snake. Over the intercom the *Tunny*'s watch personnel in the conning tower could hear the shouts and curses of the SEALs as they tried to avoid being bitten while the escape chamber was drained. The SEALs managed to kill the sea snake. But they did not see the humor of the event as did those listening over the intercom.

The *Tunny* was relieved in her troop transport role in 1969 by the *Grayback* and was decommissioned at Mare Island. Subsequently she was used as a target for a Mark 37 torpedo fired by the USS *Volador* (SS 490) off San Diego on 19 June 1970. Like the *Barbero* earlier, the *Tunny* was struck in the stern but refused to sink; she had to be "put down" by a destroyer's 5-inch guns.

The *Grayback* and *Growler* were newer and in 1959—one year after they were completed—the Navy began feasibility studies for converting them to torpedo-attack submarines when the Regulus missile program ended.[2] Two schemes were "developed based on the assumption that an alternate mission cannot be developed . . . which would utilize the missile hangars." The first scheme involved reverting to the attack submarine configuration originally planned; the second would provide a conformal array, the BQS-4 sonar, and other features for the torpedo-attack submarine role. The second option, which would have provided a more-capable attack submarine, was cheaper ($4.5 million versus $8 million for the first scheme) and was recommended by the chief of the Bureau of Ships. In the event, neither submarine was converted to a "straight" SS configuration.

In early 1967 the *Grayback* began conversion to a troop transport/special operations submarine at the Mare Island shipyard. Her Regulus missile equipment was removed and her twin bow hangars were converted for the stowage of Swimmer Delivery Vehicles (SDVs). They could be launched and recovered while the *Grayback* was submerged. A decompression chamber also was fitted in the submarine During her conversion the *Grayback* was lengthened by 12 feet and re-engined. Also, her sail was heightened another ten feet to improve ship handling characteristics as needed to launch and recover swimmer delivery vehicles while at periscope depth. A diving medical officer was assigned to the submarine's wardroom because scuba operations would be standard for launch and recovery of SDVs; both SEALs and the *Grayback*'s launch/recovery crews used scuba gear. She was commissioned as LPSS 574 on 9 May 1969.[3]

There were plans to convert the *Growler* similarly to a transport submarine, but *Grayback*'s conversion costs soared from a prior estimate of $15 million to more than $30 million. In addition, unanticipated ship repair costs caused by the Vietnam War mounted; accordingly, the plans for the *Growler*'s conversion to an LPSS were dropped. (The *Growler* eventually went to New York City for public display at the *Intrepid* Air and Space Museum; she remains in essentially the same configuration as during her Regulus operations.)

Problems in the War Zone

The *Grayback* transferred to Subic Bay and relieved the *Tunny* in 1969. Home-ported in the Philippines, she operated off South and North Vietnam with U.S. Marines and SEALs, and with South Vietnamese commandos until the end of American involvement in the war, in 1973. In early 1972 she took part in a failed prisoner-of-war rescue attempt—Operation Thunderhead. The plan involved an escape by several American prisoners from a North Vietnam prison and their movement by boat down the Red River, which led into the northern Gulf of Tonkin.

The *Grayback*'s transit into the Gulf of Tonkin for the escape was unknown to most Seventh Fleet forces conducting combat operations in that area. The water in the gulf is very shallow, generally less than 200 feet, which meant that the *Grayback* could not go deep enough to clear the keels of deep-draft ships and so was forced to stay at periscope depth during her entire transit. The *Grayback* penetrated submerged into the northern Gulf of Tonkin, dodging U.S. warships, and "bottomed" in very shallow water near the mouth of the Red River. *She remained there, on the bottom in about 65 feet of water, for 13*

The *Grayback* as the transport submarine LPSS 574, seen off Subic Bay in the Philippines. Her twin hangars were converted for supporting SEALs and their equipment, and her Regulus launcher was deleted. The three fin-like antennae are for the AN/BQG-4 PUFFS—Passive Underwater Fire Control Feasibility System. *U.S. Navy*

Swimmers handle a rubber landing craft in front of the twin hangars of the *Grayback* in her transport configuration. A similar conversion of her near-sister submarine *Growler* had been planned, but funds were too tight in the aftermath of the Vietnam War to proceed with the project. *U.S. Navy*

days. Each night she raised her air-intake mast and snorkeled to recharge her batteries, still sitting on the bottom.[4]

For the rescue operation the *Grayback* carried four swimmer delivery vehicles, a SEAL platoon, and underwater demolition personnel. The last would operate the SDVs, insert the SEALs ashore in North Vietnam, and set up an observation post to assist the escapees to rendezvous with the *Grayback*. The submarine launched an SDV on the second night after her arrival; the SEALs intended to scout the shore. However, inshore currents in the area were so strong that the SDV could not return to the *Grayback* before its battery power was exhausted. The SDV could make a maximum of only four knots on its battery, and the current encountered was about two knots. The four riders had to abandon the SDV and tread water. The *Grayback* notified her only authorized support ship, the cruiser *Long Beach* (CGN 9) operating farther south in the gulf, when the SDV did not return. A helicopter from the cruiser located the SDV riders in the water about ten miles south of the *Grayback*'s position and rescued them, taking them back to the *Long Beach*.

The SEAL platoon leader, Lieutenant Melvin Dry Jr., was one of the four lifted to the *Long Beach*. He was anxious to return to the *Grayback* to continue the mission, so a night helicopter transfer of Dry and his teammates to a point in the water near the *Grayback* was attempted.

It, too, went amiss. They were dropped from too high an altitude and at too high a speed. Dry was killed upon impact. His team treaded water for several hours, supporting his body until another helicopter rescued them.

Though concerned at the loss of the first SDV, the *Grayback*'s commanding officer, Commander John D. Chamberlain, decided to try another SDV launch to restore the confidence of his crew and the special forces on board. The SDV was to launch, proceed west for about 500 yards, and then return to *Grayback*, recovering into a net stretched from the hangar position in the bow back to the sail. In the center of the net was an acoustic "pinger," a sound source to home in on.

The SDV flooded immediately after launch. The operators and passengers managed to reach the surface, but no one on board the *Grayback* was aware of the problem. There were no communications between the SDV and the submarine once the vehicle departed the hangar. When the SDV failed to return as scheduled, the *Grayback*'s commanding officer again notified the *Long Beach*. Another helicopter located the swimmers and pulled them up to safety. With that second failure, Commander Chamberlain decided that no more SDV launches would be made. Instead, if the escapees were sighted the *Grayback* would send SEALs to the beach in inflatable rubber boats to assist. Unbeknownst at the time to the *Grayback* or to the embarked SEALs, the attempted prison escape had been abandoned.

Later, when the *Grayback* was under way, snorkeling at night, her snorkel mast and periscope were mistakenly taken under fire by the frigate *Harold E. Holt* (FF 1074). The *Holt* had detected a small radar target and, not having been informed of the *Grayback*'s presence in the area, assumed it was a North Vietnamese torpedo boat and engaged with her 5-inch gun. The watch officer at the *Grayback*'s periscope was startled, but the submarine escaped without suffering any damage.[5] The *Grayback* again called the *Long Beach* by radio to request that the shooting cease.

After the end of the Vietnam War the *Grayback* continued to operate in the Western Pacific, frequently with special forces of allied nations as well as of the United States. Finally, the *Grayback* was retired, as newer, larger submarines assumed the special operations–transport role.[6] She was decommissioned on 15 January 1984. The submarine was sunk as a target by gunfire from several surface ships, including the battleship *New Jersey* (BB 62), in the Philippine Sea in August 1986.

The Special-Mission Submarine

The nuclear-propelled *Halibut* completed her seventh and final Regulus missile patrol—and the last Regulus missile patrol—in May 1964. The *Halibut* went into the Mare Island yard in February 1965, where her Regulus missile equipment was removed. Although relatively new—completed in 1960—the *Halibut* was considered too large, too slow, too noisy, and her sonar not sufficiently advanced to be employed effectively as a torpedo-attack submarine. Nevertheless, on 15 April 1965, she was reclassified as an attack submarine (SSN). This was done because Admiral H. G. Rickover, then head of the Navy's nuclear propulsion program, did not want nuclear-propelled submarines designated as "auxiliaries"

The *Halibut* then participated in the evaluation of the new *Permit*-class attack submarines, a program conducted by ComSubPac.[7] The *Permit*-class evaluation pitted the new submarines, with their long-range BQQ-2 passive sonars, against nuclear and diesel-electric submarines to determine detection ranges of submarine targets and to develop suitable tactics for search and attack. The results were factored into ComSubPac planning for wartime campaigns against Soviet submarines.

Subsequently, the Navy's Deep Submergence Systems Project, established in 1964 to develop advanced submarine escape and rescue systems as well as deep-ocean search and recovery capabilities, secretly funded the conversion of the *Halibut* to a "special mission" submarine.[8] The designers were careful to make a minimum of externally visible changes to help disguise the *Halibut*'s new role. The submarine was modified at the Pearl Harbor Naval Shipyard during a $70 million "overhaul" that lasted from February to September 1965; additional modifications were made at Mare Island and the Keyport (Washington) naval base. Her new features included:

- Facilities to enable the submarine to stow, release, tow, and recover "Fish" towed sensor and camera devices
- A darkroom photographic facility to develop and print photography obtained by the "Fish"
- A heightened sail structure to house additional surveillance antennas
- A thruster device installed on top of the hangar to improve maneuverability.[9]

The "cover" for the last two changes was that the submarine would be used to support the development of submarine rescue devices.

The *Halibut* as a special-mission submarine—designated SSN 587—with a purported "DSRV Test Vehicle" installed aft. In reality, the structure was a divers' habitat for use in the covert tapping of Soviet communication cables in the Sea of Okhotsk. "DSRV" indicated Deep Submergence Rescue Vehicle. *U.S. Navy*

The "Fish" was a towed "body" about 12 feet long and weighing two tons that contained cameras, strobe lights, and sonar for detecting seafloor objects. A tunnel-like chute installed in the bottom of the *Halibut*'s large bow hangar—the "Bat Cave"—permitted the launching and retrieval of the Fish while the submarine was submerged. Developing the Fish and its lights, cameras, sonar, etc., that could *survive,* let alone successfully operate, at depths to 20,000 feet was exceedingly difficult (the *Halibut*'s operating/test depth was only 700 feet) and very expensive. The 20,000-foot capability covered 98 percent of the ocean floor.

The Fish was designed to be towed for some six days and then winched back up into the submarine, cruising at a depth of about 200 feet, a process that took several hours. The Fish depth could be easily and accurately controlled by reeling cable in or out and by slightly changing speed. Once the Fish was back in the Bat Cave, the camera film would be extracted for on-board developing and the Fish's batteries would be recharged. The *Halibut* normally carried two Fish.

The submarine's hangar itself—originally designed to house four Regulus II missiles—was almost 30 feet wide, 50 feet long, and 30 feet high. When she had been a missile submarine, crew said that if the racks for torpedoes and missiles were removed, they "would have a great basketball court." But, one officer replied, "No, we don't play basketball in there; we're liable to hurt the birds."[10]

A plan of the *Halibut* configured as a special-mission submarine—intended primarily to locate objects clandestinely on the deep ocean floor. Note the extensive modification of her forward Regulus missile hangar. *Courtesy of Michael White*

The rebuilt hangar had three levels. It contained berthing space for the technicians who would be embarked for special missions, a computer area, photographic darkroom, and stowage and handling gear for the two Fish. (The *Halibut* retained her four forward and two stern 21-inch torpedo tubes and carried torpedoes.)

The reconfigured *Halibut* first tested the Fish system off Hawaii, searching for a pre-positioned target on the ocean floor. One of the cable strands broke and created a snarl that prevented normal recovery of the Fish. As the crew and on-board specialists were trying to correct the situation the Fish was lost, probably snagged on the ocean floor and torn away. Next came the *Halibut*'s first operational mission: to locate and examine the re-entry vehicle from a Soviet missile test in the Pacific in February 1968. Unfortunately, when the *Halibut* launched the Fish during an evaluation prior to the operation, the $5 million device slid out of the chute … and was lost; the wire cable had not been properly attached! Another *Halibut* Fish had been shipped, but inadvertently sent to South Vietnam. It was finally delivered in time for the mission but failed to locate the missile re-entry body.

When the *Halibut* left the missile target area—without Soviet detection—there was a problem winching in the tow cable, and the submarine had to surface at night and put men on deck to deal with it. One man went overboard when a "rogue wave" swept over the submarine. The maneuvers to rescue the sailor required the *Halibut* to "back emergency," which probably put the Fish on the ocean floor even though it was being reeled in as fast as possible. The sailor was recovered. The Fish was recovered.

According to Captain Edward Moore, commanding officer of the *Halibut* from February 1967, "during these early missions we had become quite good at controlling both ship and Fish depth, and in searching for targets, but we had not yet learned how to accurately position the Fish for photographs."[11]

During the summer of 1968, the *Halibut* would covertly locate the sunken remains of the Soviet Golf II–class, diesel-propelled, ballistic missile submarine *K-129*, which had been lost in April 1968 northwest of the Hawaiian Islands with all 99 men on board. The *K-129* had suffered an accidental missile ignition while on a deterrent patrol. An operation to locate and possibly recover the remains of the Soviet submarine was mounted. For it the *Halibut* carried 13 officers, 123 enlisted men, and six technical specialists as she departed Pearl Harbor. The *Halibut* sought the "target object"—as the *K-129* wreckage would be called in official documents—from late April to late May 1968. (A code name used by some Navy offices for the search was Velvet Fist; later press reports erroneously labeled it Project Jennifer.)

Ultimately the *Halibut* succeeded in locating the remains of *K-129*, leading to a covert recovery effort funded and directed by the Central Intelligence Agency. The recovery—Project Azorian—was conducted during the summer of 1974, employing the "cover" of a Howard Hughes company to mine seafloor manganese nodules with the specially built ship *Hughes Glomar Explorer*. The effort was partially successful, although the primary target of the operation—the submarine's one remaining nuclear-armed missile—was not recovered. (A subsequent plan to send *Glomar Explorer* back to the scene for the missile was aborted when the Soviets learned of the initial recovery effort.)

★   ★   ★

In October 1971, the *Halibut* covertly probed the Sea of Okhotsk to locate a Soviet underwater communication cable that ran across the Sea of Okhotsk from the massive naval complex at Petropavlovsk on the Kamchatka Peninsula to other points in the Soviet Far East. The base communicated with the rest of the Soviet Union by air, by sea, and using seafloor cables.

The *Halibut* bottomed alongside the cable in about 400 feet of water and "locked out" Navy divers, who attached an electrical induction apparatus to it. The divers operated from a "pod" habitat attached to the stern of the *Halibut*. Once locked into the pod, the divers pressurized it and, using saturation diving techniques, remained at the 400-foot working depth for long periods with no need to decompress until the mission was completed. Food and drink were transferred directly into the pod from the submarine.[12] (The saturation diving was part of the Deep Submergence Systems Project's effort to enable diver to work for sustained periods at depths to 1,000 feet.)

The induction device recorded cable traffic, which was especially valuable because ballistic missiles test-fired from the Tyuratam missile complex in the central Soviet Union flew to a target area east of the Kamchatka Peninsula. Very valuable intelligence data on missile impact accuracy was routinely transmitted back to Moscow, initially through the cable. In addition, the submarine base at Petropavlovsk—itself a former Regulus missile target—generated considerable cable traffic for the *Halibut*-planted device to intercept. The *Halibut* conducted several of those clandestine "bugging" missions, each time leaving a new long-life, battery-powered device and retrieving the old one, with its previously recorded material.[13]

Within a few years the *Halibut* was outdated for special missions, for which newer submarines had become available. The *Halibut* was decommissioned on 30 June 1976, "mothballed" at the Keyport/Bangor submarine base in Washington in that year, and later scrapped.

Awards and Pins
A very subtle clue to the *Halibut*'s classified operations was the large number of Navy enlisted divers who were awarded the Legion of Merit for unspecified actions. The Legion of Merit often was awarded to the commanding officer of a submarine for a successful covert surveillance mission, but rarely to enlisted personnel. In general, steps were taken to preclude inviting attention to special operations by awards for successes. Such awards were not publicized in any fashion; they never appeared in Bureau of Personnel announcements or in the *Navy Times* newspaper.

As noted above, when the *Halibut* returned to Pearl Harbor from the final Regulus deterrent patrol on 14 July 1964, there were no press releases, no public relations campaign. There also were no special submarine patrol badges for Regulus crewmen. A distinctive Polaris Patrol Pin was established in 1969 for all Polaris submarine sailors to acknowledge their arduous duties; it was awarded to each crew member—officer and enlisted—who made a Polaris deployment.

In 1970, then-Commander John O'Connell, in the Submarine Warfare Division of the Office of the Chief of Naval Operations, originated a request to extend eligibility for the deterrent patrol pin to former Regulus crewmen. The memorandum was returned by his seniors without comment or acknowledgment. There the matter sat for almost 27 years, until in April 1997, Vice Admiral Richard W. Mies, then Commander, Submarine Force Atlantic Fleet, notified the Bureau of Naval Personnel that the personnel who had participated in Regulus missile deterrent patrols were now eligible to wear the submarine deterrent patrol insignia.[14] Thus, some recognition at last came to the several hundred officers and sailors who carried out the 41 Regulus deterrent patrols, which had begun before the first Polaris submarine entered service.

With all of the Regulus missile-launching submarines removed from that role, the radar-equipped guidance submarines, both nuclear and diesel-electric, had their special equipment deleted and went back to standard attack submarine duties, except for one boat. In addition to attack submarine missions, the venerable *Carbonero* undertook an additional role as a test platform for the submarine delivery of biological agents, a program given the code name Project 777. She was active in those trials from 1964 to 1966 in the Hawaiian area. The submarine carried harmless biological agents in a special tank in her forward superstructure. She dispensed the agents through a false radio antenna while at periscope depth, and stations ashore measured the extent of their spread.

The "launching" of biological agents from a submarine was another form of attack that might be used against an enemy's homeland—but it was not pursued further. (The U.S. Navy ran such simulated biological attacks on coastal cities—including San Francisco—from 1949 until 1969. These tests were conducted to help develop both defenses against such attacks and to contribute to the development of such "retaliatory" biological attack capabilities. Some of the agents, although non-dangerous by design, may have caused some injuries to the target populations.)

Supersonic Cruise Missiles

THE U.S. NAVY ORIGINALLY PLANNED to have the supersonic Regulus II missile operational in 1953 and the supersonic Rigel missile entering service two years later. The "ultimate" submarine-launched cruise missile—the supersonic Triton—initially was planned to be operational in 1960.[1]

During the late 1940s and into the 1950s, cruise missile technology was well ahead of ballistic missile technology. In addition, ballistic missile technology at the time depended on liquid-fuel rocket motors. The U.S. Navy was determined to avoid taking liquid-fuel missiles to sea because of their explosive hazards. Whereas cruise missiles could be stowed in canisters external to the submarine's pressure hull, liquid-fuel ballistic missiles were so large that that the missiles—installed in vertical launch tubes—would have to penetrate the submarine's pressure hull.

In 1946, the Navy initiated the Rigel missile program. It was a submarine-launched, supersonic (Mach 2) cruise missile using ramjet propulsion. A ramjet engine uses air-speed to compress air for entry into the combustion chamber. Thus a ramjet must be accelerated by another power source, usually a rocket, to a speed at which it can operate. It is most efficient at speeds from Mach 3 to 6. Unlike a turbojet engine a ramjet cannot be used for propulsion from a dead stop.

The Rigel was to have twin Marquardt ramjet engines with multiple, solid-propellant rocket boosters for the necessary initial acceleration. The prime contractor was Grumman, which had produced a string of outstanding naval fighters as well as other aircraft.[2] The early Rigel flight-test vehicle had only one ramjet engine and a single, in-line rocket booster, to test the propulsion concept. The first FTV was launched in May 1950. The Rigel was to have an initial range of 500 nautical miles; its guidance involved a modified Loran system. Two guidance submarines would serve as "beacons" to be interrogated by the missile to determine if it was on the correct flight path to the target. When the target area was reached the missile would enter either a preprogrammed or a ballistic path to impact. The payload envisioned was the W5 nuclear warhead, with a specified accuracy (CEP) of 600 yards.

There were serious problems during the Rigel vehicle flight tests. By October 1952, 11 flight test vehicles had crashed. The Rigel development program was cancelled in August 1953, because of these test vehicle failures. The technology of that day was inadequate to support such an advanced missile.

Seeing an opportunity to provide a solution to the Navy's missile goal, the Chance Vought company stepped in and proposed that the Regulus I subsonic missile be upgraded to supersonic speed and provided with additional fuel for increased range. This so-called Regulus II could fill the Navy's cruise missile gap created by the Rigel cancellation. The Bureau of Aeronautics put together a new program in which the Regulus II replaced Rigel in the submarine-launched cruise missile program, while the Triton remained as the third generation for planning purposes.[3] Thus, by default, the Regulus II became the planned successor to the Regulus I. Under this plan the Regulus II was to become operational in 1957 and the more advanced Triton cruise missile in 1965.

Regulus II Takes Off

The Regulus II cruise missile now took center stage in Navy strategic missile plans. Chance Vought had long been aware of the need for an upgraded version of the Regulus I missile and had begun a study of a supersonic variant in June 1951, only three months after the first flight of a Regulus I flight test vehicle. The company called the advanced missile design the V-379, later the Regulus II. The proposed cruise missile was a giant leap beyond the subsonic Regulus I, estimated to have a range of more than 1,000 nautical miles, supersonic cruise speed, and an inertial navigation system with a nuclear warhead. (In congressional testimony Admiral Arleigh Burke confirmed a 1,200-mile range for the Regulus II.[4])

In June 1952, the Bureau of Aeronautics put out a formal request for proposal for a supersonic variant of the Regulus I missile. Chance Vought submitted its proposal for the Regulus II missile that December, but not until September 1953 did BuAer approve the production of four flight test vehicles. In February 1955, the first FTV was delivered to Edwards Air Force Base.

Nearly four years of design work and wind tunnel testing of models had preceded the first Regulus II tests at Edwards. Experience with the Regulus I helped the Chance Vought engineers to carry out ramp and reliability tests of the new missile, followed by low-speed and high-speed taxi trials. On 29 May 1956, the first flight test vehicle began its takeoff roll and became airborne. That first test took the missile to 10,890 feet and a speed of 356 mph. After almost 33 minutes of flight the FTV was successfully landed under the control of a TV-2D Shooting Star chase aircraft.

The high speed of the Regulus II missile put a strain on the available chase and control aircraft. Subsequently, the Douglas F4D Skyray and Chance Vought F8U Crusader fighter aircraft were employed in that role, principally the Crusader. (Unlike the two-seat TV-2D, these were single-seat fighters.)

In August 1956, on its seventh flight, the first FTV crashed and was lost when a throttle failure caused the missile to stall during its landing sequence. The missile had previously reached an altitude of 35,000 feet and a speed of Mach 1.5. In October an FTV reached 54,000 feet and Mach 1.6.

High-speed pitch oscillations caused the loss of two vehicles during subsequent test flights. Modification of the yaw gyro, controlling left and right movement, solved the problem. The first seven missiles tested were powered with the Wright J65-W-6 turbojet engine. Its manufacturer used aluminum turbine blades, which limited engine performance to 35,000 feet and Mach 1.8 except for short periods due to inlet temperature limitations. The subsequent missiles had the General Electric J79 turbojet engine, which was used by the McDonnell F4H Phantom and Douglas A3D Skywarrior, both in series production at that time.

Rather than the twin booster rockets of the Regulus I to launch the missile, the Regulus II used a single booster. In November 1957, the first boosted launch of a Regulus II missile took place. That missile reached 35,000 feet and Mach 1.1 and was successfully recovered, although the hot engine exhaust destroyed the braking parachute upon landing.

Three guidance systems had been proposed for the Regulus II missile: Regulus Inertial Navigation (RIN), the Trounce IB radar, and Automatic Terrain Recognition and Navigation (ATRAN). The latter two never flew in the Regulus II. RIN was built by the AC Sparkplug firm and was a self-contained system. Its development had begun in 1955 as an improvement for Regulus I guidance, but became the primary navigation system for Regulus II. (It was never backfitted into the Regulus I missile.)

In January 1958, the first RIN-controlled Regulus II flight took place. It and the second RIN flight about six weeks later were failures: the primary guidance system failed shortly after both launches. In each case, control was handed over to ground radar, and the missile was recovered successfully.

In May 1958, the first all-Navy launch of a Regulus II took place, with a GMU-55 launch team. That July a Regulus II missile sustained Mach 2 speeds at altitudes from 46,000 to 52,000 feet. The highest speed attained during the 37-minute flight was Mach 2.1. Later that month the first terminal dive was attempted—and failed: the missile broke up after the dump signal was transmitted and the missile began its dive. Wind tunnel tests had indicated that additional stability during the terminal dive maneuver could be achieved by adding a small lower ventral fin. The fin solved the problem. A successful terminal dive test was conducted on 1 November 1958, validating the modification.

The *Grayback* in September 1958, with a Regulus II on her launcher. The missile was twice the size of the Regulus I. The *Grayback* launched one Regulus II, the only submarine to launch that missile; the only other at-sea "Reg II" launch was from the former LST *King County*. *U.S. Navy*

The USS *King County* (AG 157) was the former tank landing ship *LST 587*, extensively modified to serve as a test bed for the *Halibut*'s Regulus II hangar and launcher arrangement. When that program ended the *King County* continued to serve as a missile and space tracking and support ship. *U.S. Navy*

The *King County* launching a Regulus II missile on 10 December 1958—her only launch of a "Reg II" missile. As the *LST 587* the ship saw service in the Western Pacific during World War II (1945) and in the Far East during the Korean War (1950–1953). *U.S. Navy*

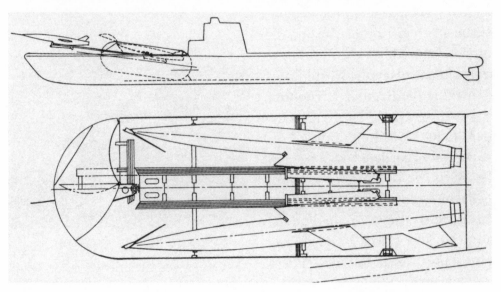

A four-missile magazine/launchers intended for advanced Regulus II submarines.
© *A. D. Baker III*

The USS *Grayback* launched the first Regulus II missile to be fired from a ship on 16 September 1958. That was the only "Reg II" to be launched from a submarine and the penultimate missile launched at sea. The landing gear of that missile failed to deploy, but a successful wheels-up landing was made at Rosemond Dry Lake in California.

The second—and last—launch of a Regulus II from a ship occurred on 10 December 1958. The launching ship was the USS *King County* (AG 157), a tank landing ship modified to duplicate the stowage and launching arrangements for the Regulus II planned for the *Halibut*. The *King County* launch, conducted by GMU-55 personnel, was completely successful.[5] The era of the Regulus missile had ended.

Prior to those successful Regulus II launches, the Chief of Naval Operations, Admiral Burke, in January 1958, published his plan for "The Navy of the 1970 Era":[6]

52 MISSILE LAUNCHING SUBMARINES, ALL NUCLEAR POWERED
40 with POLARIS or a successor, 1500-mile or greater range
12 with [guided] missiles, 1000-mile or greater range.

Death of a Missile

However, the Department of Defense Comptroller's office was beginning to look at submarine-launched cruise and ballistic missiles as equivalent and therefore duplicative efforts. The Office of the Secretary of Defense wanted to force the Navy to make a choice between what it perceived as two competing weapon concepts. Regulus II tests and trials were ongoing, and the missile seemed to be moving closer to acceptance into service, but in Washington some hard financial and policy realities were being faced.

On 12 December 1958, in a move that was a surprise to most of the Navy, Secretary of the Navy Thomas S. Gates cancelled the Regulus II program. All U.S. Navy cruise missile development was halted in favor of the now promising solid-fuel Polaris fleet ballistic missile. Available Regulus II funding was transferred to the Polaris project.[7]

Soon after, the personnel of Guided Missile Unit 10 were waiting for the 0800 muster formation to start off their working day at the Pearl Harbor Submarine Base. Lieutenant "Doc" Coleman, a former warhead officer at GMU-10, had just returned from the Regulus missile course at the Guided Missile School in Dam Neck, Virginia, and was about to embark upon his new duties in the missile department. He struck up a conversation with a GMU-10 officer. Coleman casually remarked that the Regulus II program had been cancelled. The effect was explosive. Coleman was immediately taken up to talk to the officer-in-charge, Lieutenant Commander Samuel Bussey, to repeat his statement. Bussey got busy on the telephone to officials at Submarine Squadron 1 and Submarine Force Pacific Fleet to ascertain what was happening.

Unaware of the fiscal program difficulties, the two shore-based Regulus guided missile units had been preparing to expand their facilities to accommodate the much larger and more complex Regulus II missile. GMU-10 was heavily engaged in planning a move to the Naval Ammunition Depot at the West Loch of Pearl Harbor. Telephone calls to Washington confirmed the story—the Regulus II program was officially cancelled, although the decision had not yet been announced by the Navy Department.

The existing "Reg II" missiles continued to be launched by GMU-55, primarily as targets and for training. The last flight of a Regulus II occurred on 13 December 1965, from Point Mugu. That missile was launched and recovered for the tenth time. During that final flight it was fired at five times by ships' anti-aircraft guns as it reached a speed of Mach 2 and an altitude of 58,000 feet.

★   ★   ★

For several years, events had been occurring behind the scenes that would cause the end of the strategic cruise missile in the U.S. Navy. In February 1955, the Technological Capabilities Panel, otherwise known as the Killian Committee, had recommended development of a sea-based, liquid-fuel, intermediate-range ballistic missile. The panel had been was established by President Dwight D. Eisenhower in 1954 to examine the possibility of a surprise attack on the United States by Soviet bombers or missiles with nuclear weapons. James Killian, who led the panel, was the first presidential science advisor. (He would later become president of the Massachusetts Institute of Technology.)

The development of such a weapon was supported by the Naval Research Laboratory, the Bureau of Aeronautics, and the Assistant Secretary of the Navy (Air). However, Rear Admiral John H. Sides in the Office of the Chief of Naval Operations strongly opposed it on safety grounds, recalling the disastrous Operation Pushover tests in 1948. In Pushover, conducted to determine the effects of an accident with a liquid-fuel missile on board ship, V-2 ballistic missiles were made to fall on a simulated ship's deck. The results had been catastrophic. (The Navy did successfully launch a V-2 from the flight deck of the carrier *Midway* on 6 September 1947.[8])

Nevertheless, Admiral Burke approved participation in the Jupiter project, an Army-developed intermediate range ballistic missile, to be taken to sea, under the new Fleet Ballistic Missile (FBM) project, on board surface ships. Again there was opposition within the Navy's leadership, this time major and widespread, stemming in large part from experience in the aircraft carrier/B-36 bomber controversy of the late 1940s and the expected high cost of a submarine missile program. The Navy had lost the earlier controversy with the first "super carrier," the *United States* (CVA 58), having been cancelled and the Air Force's B-36 strategic bomber entering in production.[9] Senior Navy officers were not anxious to get into another dispute with the Air Force, which opposed the Navy's getting into the strategic attack arena with submarine-launched ballistic missiles.

Admiral Burke set up a new agency, the Special Projects Office, under Rear Admiral William F. Raborn. Burke realized that a sea-based ballistic missile capability would be seen within the Navy as a threat to naval aviation's nuclear weapon delivery capabilities. Thus his selection of Raborn to head the new office: Raborn's qualifications were impressive, but it did not hurt that he was a naval aviator and had previously commanded an aircraft carrier.

Funding for the new weapon system also fell into channels different category from normal Navy weapons procurement. For the FBM program, Admiral Raborn submitted his funding requests directly to the service secretaries, in their capacities as members of the Joint Army-Navy Ballistic Missile Committee. If favorably endorsed by the committee, the request went directly to the Office of the Secretary of Defense. If approved at that level the funds would be disbursed directly to the Special Projects Office.

As noted above, the Defense Department comptroller viewed the Navy's submarine-launched cruise missile program and the fleet ballistic missile program as duplicative. In December 1955, the Office of the Secretary of Defense had asked the Navy to make a choice between the two programs. Admiral Burke refused to do so.[10] Accordingly, in July 1956, the comptroller had issued a ruling that approved a budgetary proposal by the Ballistic Missile Committee that required the services to expend the authorized money exactly as had been proposed. He also told the Navy to find the requested $25 million for the FBM program within its fiscal year 1957 budget.

In August 1957, Admiral Burke approved the construction of three submarines for the Regulus II missile (SSGN 594–596). Further, in April 1958, he approved the modification of six guided missile cruisers then undergoing conversion to carry four Regulus II missiles each:

CG 10 *Albany*	CG 13 (ship not designated)
CG 11 *Fall River*	CG 14 (ship not designated)
CG 12 *Chicago*	CG 15 (ship not designated)

These conversions, involving former 8-inch (203-mm) gun heavy cruisers (CAs), were in addition to the newly built, nuclear-propelled cruiser *Long Beach*.[11]

At that same time, two new factors were working to threaten the future of the submarine-launched cruise missile program. The first was the launching by the Soviet Union on 4 October 1957 of the *Sputnik I* satellite, the first artificial satellite to be put into Earth orbit. It only weighed some 160 pounds, but it was followed into orbit in November of the same year by *Sputnik II,* a 1,120-pound craft. Although these weights did not approach that of a satellite of the size required for a nuclear warhead, it was clear that Soviet ballistic missile technology was more advanced than had been thought by American officials. Could a Soviet Intercontinental Ballistic Missile (ICBM) be far behind? (The first U.S. attempts to launch a satellite had failed. The first U.S. satellite to orbit the Earth—*Explorer 1*—weighing 30.8 pounds was launched on 31 January 1958.)

The second element was the Eisenhower administration's effort to control the defense budget. A $38 billion Defense Department ceiling was established. Regulus I missile procurement ended in 1958 as programmed, and purchase of planned Regulus II missiles was reduced in January 1958.[12]

At about this time, because of a breakthrough in solid-propellant rocket technology and the development of smaller nuclear warheads, Admiral Raborn recommended shifting from the Army-Navy, liquid-fuel Jupiter missile to the solid-fuel Polaris fleet ballistic missile.

That same year, the Navy's budget problems came to a head: there was not enough money available to carry out all shipbuilding and conversion plans that had been tentatively approved. Nine planned warships were cancelled, for a savings of about half a billion dollars; heavy cruiser conversions to missile ships were delayed; and the Regulus II missile, planned for the fiscal year 1960 budget, was deferred. The new FBM—soon to be named Polaris—offered several advantages over the Regulus II:

- The Polaris missile was submerged launched.
- The Polaris ballistic missile was less vulnerable to intercept than the (aerodynamic) cruise missile.
- The Polaris A-1 missile had a slightly greater range than Regulus II with the promise of longer ranges for later variants.
- A Polaris submarine could carry 16 missiles compared to four for the Regulus II submarines.

The upshot was that as Raborn had recommended, the Navy withdrew from the joint Army-Navy Jupiter program and embarked on the solid-fuel ship- and submarine-launched ballistic missile. On 19 November 1958, two days after an Air Force Atlas ICBM completed the first full-range flight, the Office of the Secretary of Defense let the Navy know that development of the Regulus II cruise missile would no longer be supported. The Chief of Naval Operations' budget committee did not protest this action. The president of the Chance Vought made a personal appeal to the Secretary of the Navy to retain the cruise missile effort, but he was rebuffed.

Accordingly, Secretary of the Navy Gates cancelled the Regulus II program.[13] But interest in the Regulus II missile continued; several members of Congress asked pointed questions about why the weapon was cancelled. In January 1959, Secretary of Defense Neil McElroy went on the record to explain to Congress the reasons:

The Regulus II is a good weapon concept and its development was progressing satisfactorily. However, the Polaris system promises to be far superior in overall effectiveness. Since this system has now progressed to a point where we can have confidence in its early operational availability, the Regulus II is no longer of the same importance. Considering the extremely high costs involved in developing, producing, operating, and maintaining the training and logistics support for two distinctly different missile systems, both designed for similar missions—we decided to concentrate our efforts on Polaris, the more advanced of the two, and drop the Regulus.[14]

There was, briefly, hope for other-service use of the Regulus II, both before and even after its cancellation by the U.S. Navy. In 1956, the U.S. Air Force informally discussed acquiring the Regulus II missile as a strategic strike weapon to be carried on B-52 Stratofortress bombers. Several European NATO nations also expressed interest in obtaining the Regulus II as a ship- and land-launched nuclear strike weapon. In April 1958, the United States released preliminary information about the Regulus II system to NATO military officials. In March 1959, three months after the cancellation of the U.S. missile production, Chance Vought proposed to NATO with BuAer's concurrence a land- and sea-based deterrent Regulus II force. The French, German, and Italian armed forces initially displayed some interest.

The French government appeared to be the most interested in the weapon, for the *Force de Frappe*—France's strategic deterrent force. It considered both sea and land basing and procurement of some 20 to 30 missiles.[15] At one point in 1958 the French Navy considered launching the missile from its two aircraft carriers. In the event, the French developed and deployed land-based ballistic missiles, land-based bombers, and submarine-launched ballistic missiles with nuclear warheads for the strategic deterrent role. There was no foreign Regulus II acquisition.

At the time of the cancellation of the Regulus II program in 1958 there were 24 fleet training missiles and 23 tactical missiles available. All were reconfigured as KD2U-1 drones, with target beacons, miss-distance recorders, and in some missiles Luneburg lenses to facilitate radar acquisition, simulating Soviet bomber formations. These remaining 47 Regulus II missiles, save one, were expended as targets for air defense systems testing.[16]

No Third-Generation Missile

The Triton missile development had started in the late 1940s. It was a product of Johns Hopkins University's Applied Physics Laboratory, which had developed the Navy's Terrier, Talos, and Tartar surface-to-air missile programs. By 1950, the Triton was envisioned as a 2,000-n.mile missile, traveling at speeds of Mach 1.6 to 2.5 at an altitude of 80,000 feet. The missile would use inertial guidance supplemented by a day-time star tracker and employ radar map-matching for terminal homing. The warhead weight was to be about 1,500 pounds, although no specific nuclear warhead was indicated in the early stages of development. The desired accuracy (CEP) was specified as 600 yards.

Envisioned as the U.S. Navy's third-generation submarine-launched cruise missile, the new Triton began full-scale development in 1955, but the missile never reached the production stage.[17] The Triton project was cancelled in 1957, primarily for fiscal reasons. No Triton test vehicles were flown.

The end of the Regulus II program marked the end of strategic cruise missiles in the U.S. Navy for more than a decade.

Air Force Strategic Cruise Missiles

THE U.S. AIR FORCE INITIATED A PROGRAM of land-launched strategic cruise missiles shortly after World War II, again because available cruise missile technology offered the promise of superior range performance compared to ballistic missiles. While the Navy soon was in competition with the Air Force for the development of strategic (nuclear) attack weapons, the idea was voiced periodically that Air Force cruise missiles could be adapted for shipboard use. Further, there was competition between the services for cruise missile development and deployment to the extent that there was for land-based and sea-based ballistic missiles. Thus, the Air Force's land-launched cruise missile program was related to the Navy's efforts in that field.[1]

The Navaho Missile

The first land-launched strategic cruise missile sponsored by the U.S. Air Force was the XSM-64 Navaho, the "SM" indicating strategic missile. Although this missile never reached operational status, it bore considerable fruit in various technologies that enabled later cruise missiles and ballistic missiles to be extremely accurate weapons. The Navaho was a ballistic rocket that boosted a supersonic cruise missile high into the atmosphere. The design was highly attractive because the cruise missile's air-breathing ramjet engine would not have to carry its own oxidizer as would a ballistic missile, thus reducing the weapon's weight.

The Navaho development program had three stages: (1) a study of a "winged V-2" concept based on the German ballistic missile; (2) replacement of the V-2 rocket engine with a supersonic ramjet; and (3) determination of the size and thrust of a rocket booster necessary to launch the winged V-2.

In April 1946, the Army Air Forces approved a first segment of the Navaho program, the MX-770—a 175- to 550-mile surface-to-surface missile. In July 1947, a ramjet engine was added, to achieve a proposed 1,500-mile range. By March 1948, the program was focused on a 1,000-mile test missile, a 3,000-mile test missile, and a 5,000-mile operational missile. Subsequently the Air Force also considered the concept of a B-36 strategic bomber carrying and launching the Navaho missile (it dropped that idea in 1951).

North American Aviation began preliminary design work on the missile in January 1947. The first Navaho flight test vehicle—essentially a technology demonstrator, designated X-10—flew in October 1953. It was 70 feet long, with a 28-foot, delta-shaped wing and a V-tail configuration. The vehicle had radio control and retractable landing gear for recovery. The 11 X-10 vehicles made 27 flights, of which the 19th reached a speed of Mach 2.05, a record at the time for an aircraft, manned or unmanned.

Next in the program was the G-26, a nearly full-size Navaho vehicle. It was vertically launched with a liquid-fuel rocket booster and was intended to reach about 50,000 feet and a speed of Mach 3 before the booster was discarded and a pair of ramjet engines ignited. Four G-26 test launches were made from Cape Canaveral, Florida. None was successful.

The G-38—later designated XSSM-64A—was the final experimental version of Navaho. This was a slightly larger and improved version of the G-26. None was launched: the Navaho program was shut down on 13 July 1957, primarily because of competition within the Air Force ballistic missiles for available missile funding.

Despite its failure to reach operational status, the Navaho introduced several new technologies that would contribute significantly to other Air Force and Navy missile programs. The Air Force's air-launched missile Hound Dog was later derived from the Navaho, while Navaho-derived liquid-fuel rocket engines were to be used in the Atlas, Thor, and Titan ballistic missiles.

An X-10/SM-64 Navaho test vehicle in flight. The North American strategic cruise missile was one of two weapons of this type that was produced by the United States. A nuclear-powered missile of this kind was considered by the United States but not built; Russia was reported to be developing such a nuclear-powered weapon when this volume went to press. *U.S. Air Force*

An XSM-64 Navaho coupled to its liquid-fuel booster rocket is launched from Patrick Air Force Base in Florida. The Navaho program was considered a failure, although it provided several advances in missile and navigation/guidance technology. *U.S. Air Force*

Further, the Navy installed the Navaho N-6 autonavigator, an inertial guidance system, in the *Nautilus* (SSN 571), the world's first nuclear-propelled submarine, in April 1958. Employing that system, she became on 3 August 1958 the first ship to reach the North Pole. Later systems derived from that inertial navigation technology would be placed in ballistic missile submarines to provide extremely accurate navigation for submerged missile launch.[2] For a "failure," the Navaho was a remarkable success from the viewpoint of technology development.

The Snark Missile

The Snark, the second Air Force supersonic strategic cruise missile, bore more fruit, albeit a little bitter. An intercontinental-range missile, it was designed to strike targets in the Soviet homeland with the W39Y1 warhead—a 3.8-megaton nuclear warhead.[3]

The Snark had a troubled development history. Requirements first were laid out in 1946, then cancelled, and then in 1947 reinstated. Northrop was the prime contractor for the missile, which initially was to be powered with the same Allison J33 turbojet engine that was used in the Matador and Regulus missiles. A pair of rocket boosters was to launch the missile.

The engine was underpowered for the size of the missile, the Snark being 69 feet, 11 inches long, and weighing some 25 tons (plus rocket boosters). The long, sleek configuration of the Snark, with sweptback wings, led to descriptions of it as a "pilotless" bomber. Compared to a contemporary bomber, in fact, and beyond alleviating the need for a trained crew, the Snark offered low investment and operating costs, a small radar cross section, and a relatively large nuclear warhead.

The first Snark test vehicle launch, in December 1950, was a failure. In April 1951, the second launch achieved a flight lasting only 38 minutes—another failure. From 1953 to 1958, the guidance system was "flight tested" 196 times on B-45 Tornado and B-29 Superfortress bombers. The general conclusion was that the guidance system worked—"but not for long."[4]

In June 1950, the Air Force changed the requirements for the missile to include:

- Supersonic dash at the end of the 5,500-nautical mile mission
- A payload of 7,000 pounds (later reduced to 6,250 pounds)
- Accuracy (CEP) of 1,500 feet

The existing Snark cruise missile could meet none of these requirements.

Flight tests of the Northrop Model N-25 flight test vehicle ended in March 1952, after 16 test missiles had flown a total of 21 times. The maximum speed achieved was only Mach 0.9. Northrop responded to the change in requirements with the N-69 Super Snark, a scaled-up N-25. The J71 jet engine was used in the Snark *A, B,* and *C* versions; the Pratt & Whitney J57 jet engine—generating 11,000 pounds of thrust—was chosen in December 1953 for the series *D* production model.[5] Two underwing auxiliary fuel tanks could be fitted. (The redesigned "Super Snark" was given the military designation SM-62.) The test missile variant had two centerline retractable landing skids and a drag parachute, for recovery.

The first N-69, launched on 6 August 1953, failed, as did the next four missiles. On 3 June 1954, a flight of 3½ hours took place, but the missile exploded upon landing. Flight tests were completed in May 1955, two years *after* the tentative missile in-service date. On 2 October 1956, the first successful recovery took place, on the 31st flight of the N-69.

The N-69 Super Snark was intended to complete its mission with a terminal dive toward the target. In May 1955, wind tunnel tests showed that the technique would not work. In July the Air Force accepted a different delivery concept: the nose section with the nuclear warhead would detach from the missile and follow a ballistic trajectory to the target, while the remainder of the missile pitched up to avoid collision with the warhead. Earlier, in mid-1954, the Air Force had reduced the required CEP to 8,000 feet, reflecting the large, thermonuclear warhead of the missile.

The *D* model of the missile was equipped with a stellar-inertial system and additional pylon fuel tanks. In October 1956, the first stellar-guided flight took place.[6] Flights of Snarks to a range of 2,100 miles soon were achieved with greater ranges in the offing, but the CEP averaged 20 miles—too great a distance for even a large, 3.8-megaton warhead. Further, the probability of successful launch was only 0.35, and only one in the final ten missile test flights reached the planned range of some 5,000 miles.[7] Frequent crashes off Cape Canaveral led to that sea area's being humorously termed "Snark-infested waters."

On 5 December 1956, a test Snark was launched from Cape Canaveral; the missile was to fly to a point near Puerto Rico, make a turn, and return toward the cape. En route, radar tracking indicated that the Snark was drifting to the right of its flight path. Then the missile began ignoring commands sent by ground controllers. Subsequently "destruct" signals from several radar tracking stations along its flight path were ignored. Fighter aircraft were scrambled from Ramey AFB in Puerto Rico in an effort to destroy the missile, but they were too late to intercept it. The Snark disappeared over the Atlantic. Twenty-six years later, in 1982, a farmer found the errant missile in a forest in northeastern Brazil. (Later model Snarks were provided with a second power bus in an attempt to prevent similar "escapes.")

Presque Isle in Maine was designated as the first operational Snark base in March 1957. The following December the Air Force's 556th Strategic Missile Squadron was activated at Patrick Air Force Base in Florida, and that June the first Snark launch by an Air Force missile crew took place there. The first Snark missiles were deployed to Presque Isle in May 1959.

Only six months later, however, in November, the head of the Air Force's Strategic Air Command (SAC) recommended cancellation of the Snark cruise missile program. The first Atlas D ICBMs—the first U.S. weapon in that category—had become operational in September of that year. Air Force headquarters rejected the SAC proposal,

A Snark intercontinental-range cruise missile being prepared for flight at Cape Canaveral, Florida. The twin booster rockets and external fuel tanks are visible beneath the wings. The Snark was operational with the Air Force—for a very brief period. *U.S. Air Force*

An SM-62 Snark test missile in flight. This was the only land-launched, strategic cruise missile to be deployed by the United States—albeit for a brief period. The U.S. Air Force and Defense Department leadership preferred ballistic missiles over cruise missiles in the strategic strike role because they could reach targets faster and were less vulnerable to interception. *U.S. Air Force*

however, and Snark was placed on launch alert to strike targets in the Soviet Union on 18 March 1960.

Nevertheless, President John F. Kennedy ordered the Snark program cancelled shortly after taking office in January 1961. He declared that the Snark "was both obsolete and of marginal military value relative to ballistic missiles." Kennedy's Secretary of Defense, Robert S. McNamara, favored ballistic missiles over land-launched cruise missiles as well as over manned strategic bombers. Accordingly, the Snark program ended and the alert missiles at Presque Isle were deactivated on 25 June 1961.[8]

The Matador Missile

Meanwhile, the Army Air Forces' JB-2 version of the German V-1 cruise missile was morphing into the Matador cruise missile, in a program that began as research and development project MX-771. Somewhat similar to the Navy's Regulus cruise missile, the Matador used the same Allison J33 turbojet engine and the same nuclear warhead (the W5, with 40 to 50 kilotons of explosive power). Matador was launched with one solid-fuel rocket booster, its transport vehicle serving as the launcher. Matador guidance involved ground-based radar operators who tracked and guided the line-of-sight missile at an altitude of 40,000 feet to a maximum range of about 225 miles. To attack, a ground controller radioed a dive signal, causing primer-cord explosive to blow off the wings; the missile then would dive on the target.

The Air Force began flight testing the Matador prototype—at the time designated XB-61—at Holloman air base in New Mexico, with the first launch on 20 January 1949. (Later the designation TM-61 was assigned, the "TM" indicating tactical missile.) The first Matador service test version was launched from Cape Canaveral the following year. There were several crashes, for various reasons; the Air Force ascribing most of the problems to the Martin Company's design and production processes. The Matador survived the development phase, however, and went into production.

In late 1954 the Shanicle guidance system was introduced in the Matador TM-61C version as an addition to the existing radar-tracking system. Shanicle employed a hyperbolic grid system, with one transmitter providing azimuth information and a second transmitter for range. Although the missile had enough fuel for a range of about 700 miles, both Shanicle and its radar-guidance systems were limited to the line of sight, meaning an operational range of only about 200 miles. However, Shanicle did enable one operator to direct several missiles simultaneously.

Meanwhile, in October 1951, the 1st Pilotless Bomber Squadron, with Matador cruise missiles, was activated at Patrick AFB. The squadron deployed to Bitburg Air Base in West Germany in March 1954.

The Matador was intended for use against targets with heavy air defenses that might defeat Allied manned aircraft. It also could be employed at night or in weather bad enough to preclude manned aircraft from attacking. The Matador was road mobile and thus—in theory—more survivable than manned aircraft operating from fixed and hence easily targetable air bases. However, up to 25 support vehicles were required per Matador "launch element," each with four missiles and one launcher per element. Each Matador squadron originally had six launchers, later increased to eight; it took about one and a half hours and a mobile crane to transfer a missile from its transportation trailer to the mobile launch ramp.[9] The overall reliability of the TM-61C was 71 percent, and the reported CEP was 2,700 feet.[10] The Matador was designed with a chemical warhead delivery capability, although it was deployed only with the W5 nuclear warhead.

An Air Force Matador cruise missile on a zero-length launcher. The U.S. Air Force sponsored several cruise missiles for the nuclear strike role—theater and strategic—in the early years of the missile age. *Martin Marietta*

Parachutes provided for the recovery of a Matador cruise missile after a training flight. Note the air bags under the fuselage. Nearing the ground the parachutes will fall away and the air bags will inflate. *Martin Marietta*

A Matador cruise missile on a zero-length launcher in an undisclosed European NATO country during a training exercise. Note the booster rocket under the missile's tail. Air Force security troops are in the foreground as the missile is prepared for launching. *Martin Marietta*

The TM-61B version of Matador was an attempt to improve some of the limitations of the TM-61A and the *earlier* TM-61Cs. The *B* model had a folding-wing configuration, a towed zero-length launcher, and a map-matching guidance unit. Development work on Matador B began in 1957, and production started late that year. The Air Force decided that the differences between the earlier Matadors and the "new missile" were significant enough to warrant a new name for the latter: the TM-76 Mace cruise missile.

Matador missile squadrons operated under the Air Force's Tactical Air Command; the missiles were considered "tactical" nuclear weapons, as opposed to the "strategic weapons" under the cognizance of the Strategic Air Command. In Europe, Matador and the later Mace missile squadrons were part of the NATO-controlled nuclear delivery capability, although the missiles and their warheads always were in U.S. custody. The Matador was deployed only in West Germany, at three bases, from 1954 until 1962.

The Mace Missile

The TM-76 Mace A—beginning life as the TM-61B Matador—was some five feet longer than Matador, providing space for additional fuel to enable a range of 800 miles. It also had the W28 warhead with a 1.1-megaton yield—a significant increase over the

W5. Another major change was the introduction of the Automatic Terrain Recognition And Navigation (ATRAN) and a radar map-matching navigation device. The second version—the Mace B—had an inertial navigation system and an increased range of approximately 1,500 miles, placing targets inside the Soviet Union at risk from launch locations in West Germany.

Mace B inertial guidance system needed to know its exact launch point to compute the route to the target, so the weapon had to be launched from a predetermined position. This consideration led to the development of hardened (protected) launch sites, unlike Mace A or Matador.

In 1959, the Air Force deployed the first Mace missiles to Europe, fully replacing the Matador by 1962. At peak strength there were six missile squadrons in Europe, with just under 200 Matador and Mace missiles. Matador and Mace training flights were conducted at the U.S. Wheelus airfield in Libya.

A Mace cruise missile launches from Holloman Air Force Base in New Mexico during a training exercise. The booster rocket is clearly visible under the rear of the fuselage as the missile leaves the zero-length launcher. *Martin Marietta*

In April 1969, the last Air Force cruise missile unit in Europe, the 71st Tactical Missile Squadron, was deactivated. The U.S. Army's Pershing II Intermediate-Range Ballistic Missiles (IRBMs) took over the Quick-Reaction Force nuclear alert role.

In the Far East, beginning in 1957, Matador and later Mace cruise missiles were deployed in South Korea, Okinawa, and Taiwan. Air Force personnel arrived on Taiwan with the missiles in December 1957, and the W5 warheads followed in January. In May 1958, the first Matador demonstration launch in the Far East—a TM-61C missile—was made from Taiwan, conducted in the presence of President and Madame Chiang Kai-shek.[11] Nuclear-armed Matador missiles were maintained on alert in Taiwan until 1962. Their targets were in mainland China. In South Korea the Matador TM-61C missiles were operational from January 1959 to March 1962. Also, in December 1961, Mace missiles were deployed on Okinawa. Those weapons were operational until December 1969.

The era of Air Force–operated land-based cruise missiles in the U.S. nuclear arsenal came to an end in 1969, when the last Mace missiles were retired. The Matador and Mace missiles were replaced from the late 1960s by nuclear-armed land-and carrier-based tactical aircraft as well as by ballistic missiles. Thus the Air Force land-based cruise missiles survived several years longer than the Navy's initial cruise missile program—the Regulus I.

. . . and the Pluto Project

One other strategic cruise missile reached an advanced stage of development in the United States during the Cold War—the *nuclear-propelled* Pluto. The Pluto Supersonic Low-Altitude Missile (SLAM) was an ambitious program to develop an "unmanned bomber" powered by a nuclear ramjet engine. SLAM has been described as a "locomotive-size missile that would travel at near treetop level at three times the speed of sound, tossing out hydrogen bombs as it roared overhead."[12] The name Pluto originally was assigned to the missile's nuclear ramjet engine; however, in practice it referred to the entire program.[13]

The critical component of the program was the missile's nuclear ramjet engine. Ramjet technology offered the promise of high speeds for a large vehicle, while nuclear technology could provide the "fuel" necessary for intercontinental ranges. The ramjet was to propel the aircraft at Mach 3 speeds, with air temperature at entry to the engine almost 1,000° F and at exit (exhaust) 2,200° F. The engine size and weight as well as nuclear-radiation issues were major constraints on the project.

On 1 January 1957, the Lawrence Livermore National Laboratory in California was selected to develop the nuclear engine. After extensive efforts, on 14 May 1961, at Jackass Flats, Nevada, the world's first nuclear ramjet engine—the ToryIIA, mounted on a railroad car—was tested for 45 seconds. This was a scale model, mounted on a rail car so it could be retrieved by remote control into a protective shed, where it could be fueled and maintained, also by remote control. Three years later, on 20 May 1964, the ToryIIC nuclear ramjet was run for five minutes at full power, producing 513 megawatts and the equivalent of more than 35,000 pounds of thrust.

It was envisioned that the Pluto missile would have preset guidance coupled with Terrain Contour Matching (TERCOM). The payload would be some 5,500 pounds of nuclear warheads ranging from one of 26 megatons to 42 of five kilotons.

Despite successful engine tests, the rapid development of ICBMs and the operational problems associated with what was essentially an unmanned nuclear-powered bomber led to the decision, on 1 July 1964, to cancel the Pluto program. The entire effort to date, costing some $320 million by the end of fiscal year 1964, had been related to engine development. The engine weighed 14,410 pounds.

The missile's airframe was not developed.

A half-century later, Russia was developing the Burevestnik nuclear-powered cruise missile. It was a weapon cited by President Vladimir Putin as carrying a thermo-nuclear warhead with "unlimited range."

Land-based strategic cruise missiles—missiles that could strike the Soviet Union and mainland China—were in vogue for several years early in the Cold War. That interest would be resurrected in the 1970s in the context of Intermediate-range Nuclear Forces (INF) weapons that again would be forward-deployed in allied countries.

The Soviet Perspective I

THE U.S. NAVY INITIALLY DEVELOPED CRUISE MISSILES for attacking the Soviet homeland; only a decade later did it turn to ballistic missiles for the strategic attack role. The Soviet Navy initially undertook the development of submarine-launched *torpedoes*, as well as cruise and ballistic missiles with nuclear warheads, for the strategic attack role—and vigorously pursued both types of missiles from the outset of the Cold War (1946–1991).

The Soviet Union detonated its first atomic bomb on 29 August 1949, little more than four years after the first U.S. nuclear detonation. Immediately the development and production of nuclear weapons was initiated. The critical issue for the Soviet political-military leadership, however, was how to deliver those nuclear weapons against targets in the United States.

The first Soviet nuclear delivery platform was the Tupolev Tu-4 long-range bomber, given the NATO designation Bull. This four-piston-engine aircraft, which entered operational service in 1947, was a direct copy of the U.S. B-29 Superfortress.[1] The Soviet regime sought to have multiple means of attacking the West, however, and in 1949–1950 two nuclear-armed torpedo programs were initiated. These efforts were undertaken without coordination with the Navy! Rather, the programs were formalized under the Ministry of Medium Machine Building, which was responsible for all nuclear weapons development.[2] The weapons were the large T-15, for use as a strategic attack weapon by nuclear-propelled submarines, and the T-5, of conventional torpedo size for use in the anti-ship role by diesel-electric submarines. The T-15 torpedo—the first nuclear weapon employed by the Soviet Navy and the product of one of the most ambitious submarine weapon projects ever undertaken—was intended as a strategic attack weapon to be used against major Western bases, such as Gibraltar and Pearl Harbor. As for Western cities, aside from those considered to be too far inland, it was expected that their seaward approaches would be too well protected.

The submarine carrying a T-15 would surface immediately prior to launching the torpedo, determine its precise location by stellar navigation and use radar to identify coastal landmarks. The torpedo was to carry a thermonuclear (hydrogen) warhead a distance of some 16 n.miles. The T-15 was to have a diameter of just over five feet (1,550 mm) and a length of almost 79 feet. The 40-ton underwater missile would be propelled underwater to its target by a battery-powered electric motor at about 30 knots. Like the missile, the firing submarine was being developed under the aegis of the Ministry of Medium Machine Building.

The first Soviet nuclear-propelled submarine—Project 627, given the NATO code name "November"—was designed to carry one T-15 "land attack" torpedo plus two conventional torpedoes for self-defense. However, following Josef Stalin's death in March 1953, there was a total reappraisal of Soviet defense programs. The Commander-in-Chief of the Navy, Admiral Nikolai Kuznetsov, was aware that a nuclear-propelled submarine was being developed, but so great was the secrecy of nuclear programs in the Soviet Union that he was given no information about its payload, a single, giant nuclear torpedo. When in July 1954 the design was completed and Kuznetsov was briefed, he is reported to have declared, "I don't need that kind of boat."[3] The T-15 project was cancelled, and the November was redesigned as a torpedo-attack submarine of more conventional design—still, the Soviet Navy's first nuclear-propelled undersea craft.[4]

The Soviet Navy's strategic strike weapons would be nuclear-armed cruise and ballistic missiles. Later, in the 21st century, Russia would develop nuclear-armed, underwater drones to be carried by specialized submarines for attacks against Western coastal cities (see below).

The First Cruise Missiles

Almost concurrently with the U.S. Navy development of the Regulus attack missile, the Soviet Navy was working on the P-5 missile system, later given the NATO designation SS-N-3 Shaddock. However, whereas the U.S. Navy would consider the Regulus only as a land-attack weapon, the Soviet Navy would employ later variants of the Shaddock as an anti-ship weapon as well. Indeed, in the 1960s and 1970s the submarine-launched Shaddock was considered to be a major—if not *the* major—threat to U.S. Aircraft carriers. Further, the Soviets continued to develop and employ cruise missiles during the U.S. Navy's *strategic* cruise missile hiatus in the decade between the Regulus I and Tomahawk land-attack weapons.

The Soviet Union had not been a target of German V-1 cruise missiles, although there were reports of German planning for a suicide force to attack Soviet cities using *piloted* V-1 missiles, carried toward their targets by long-range bombers.[5] In July 1944, however, Great Britain provided a damaged V-1 to Soviet officials, and by the end of the war work was under way on cruise missiles at several aircraft design bureaus.

During the war Vladimir N. Chelomei, already a recognized mathematician and scientist, had worked on the development of pulse-jet engines similar to that used in the V-1 missile. He was put in contact with Georgi Malenkov, a member of the State Defense Commission and a close associate of dictator Josef Stalin, to tell the politician that he could build a weapon similar to the V-1. Malenkov met with Chelomei on 14 June 1944 and supported the proposals of the 30-year-old designer. Chelomei was given the resources to pursue cruise missile development, and a year later he created the V-1 analog—designated 10X and named *Volna* (wave). The missile was to be carried and launched by bomber aircraft. Air-launched variants included the 14X and 16X designs. Development was also initiated of ground-launched and ship-launched versions of the missile, the latter designated 10XN. Design work began to modify a World War II–era Type XIV series submarine to launch the missile, but that project was halted in 1953.

★   ★   ★

Nikita Khrushchev, who emerged as head of the Soviet regime after the death of Josef Stalin in 1953, authorized the opening of a design bureau for strategic cruise missiles under Chelomei. In the United States, aircraft manufacturers also design aircraft, often also tactical and strategic missiles. In contrast, the Soviet Union established (and Russia continues to employ) bureaus specializing in the design of aircraft and missiles, as well as others designing surface ships, submarines, tanks, artillery, etc. These bureaus are separate from the manufacturing facilities, which enables them to be more innovative—that is, not tied to a particular factory or shipyard that might not be the best to produce their designs. Further, there were multiple aircraft, missile, and submarine design bureaus, etc., bringing the benefits of design competition.

The Soviet/Russian aircraft design bureaus such as Antonov, Beriev, Ilyushin, MiG, Sukhoi, Tupolev, and so on, have long been known in the West.[6] Less known—indeed, for a long time highly classified—were the identities of the missile designers and the missile design bureaus.

★   ★   ★

In 1952–1953 design work began on submarine Project 628, an updated version of the large, World War II–era K-class submarine that would be configured to conduct experimental launches of Chelomei's 10XN Volna cruise missile. The missile was powered by twin ramjet engines and was launched by the surfaced submarine from a ramp with the aid of a single booster rocket.

In 1953, the U.S. Central Intelligence Agency observed, "With respect to guided missiles, there is no evidence that the Soviet Union has any guided missiles available for operational use. On the other hand [redacted] the Soviet Union has been conducting an intensive research and development program and has exploited German progress in this field. [redacted] [T]he Soviet Union has produced at least experimental quantities of the V-1 type missile."[7]

Subsequently, land launchers for the 10XN missile were reported by Western intelligence being installed near Leningrad and Vladivostok, but it did not enter ground or naval service; the air-launched 10X did become operational with the Soviet Air Forces in 1953.[8] It was rejected for naval service because of guidance limitations, the high fuel consumption of available ramjets, the fact that supersonic missiles were by then in development, and the disbanding of Chelomei's design bureau in December 1952 because of political intrigue within the defense industry. Artem Mikoyan, the chief designer of the MiG-series fighter aircraft, proposed a competing cruise missile, and Chelomei's design group—Plant No. 51—became a branch of Mikoyan's OKB-155 design bureau.[9]

Land-Launched Cruise Missiles

Meanwhile, Sergey Pavlovich Korolev, a missile designer who in 1938 had been imprisoned for almost six years in the Stalinist purges, also began work in the cruise missile field.[10] In 1952, while participating in ballistic missile projects—derived from the German V-2—he started developing a strategic cruise missile analogous to the U.S. Navaho. Korolev's bureau "began to take a look at a [cruise missile] design as a fallback in case its own ballistic missile designs continued to be stymied."[11]

Korolev's initial goal was a test vehicle that could carry a half-ton payload more than 800 miles.[12] However, in April 1953, when it was learned that the Americans were developing the Atlas ICBM, the cruise missile project was taken out of his hands so that his bureau could concentrate on ballistic missiles (and, subsequently, on space projects). Two of the aviation bureaus were directed to continue the development of strategic cruise missiles, those directed by, respectively, aircraft designers Vladimir M. Myasishchev and Seymon A. Lavochkin. Their strategic cruise missiles were identified as, respectively, *Buran* (blizzard) and *Burya* (storm). Neither the Myasishchev nor Lavochkin design bureaus had experience in missile development, although the former had acquired key engineers who had been engaged in missile work at the Chelomei group.[13]

The more significant of these two projects was the Burya, a land-launched, strategic cruise missile similar in concept to the U.S. Snark and Navaho, but more ambitious. This Soviet effort—also known as "Object 350"—was undertaken in cooperation with the Korolev's ballistic missile design team. Burya dated from a 1947 session of the Presidium of the Central Committee of the Soviet Union to discuss missile problems. When "trans-Atlantic" weapons came up, the Presidium decided to initiate an intercontinental missile program. Strategic cruise missiles were to be deployed simultaneously with ballistic missiles.

Because the Buran and Burya were to be supersonic cruise missiles, the Soviets pressed the development of ramjet propulsion and lightweight titanium metal. Titanium welding was introduced in the Soviet Union at that time, apparently in part to support these missile projects. Subsequently the Soviet Union created the world's largest titanium metal industry, primarily in connection with production of advanced missiles, aircraft, and submarines.[14] Progress also was made in missile coatings, insulation, and other technologies because of the demands of the missiles' flight profiles.

The Burya was to have a nuclear payload of up to 5,500 pounds and a missile launch weight of almost 210,000 pounds, including two liquid-propellant rocket boosters. The missile had a cylindrical body; a stub, mid-body delta wing, with a 70-degree leading edge sweep and a straight trailing edge; and a cruciform tail assembly. The missile was launched from a vertical position. Its flight profile was to be controlled by an automatic astro-navigation system. As the missile neared its target the autopilot would cause it to dive, at which point the warhead was to be released. The Burya was to have a maximum speed of just over Mach 3 and a range of some 5,000 miles—*a very ambitious project!*

Manufacture of the Burya missile began in the central Soviet city of Kuibyshev. The first launch of a test vehicle occurred in late 1957. This and several subsequent tests failed. According to one Russian account, "The specialists had to tackle a lot of problems they had never faced before and time was pressing."[15] Meanwhile, Korolev's R-7 *Semyorka* (seven) intercontinental ballistic missile had been successfully launched at Tyuratam (in Kazakhstan) on 21 August 1957; Khrushchev cancelled the rival strategic cruise missile programs that November.[16]

Myasischev's Buran missile—designated "M-40"—was cancelled outright, because none had been completed, let alone flown.[17] It was very similar to the U.S. Navaho strategic cruise missile.

Lavochkin's Burya was allowed to continue flight testing, as several missiles had been produced. The first test flight, on 1 August 1957, failed shortly after launch. The Burya's first successful test flight occurred in December 1958. During 1957–1960 there were 17 Burya launches, of which only four were considered successful. Burya vehicle test flights achieved speeds of about Mach 3 and reached ranges of just over 4,000 miles. Meanwhile, the development of ballistic missiles continued at a rapid pace. The Burya project formally was cancelled in February 1960, although development work on a photo-reconnaissance version of the missile continued until early 1961.

Weapons historian Steven Zaloga wrote, "The Lavochkin Burya was a significant technical achievement due to its advanced ramjet propulsion, its pioneering technologies in materials that could withstand the heat of high supersonic flight, and its novel astro-navigational guidance system. But such cruise missiles offered nothing over ballistic missiles. In particular, they were viewed as far more vulnerable to American air defenses than ballistic missiles due to their slow terminal speeds."[18]

Thus, as in the United States, land-launched strategic cruise missiles were abandoned by the Soviet leadership in favor of ballistic missiles. However, interest in strategic cruise missile launched from submarines would continue in the Soviet Union. Also as in the United States, consideration was given in the Soviet Union to a nuclear-powered, ramjet cruise missile, a concept that ultimately was not pursued in either country.

★   ★   ★

The 1952 decree closing Vladimir Chelomei's design group had been one of the last such documents signed by Stalin, who died in March 1953. At his death Malenkov gained considerable power, and Chelomei soon had the support of Khrushchev as well. Chelomei was able to reestablish his design group, which in June 1954 became special design group SKG-10 and then, in August 1955, OKB-52. (Khrushchev's son, Sergei, an engineer, worked at that bureau.)

Chelomei also was garnering support from the military establishment by his successes with naval cruise missiles and proposals for future missiles. Meanwhile, Myasishchev's failure with the Buran project and with his strategic aircraft designs—especially the four-turbojet, supersonic M-50 bomber—led Khrushchev to close his design bureau. Chelomei took over Myasischev's facility at Fili, outside of Moscow, as well as many of the bureau's talented aviation engineers. Such tumult was common within the communist defense-industrial establishment.

A still further refinement of the V-1 design by Chelomei was the 15X missile, based on the availability of the Rolls-Royce Nene centrifugal-flow turbojet—which had been provided by Britain's Labour government to the Soviet Union for *civil aviation use*. This engine, which became the power plant for the famed Mikoyan-Gurevich MiG-15 turbojet fighter aircraft, and an advanced point-to-point guidance system gave promise of an effective submarine-launched strategic weapon. The submarine would—it was hoped—transit to a pre-selected launch position with the missile in a launch container either being towed or fitted on the deck of the submarine.[19]

In 1950, design bureau TsKB-18 began work on a cruise missile submarine propelled by a closed-cycle steam turbine that had been developed by the Germans during the war.[20] That Soviet submarine (Project 624) was to have had a submerged displacement of 2,650 tons and carry the *Lastochka* (swallow) cruise missile. Developed by aircraft designer Lavochkin, the missile was to have a range against shore targets of 160 n.miles. However, development of both the missile and the submarine was soon halted.

The Shaddock Missile

Chelomei in 1954 conceived of ship-launched missiles with wings that would automatically extend shortly after launching. This approach would enable the missiles to be carried in containers approximately the same size as the missile's fuselage and booster rockets. Also, aerodynamic and engine improvements made possible the elimination of a launch ramp, permitting the missile to be launched directly from the canister. Chelomei applied this concept to the 20X missile, which, upon provision of more-flexible guidance systems, become the P-5, or Shaddock (discussed above).

The deck-mounted canister, performing both the storage and launch functions, would be broadly adopted by the Soviet Navy, simplifying installations in surface ships as well as on submarines. This was in sharp contrast to the U.S. Navy's method, which looked at the Regulus canister as simply a hangar, from which the missile had to be manually extracted and placed on launch rails, where its wings were unfolded, and other manual functions were performed before launch.

In 1955, the decision was made to produce both Chelomei's P-5/Shaddock cruise missile and the P-10 cruise missile, being developed by OKB-48 under seaplane designer Georgiy M. Beriev. Both missiles were intended for strikes against Western land targets with nuclear warheads.

A Zulu (Project 611) diesel-electric submarine was modified in 1955 to test launch the P-10. As with the U.S. Regulus, the missile was housed in a hangar; it would be extracted from the hangar, its wings extended, and then launched. The hangar was on the deck casing *aft* of the conning tower, but the missile launched *forward*, over the bow. During the fall of 1957 four P-10 missiles were launched from the submarine, but work on this weapon was halted due to the successful tests of the P-5 missile, which was supersonic (Mach 1.2), had a range of 300 nautical miles, and incorporated other advantages when compared to the P-10.[21]

In 1957, the Whiskey diesel-electric submarine *S-146* was modified to conduct tests of the P-5 missile (the submarine redesignated Project P613). The missile canister on this submarine too was placed behind the conning tower, and, again, the missile was launched on the surface and flew forward, over the bow. Following P-5/Shaddock tests at the Kapustin Yar test range in the southern Soviet Union in 1956, the first P-5 missile was launched from *S-146* on 22 November 1957, in the White Sea.

In 1959, after extensive tests the P-5 system became operational and was installed in submarines as well as on surface ships.[22] All work was halted on competing surface-to-surface cruise missiles. Of particular significance in the latter decision was not just the P-5 missile, but also its innovative container-launcher concept.

★   ★   ★

Four Whiskey Twin-Cylinder (Project 644) submarines were delivered to the fleet in 1960, each with paired missile canisters aft of the conning tower that elevated 15 degrees to fire aft, over the stern. The time from the submarine's surfacing until it launched the two missiles was estimated at five minutes.

The Project 644/Whiskey Twin-Cylinder was the first "operational" submarine to carry the Shaddock missile, following the one Whiskey Single-Cylinder missile trials submarine. These Shaddock-armed Whiskey submarines did not deploy overseas as did U.S. Regulus-armed submarines.

A Whiskey Twin-Cylinder submarine with her coupled, aft-firing Shaddock missile launchers in the raised, launching position. Unlike the U.S. Regulus missile, the Shaddock was housed in the launch cylinder with wings that extended upon launching.

These craft were extensively converted from "straight" Whiskey torpedo-armed submarines built in the 1950s. Beyond the installation of the Shaddock launch cylinders and the associated fire-control equipment, the submarines were provided with air cylinders, added ballast, and other features that made a submarine able to surface if one canister had been accidently flooded. The stern torpedo tubes were deleted, as were deck guns and reload torpedoes, providing only the torpedoes in the four bow tubes, without reloads. (Some U.S. intelligence sources contend that there were five—not four—Whiskey Twin-Cylinder submarines; some sources cite six submarines of this type.[23])

Next to be pursued was the definitive Whiskey SSG design (Project 665), known by NATO as the Whiskey Long-Bin for the craft's enlarged conning tower structure. Four forward-firing P-5/Shaddock missiles were installed in the front portion of the rebuilt, bulbous conning tower; the launch canisters were fixed at an upward angle of 14 degrees. Again, the missile could be launched from the canisters, not having to be moved onto a launching device. Between 1961 and 1963 Soviet shipyards delivered six Long-Bin conversions to the fleet. In addition to their missile-launching facilities, these submarines were lengthened some 24 feet to make room for the enlarged conning tower. Again, their two stern torpedo tubes were deleted and torpedo reloads were removed, leaving only the four torpedoes in the forward tubes.

The P-5/Shaddock land-attack missile, with a range of 300 n.miles, had a terminal speed of Mach 1.2 and an accuracy of plus or minus two nautical miles. It had a 200- or 350-kiloton nuclear warhead and could carry instead a conventional warhead. These submarines provided the Soviet Navy with valuable experience and training in cruise missile submarine operations. Unlike the two converted fleet boats used by the U.S. Navy in the Regulus program (*Barbero* and *Tunny*), the Soviet Twin-Cylinder and Long-Bin submarines did not undertake long-range missile patrols.

(On the night of 26–27 January 1961, the Whiskey Twin-Cylinder submarine *S-80* foundered because of a snorkel failure with the loss of all 68 men on board. The wreck was discovered by fishermen in 1968 and subsequently salvaged.)

The Project 665/Whiskey Long-Bin was the ultimate configuration of the prolific Whiskey class to carry the Shaddock cruise missile. This Long-Bin submarine was moored with the *Sverdlov*-class light cruiser *Oktyabrskaya Revolutsia*; a Project 641/Foxtrot was moored between the missile submarine and the cruiser.

A Whiskey Long-Bin submarine in port with signal flags rigged for a Soviet holiday. Note the huge conning tower, which housed four, forward-firing Shaddock missile tubes. These submarines did not forward deploy to the extent that the analogous U.S. Regulus submarines did.

Shaddock Proliferation

The success of the Shaddock missile led to the cancellation of several other sea-launched cruise missile projects that were intended primarily for the land-attack role. In 1956—two years before the first Soviet nuclear-propelled submarine went to sea—design work began on the Project 659 (NATO Echo I) boat. This missile submarine would have the same reactor plant as the first Soviet nuclear submarine (Project 627/November SSN) but would not have the November's advanced hull shape. Rather, the Echo I and the later Projects 651/Juliett SSG and Project 675/Echo II SSGN, as well as the Project 658/Hotel SSBN submarines, had conventional hull designs to enhance their stability on the surface while launching missiles.

The first Echo I, the *K-45*, was laid down on 28 December 1958 and placed in commission on 28 June 1961.[24] Through 1963 four more nuclear-propelled submarines of this type were built, all at the Leninskiy Komsomol Shipyard at Komsomolsk-on-Amur in the Far East. These submarines had a length of 364¾ feet and displaced 4,976 tons submerged. Missile armament of the submarines consisted of six P-5/Shaddocks in paired launch canisters mounted on the deck casing and elevated 15 degrees to launch forward. The Echo I also were armed with torpedoes.

The early Shaddock cruise missile system had a number of deficiencies, among them low accuracy and the necessity for the submarine to remain on the surface for about 20 minutes to prepare the missiles for launch. Accordingly, from 1958 to 1961 the Chelomei bureau developed a new system, designated P-5D. It had increased range and a higher probability of penetrating air defenses to reach its target. A Whiskey Twin-Cylinder submarine was refitted to test the missile, and the P-5D was accepted for service in 1962.

The Chelomei bureau now developed the P-7 missile, based on the P-5 and P-5D weapons but intended to have almost twice their range—that is, approximately 540 nautical miles. Flight tests took place from 1962 to 1964, and a Whiskey SSG was again to be used as an at-sea test platform. However, the P-7 missile did not become operational in submarines because the role of cruise missile submarines shifted from strikes against land targets to the anti-ship warfare (see below).

(Chelomei in 1959 began developing designs for ballistic missiles and spacecraft. He initiated several successful weapons that competed with the projects of Sergei Korolev and Mikhail Yangel, the leading Soviet ballistic missile designers of the era.[25])

The Soviet Perspective II

THE INTENSIVE SOVIET DEVELOPMENT of land-launched ballistic missiles and the problems being encountered with land-attack cruise missiles changed Soviet policy toward the latter.[1] On 14 December 1959, Nikita Khrushchev established the Strategic Rocket Forces (or Troops) as an independent military service to control all *land-based* strategic ballistic missiles. At the same time Soviet sea-based strategic forces were downgraded, and the construction of submarines with land-attack guided (cruise) missiles and with ballistic missiles was slowed precipitously. Thus, in February 1960, it was decided to halt the further development of several cruise missile programs.[2]

Of the array of strategic and antiship cruise missiles begun in the 1950s, only the P-5 and P-6 missile systems, designed by Chelomei, were placed in service on submarines in this period. However, by 1965 the Shaddock land-attack missile had been taken off of all SSG/SSGNs, which were mostly rearmed with anti-ship missiles. The five Echo I SSGNs—lacking the guidance system for anti-ship missiles—were converted to torpedo-attack submarines (SSN/Project 659T).

In the mid-1950s intensive work had been initiated on anti-ship cruise missiles concurrently with the development of land-attack missiles. The former weapons were intended primarily to attack U.S. aircraft carriers, which were armed with nuclear-armed strike aircraft and thus presented a threat to the Soviet homeland. Khrushchev in 1955 announced that "submarines armed with guided missiles—weapons best responding to the requirements indicated for at sea operations—will be deployed at an accelerated rate."[3]

The P-6 anti-ship variant of the Shaddock revealed the highly innovative directions that missile development in the Soviet Union had taken. Beyond its on-board guidance with terminal radar homing, the missile could be provided with guidance updates while in flight by a Video Data Link (VDL) system given the NATO code name Drambuie. This enabled long-range reconnaissance aircraft—primarily the Tu-95 (NATO Bear-D)—

and, subsequently, satellites to identify distant targets and relay the radar picture to the (surfaced) submarine.[4]

The Soviet Union developed two types of satellites to work in tandem to detect U.S. aircraft carriers and other surface ships: Electronic Intelligence (ELINT) satellites to detect radar emissions from ships; and, cued by the ELINT "birds," Radar Ocean Reconnaissance Satellites (RORSAT) to provide precise targeting data. The latter satellites were nuclear powered, a necessity because of the power requirements for the active radar system.

Also, a technique was developed in which the submarine launched two anti-ship missiles about 90 seconds apart. Both missiles would climb to their cruise altitude of some 9,840 feet. As they descended to a lower altitude to seek their target ship, only the first missile would activate its terminal search radar. This radar picture would be transmitted up to a Bear aircraft and relayed back to the launching ship, which would transmit updated guidance data to the second missile. This provided an optimum flight path to the second missile, while preventing the target ship from detecting it by radar emissions. Only in the final phase of the attack would the second missile activate its terminal homing radar. In this scheme—given the NATO code name Theodolite—the lead missile's transponder enabled the VDL system to identify the position of the in-flight missile as well as the launch platform, thereby establishing accurate relative positions for targeting subsequent missiles. This obviated the then-difficult task of providing the precise geographic locations of both the launch platform and the over-the-horizon target.

The first successful submarine P-6/SS-N-3a test launches were conducted by a Project 675/Echo II in July-September 1963. Modified Tupolev Tu-16RT (NATO Badger) aircraft provided the long-range targeting for the tests. The missile became operational on submarines in 1963; it was believed to be the world's first submarine-launched anti-ship missile.

In service the offboard targeting for the surface ship– and submarine-launched Shaddock anti-ship missiles initially was generated by Tu-95 (NATO Bear-D) aircraft fitted with the Big Bulge surveillance and targeting radar.[5] Subsequently, Shaddock anti-ship targeting came from satellite systems. (The Kamov Ka-25—NATO Hormone-B—helicopter also was employed for target detection and missile guidance; that coaxial-rotor helicopter went to sea on board Soviet destroyers, cruisers, and aircraft carriers that had anti-ship missiles.)

★   ★   ★

The anti-ship Shaddock could carry a conventional warhead of 2,200 pounds or a tactical nuclear weapon; deployed submarines carried both. The first P-6 missiles were installed in submarines of Project 675/Echo II and Project 651/Juliett classes. These boats also could carry the P-5 land-attack cruise missile, but few if any of the Echo II SSGNs, and no Juliett SSGs, appear to have deployed with that weapon.

★   ★   ★

Design work for Project 675—the Echo II SSGN—began in 1958; this was an eight-missile Shaddock submarine with a submerged displacement of 5,737 tons, a length

The Soviet Navy stressed surface-to-surface missiles during the Cold War. This is a Kynda-class cruiser, the first major surface missile ship of the "new" Soviet fleet. There were banks of four Shaddock missile tubes forward and amidships, with reloads in the adjacent superstructures—a total of 16 missiles. The following Kresta I class had only four Shaddock tubes with no reloads; subsequent Soviet "cruisers" stressed anti-submarine capabilities. *U.S. Navy*

of 378½ feet, and a first-generation nuclear propulsion plant. Again, the missiles were launched while the submarine was on the surface with eight stowage-launch canisters fitted in the deck casing. The paired canisters elevated 15 degrees to fire forward. The Echo II (and Juliett SSG) cruise missile submarines had an enlarged sail structure containing a large folding radar, which led to the ship's nickname "*raskladyshka*" (folding bed). When surfaced, the submarine would expose the massive radar antennas by rotating the forward portion of the sail structure 180 degrees (the NATO designation for the radar was Front Door/Front Piece).[6]

The lead Echo II, the *K-1*, was placed in commission on 31 October 1963. A total of 29 units were produced through 1968, built at the massive Severodvinsk shipyard in the north and the Leninskiy Komsomol shipyard in the Far East. Components of the cancelled Project 658 (Hotel) ballistic missile submarines are reported to have been shifted to this SSGN program when the construction of the latter had been halted.

The nuclear-propelled Project 675/Echo II was the definitive Shaddock-armed submarine, with eight missiles housed in paired storage-launch canisters. Originally intended for the land-attack role, these submarines were fitted with radars and guidance equipment for employing their missiles against surface ships.

An Echo II submarine with her forward pair of Shaddock missile canisters in the raised/launch position. This large class of 29 submarines, as well as the 16 diesel-electric Project 651/Juliett had rotating guidance/tracking radius in the forward end of their conning towers.

The Echo II SSGNs and Juliett SSGs were employed extensively in Soviet long-range operations, regularly deploying to the Mediterranean and as far as the Caribbean. The second Soviet naval visit to Cuba after the missile crisis of 1962 occurred in May 1970: the ships included two Foxtrot-class diesel submarines and an Echo II. Whereas nuclear torpedoes were carried in most if not all Soviet combat submarines by that time, the SSGNs were armed with nuclear as well as conventional Shaddock missiles. The arrival of a nuclear-propelled submarine with nuclear missiles in a Cuban port was a significant "escalation" of Soviet naval presence in the Western Hemisphere.

Diesel-Electric Submarines

The Project 651 diesel-electric missile submarine (NATO Juliett) was put into production almost simultaneously with the building of the Echo II nuclear submarines. The non-nuclear craft, 281¾ feet long and displacing 4,260 tons submerged, borrowed many design features from the highly successful Project 641 (NATO Foxtrot) torpedo-attack submarine. Its missile armament consisted of four P-6 Shaddock canisters, paired in the same manner as in the Echo SSGNs and, like them, firing forward.

The construction of non-nuclear cruise missile submarines (SSGs) apparently was undertaken at that time for two reasons. First, diesel submarines were cheaper to produce and operate, about one-third the cost of nuclear-propelled units, according to U.S. intelligence.[7] Second, the Soviets may have concluded that these diesel submarines might be needed in case of setbacks in their nuclear program, of which the difficulties with the first-generation submarines gave warning. The problems with early Soviet nuclear submarines undoubtedly influenced the decision to proceed with the Juliett program.

Seventy-two Juliett SSGs were planned at one point. In the event, only 16 were completed from 1963 to 1968, the first two at the Baltic Shipyard in Leningrad and the others at the Krasnoye Sormovo yard, inland at Gor'kiy (now Nizhny Novgorod, on the Volga River[8]). As did the Echo II submarines, these craft each had a large, rotating radar in the leading edge of their sails; one of the class later had a satellite targeting system fitted. The first few Julietts were built with low-magnetic steel. Those units soon suffered significant corrosion damage as well as cracks, hence the later submarines were of standard steel construction.

The building of diesel-electric SSGs in parallel with nuclear SSGNs also may have occurred because of limitations on the production capacity for nuclear propulsion plants. A small nuclear reactor—designated VAU-6—was developed to serve as an auxiliary power source in diesel-electric submarines. This was a pressurized-water reactor with a single-loop configuration coupled with a turbogenerator. Following land trials it was installed in one Juliett (Project 651E) during 1986–1991. The sea trials demonstrated the feasibility of the system but revealed several deficiencies. These problems later were corrected, still no additional Juliett SSGs were fitted with this system.

In 1960, on the basis of the Juliett SSG, the Project 683 nuclear-propelled submarine was designed, also to carry the P-5/P-6 missiles. This was to have been a larger craft, with more weapons, propelled (at slow speeds) by two small, 7,000-horsepower reactor plants. This design was not further pursued.

The diesel-electric Project 651/Juliett cruise missile submarine was a trim-looking craft, in some respects resembling a shrunken Echo II SSGN. There is a sonar dome visible on her bow, and her snorkel exhaust is visible at the after end of the sail structure. *U.K. Ministry of Defence*

A Juliett cruise missile submarine with her after pair of Shaddock missile launchers in the raised/firing position. The second pair of launchers is immediately forward of the sail structure.

Rather, the next Soviet cruise missile submarine was Project 670 (NATO Charlie). This submarine, which first went to sea in 1967, had the P-70 *Ametist* (SS-N-7 Starbright) anti-ship missile. Starbright was in itself a revolution in naval warfare—the world's first underwater-launched cruise missile. Each Charlie SSGN carried eight anti-ship missiles in addition to torpedoes. Seventeen submarines of that class were built through 1980.[9] Subsequent Soviet SSGNs, including the Project 661 (NATO Papa), the world's fastest submarine, also carried submerged-launch anti-ship missiles. By 1960 ten SSGNs of the Papa class were planned, but in the event only one was completed, the *K-162* (later *K-222*) in 1969. While the titanium-hulled Papa could carry eight of the new P-120 anti-ship missiles and achieved 44.7 knots on her trials, the cost was considered too great for series production, and more-capable submarines were in the offing. In the event, at the time, all of these submarines carried only anti-ship missiles—apparently with conventional and possibly nuclear warheads.

Soviet shipyards built or converted a total of 61 submarines—27 diesel-electric and 34 nuclear-propelled—armed with Shaddock missiles (see table 12-1); this was in contrast to the five U.S. submarines that went to sea armed with the Regulus cruise missile.

A U.S. intelligence evaluation of the Soviet cruise missile program in 1968 observed, "In 1963, when the [Soviet] Navy regained the strategic strike mission, the [Echo]-class program was phased out and the [Yankee]-class ballistic missile submarine program was initiated. The timing of these construction programs and the changes in mission are among the factors that indicate the Soviets do not intend to use the [Echo]-class in the primary mission of strategic strike."[10] A contemporary Central Intelligence Agency assessment argued, "The cruise-missile submarines have a primary mission against naval ships, especially carrier task forces. They could also be used against land

Table 12-1. Shaddock-Armed Missile Submarines

Project	Submarine	Number as SSG/SSGN	Completed	Shaddock Missiles
P613	SSG Whiskey mod.★	1	1957	1
644	SSG Whiskey mod.★★	4	1960	2
665	SSG Whiskey mod.★★★	6	1961	4
659	SSGN Echo I	5	1961	6
675	SSGN Echo II	29	1963	8
651	SSG Juliett	16	1963	4

★ Whiskey Single-Cylinder
★★ Whiskey Twin-Cylinder
★★★ Whiskey Long-Bin

targets, but we believe that the Soviet requirement for such employment is becoming increasingly marginal."[11]

Still, after the P-5 land-attack Shaddocks were removed from submarines, the last "beached" by 1965, concern continued among some U.S. naval officers that these submarines could pose a strategic threat to the United States. For example, late in 1968 the director of U.S. Navy strategic systems, Rear Admiral George H. Miller, stated that while the U.S. Intelligence Community's threat calculations did not address submarine-launched cruise missiles, those weapons "become doubly suspect when, under certain scenarios, the U.S. must rely on SAC [Strategic Air Command] bombers for a part of the Assured Destruction role, since the 450-nautical-mile range of the SS-N-3 cruise missile launched from the 1,000 fathom curve around the CONUS [Continental United States] could reach 20 of 34 CONUS SAC bases with a high probability of surprise attack."[12]

In time, most of the Juliett and Echo II submarines were rearmed with the P-500 *Bazalt* (basalt) missile (NATO SS-N-12 Sandbox) that enhanced their effectiveness in the anti-ship role. The missile, which became operational in 1975, had a range of some 400 n.miles with a conventional or nuclear warhead.

Launching from Land

Coastal fortifications in Russia date to the 14th century, after which, over time, they were established along the Baltic, Black Sea, and Caspian coasts. Whereas most countries— including the United States—had discarded coastal fortifications by the end of World War II, a few nations retained such installations, especially in the Baltic area. Thus, in the postwar era the Soviet Union maintained coastal artillery and by the early 1950s was adapting air- and land-launched anti-ship missiles for the coastal defense role. The forces responsible for coastal defense were (and are) a component of the Navy.

Unlike the U.S. land-based cruise missiles that were produced during the Cold War for attacking the Soviet and Chinese homelands, these missiles were deployed specifically for coastal defense. They are important to the account of land-attack cruise missiles because of their origins and their contribution to cruise missile development.[13]

In several respects the most significant of these Soviet coastal defense cruise missiles was the FKR-1—in Russian, *frontovaya krylataya raketa* (frontline combat rocket), given the NATO designation SSC-2a Salish. This weapon was adapted from the Soviet air-launched KS-1 *Komet* (NATO AS-1 Kennel), whose basic configuration was derived from the MiG-15 turbojet fighter. The FKR-1, an aircraft-launched, anti-ship missile, was powered by a reverse-engineered Rolls-Royce engine and flew at Mach 0.9 speeds for a distance of some 60 miles.[14] The missile carried a 1,320-pound conventional, armor-piercing warhead.

During the Cuban missile crisis of October–November 1962, the Soviet merchant ship *Indigirka* delivered 80 warheads for FKR cruise missiles to Cuba—*each with a nuclear payload of up to 14 kilotons*. These land-launched missiles, with a range of about 90 miles, were to be used against amphibious forces approaching the Cuban coast in the event of an American invasion attempt.[15] The presence of these weapons in Cuba was completely unknown to American political officials and military leaders.[16]

Also significant from a naval perspective, the widely proliferated P-5 Shaddock missile also was employed in the coastal defense role by the Soviet Union, as well as by several Eastern bloc and other allied nations. These land-launched weapons were designated SPU-35V *Redut* (NATO SSC-1 Sepal). The Soviet missiles were mounted on eight-wheel transporter-launch vehicles; coastal defense battalions each had an estimated 15 to 18 missiles. These weapons had a range of some 300 miles.

(Soviet and now Russian coastal defense forces have continued to operate long-range artillery as well as anti-aircraft guns and missiles to defend coastal areas. These forces also operate fixed and mobile radar installations.)

Upgrading Older Submarines
Development of the P-700 *Granit* (granite) anti-ship cruise missile (NATO SS-N-19 Shipwreck) was begun in 1967 to replace the Shaddock as a long-range, anti-carrier weapon. The Granit would be a much larger, faster, more-capable weapon, and in contrast to the Shaddock it would have the valuable characteristic of submerged launch. Being supersonic, the missile would not require mid-course guidance corrections as did the Shaddock. The new weapon's range was reported as approximately 300 n.miles with a conventional warhead and 340 nautical miles with a nuclear warhead; with an advanced turbojet engine its speed would be Mach 2.5 at altitude, slowing to Mach 1.5 as the missile approached the target at low level. The missile would be targeted against Western aircraft carriers through links to Radar Ocean Reconnaissance Satellites (RORSATs). The SS-N-19 Shipwreck also was carried by the four *Kirov*-class nuclear-propelled battle cruisers, as well as by the aircraft carrier *Admiral Kuznetsov*.

A short time later, design work on an associated cruise missile submarine began at the Rubin bureau, which had designed most of the earlier SSG/SSGNs. The possibility of placing the Granit on Project 675/Echo II SSGNs had been considered, but the size and capabilities of the missile required a new submarine, which became the Project 949 (NATO Oscar). The decision to arm the Oscar SSGN with 24 missiles—three times as many as the Echo II—meant that the new submarine would be very large. This was a third-generation nuclear "attack" submarine; after the Project 941/Typhoon SSBN, it would be the world's largest undersea craft. The missiles were placed in angled launch canisters between the pressure hull and outer hull, 12 per side. As a consequence, the submarine would have the nickname "*baton*" (loaf), by virtue of its broad beam, 59 feet—a beam that in turn would require a length of 472 feet. (Although the Oscar was not as long as U.S. Trident ballistic missile submarines, its greater beam and double-hull configuration meant that the submarine would have a submerged displacement of 22,500 tons, some 20 percent more than the Trident SSBNs.)

Aside from their 24 large anti-ship missiles, the Oscar SSGNs, which remain in service, have four 21-inch (533-mm) and four 26½-inch (650-mm) torpedo tubes that can launch a variety of torpedoes and tube-launched missiles.[17] The large size of the

Oscar and the need for a speed of at least 30 knots to engage U.S. aircraft carriers required nuclear propulsion, a twin-reactor plant producing 100,000 horsepower, according to published reports. This nuclear plant and the similar Typhoon SSBN propulsion plant are the most powerful propulsion systems ever installed in submarines.[18]

The keel for the lead ship of this class was laid down at Severodvinsk on 25 June 1978; she was commissioned on 30 December 1980, as the *Minskiy Komsomolets* (K-525).[19] Series production followed. Beginning with the third unit, the design was lengthened to 508 $\frac{1}{3}$ feet, producing the Project 949A/Oscar II variant. The additional space was primarily for acoustic quieting and the improved MGK-540 sonar. The changes increased the surface displacement by some 1,300 tons. These SSGNs—as well as other Soviet/Russian third-generation submarines—are still considered to be extremely quiet in comparison with previous Soviet-era undersea craft.

While the Granit was developed as an anti-ship weapon, the missile apparently also had a land-attack capability. The massive Oscars themselves, while developed specially for the

A nuclear-propelled Project 949A/Oscar II in rough seas in 1991. These SSGNs were the world's second largest undersea craft after the Project 941/Typhoon ballistic missile submarines. The submarine's upper rudder is topped by the towed-array sonar tube. *U.S. Navy*

The Oscar cruise missile submarine has six large hatches on each side of the outer hull with two launch tubes for the SS-N-19 Shipwreck anti-ship missile under each hatch in the original configuration; that weapon retained a land-attack capability. Some Oscar-class units have been refitted with the Kalibr missiles.

anti-carrier role, were assessed to have the potential to carry other land-attack missiles. This was confirmed in the early 21st century when several units were modified to carry the missiles of the *Kalibr* (caliber) series, with variants for the anti-ship and land-attack roles (see below).

The large size and cost of these submarines led to debates within the Soviet Navy over means of countering U.S. aircraft carriers and the need for large, specialized cruise missile submarines. As many as 20 submarines of Project 949 were being considered. When, in the early 1990s, the head of the Rubin design bureau, Academician Igor D. Spassky, was asked how many Oscar SSGNs would be constructed, his reply was, "Tell me how many aircraft carriers the U.S. Navy will have and that will be the number."[20] According to some sources, the cost of each Oscar SSGN was about one-half that of an aircraft carrier of the *Admiral Kuznetsov* class.[21] Two Russian naval officer–historians, Captains 1st Rank V. P. Kuzin and V. I. Nikol'skiy, wrote, "It is obvious . . . [that] the ideological development of the [SSGN], namely Project 949, over-stepped the limits of sensible thought and logic."[22]

Disaster at Sea

On 12 August 2000, as Russian naval forces held exercises in the Barents Sea—reportedly in preparation for a deployment to the Mediterranean—a unit of the Oscar class, the *Kursk* (K-141), suffered two violent explosions while at periscope depth. They tore open her bow and sent the giant submarine plunging to the ocean floor, a depth of 355 feet. All 118 men on board died, 23 of them in after compartments surviving for some hours, perhaps a day or two, before they succumbed to cold, pressure, rising water, and asphyxiation. The *Kursk* was the fifth Soviet/Russian nuclear-propelled submarine to be lost.[23] (The United States had lost two nuclear submarines—*Thresher*/SSN 593 and *Scorpion*/SSN 589.) The *Kursk* was the world's largest nuclear submarine to be lost and, after that of the *Thresher,* her loss was the worst such disaster in terms of casualties.[24]

The apparent cause of the disaster was a low-order torpedo fuel explosion in the foremost (torpedo) compartment, followed two minutes, 15 seconds later by the massive detonation of torpedo warheads.[25] The four previous Soviet nuclear-propelled submarines that had sunk at sea had suffered casualties while submerged, but had been able to reach the surface and remain afloat long enough for some or all of their crews to escape and be rescued by ships. The massive torpedo explosions within the *Kursk* made it impossible for the damaged hull to surface.

Post-disaster analysis indicated that the first explosion had been the equivalent of some 220 pounds of TNT and the second, 22,000 pounds of TNT.[26] (In a remarkable salvage operation, the *Kursk* was lifted from the ocean floor and towed into a floating dry dock in October 2001; subsequently she was scrapped.)

★   ★   ★

Through 1997, the Severodvinsk shipyard completed 14 Oscar-class SSGNs—2 Project 949 and 12 Project 949A submarines. These boats periodically undertook long-range operations, a concern to the U.S. Navy because they posed a major threat to U.S. aircraft carriers and other surface forces, because of their missile armament and also their stealth—their acoustic quieting made them difficult to detect and track. The massive investment in these submarines demonstrated the continuing Soviet concern about countering U.S. aircraft carriers as well as strategic missile submarines.

Two decades later, in 2017, it was announced that the eight Oscar SSGNs remaining in service would be rearmed with Kalibr missiles for the anti-ship *and* the land-attack roles.

A Change of Course

The cruise missile situation began to change radically with development of a weapon that could be launched from standard, 21-inch submarine torpedo tubes. First came the Soviet RK-55 Granat (NATO SS-N-21 Sampson), "created as an analog of the U.S. Tomahawk strategic cruise missile" for the land-attack role.[27] It had a similar, turbofan propulsion plant (plus rocket booster) and an identical control system—inertial guidance with, over land, corrections based on terrain relief. Further, this was the first Soviet naval missile developed within rigid size restrictions—the 21-inch (533-mm) torpedo tube. The missile had a subsonic speed, a maximum range of some 1,600 n.miles, and a conventional or nuclear warhead.

The torpedo tube–launched missile was one of a "family" of weapons. The Relief (NATO SSC-4 Slingshot) was a land-launched missile with a nuclear warhead. It was about to enter Soviet service in 1987 (see page 156) when it was discarded, being banned under the U.S.-Soviet Intermediate-range Nuclear Forces (INF) treaty.[28] The range of the land-launched missile was estimated in various publications at 1,550 to 1,860 miles; its length was reported as 26½ feet, including a rocket booster, its diameter just over 20 inches—an impressive weapon. The SSC-4 was to have been fired from a four-canister launcher fitted on a truck, an arrangement analogous to the U.S. Ground-Launched Cruise Missile (GLCM) derivative of the Tomahawk land-attack missile. An air-launched variant also was developed—the NATO AS-15 Kent—for carriage by the Tu-95MS/Bear-H and Tu-160/Blackjack strategic bombers.

Significantly, the land-launched missile was resurrected in the post-Soviet era, and testing began on an updated variant. In 2014, the Barack Obama administration said that these tests were in violation of the INF treaty signed by the U.S. and Soviet governments in 1987. The president sought to persuade the Russians to correct the violation while the missile was still in the test phase. The Russians ignored him and moved ahead, deploying fully operational units with the missile, which was given the NATO designation SSC-8.[29]

An SSC-8 missile battalion is believed to have four mobile launchers and a half-dozen nuclear-armed missiles. Reportedly, in early 2017 there were two SSC-8 battalions, one located at the Russian test site of Kapustin Yar in southern Russia, near Volgograd (formerly Stalingrad), and a second, operational unit. The missile is reported to have a range of at least 1,200 miles, which could easily strike Western European countries and Japan from launchers within Russian territory.

The missile was but the precursor of a new generation of Russian strategic cruise missiles.

★   ★   ★

The nuclear-propelled, strategic missile submarine *K-395,* a Project 667/Yankee completed in 1969, was taken in hand for conversion at the Severodvinsk yard to carry the SS-N-21. The mid-body of the *K-395*—which had accommodated 16 ballistic missile tubes—was replaced by a longer and slightly wider section containing 12 21-inch (533-mm), angled launch tubes in two rows, with space for up to 40 missiles or additional torpedoes. (The submarine retained her four 21-inch bow torpedo tubes.) The submarine was lengthened by an estimated 39 $\frac{1}{3}$ to 465 $\frac{3}{4}$ feet overall, with her amidships beam increased by 3¼ feet to 42 $\frac{2}{3}$.

The *K-395*'s conversion was completed in 1983. The Russians gave the program the name *Grusha* (pear) and Project 667AT, while NATO called it Yankee Notch. Additional Yankee conversions—some sources say a total of eight submarines—appear to have been planned but not undertaken because of the informal U.S.-Soviet agreement in 1991 to remove all nuclear weapons from submarines except for Submarine-Launched Ballistic Missiles (SLBMs). The SS-N-21 also was fitted in several classes of nuclear torpedo-attack submarines:

Project	*NATO*
671RTM	Victor III
945	Sierra
971	Akula
885	*Severodvinsk*★

★ The name of the first unit, used as the reporting name by the United States and NATO.

The subsequent Soviet/Russian land-attack cruise missile that could be launched from submarine torpedo tubes was the Kalibr series. It could be launched from 21-inch torpedo tubes as well as from vertical-launch tubes in surface ships and submarines, and from aircraft. The Kalibr missile "family" consists of two anti-ship, two anti-submarine, and one land-attack variants. The basic 3M-54E1 and 3M-14E most closely resemble the U.S. Navy's anti-ship and land-attack Tomahawk missiles, respectively. The 3M-14E land-attack variant uses the Glonass navigation satellite and inertial guidance, with active radar for terminal guidance against land targets that have sufficient radar contrast; the radar has been credited with a range of about 12 miles. These two missiles have solid-fuel rocket and turbojet engines that provide a cruise speed of Mach 0.9 and supersonic speeds—reported by some sources as up to Mach 3—when approaching the target. The land-attack missile has a range estimated from 930 to 1,550 miles with a conventional warhead of approximately 1,100 pounds or a nuclear warhead.

The NATO code name for some Kalibr variants is Sizzler; the 3M-54E is designated SS-N-27B. Some variants have been made available to other navies; with export missiles designated in the *Klub* (club) series.

Kalibr missiles began entering Russian service in surface ships and submarines in 2012. Sea-launched Kalibr missiles first were used in combat on 7 October 2015, when four Russian surface ships in the Caspian Sea launched 3M-14T missiles at targets in Syria.[30] Those missiles flew more than 900 miles to strike their targets. Subsequently, Russian surface ships in the eastern Mediterranean participated in further Kalibr strikes into Syria. On 9 December 2015, the Project 636.3/Kilo-class submarine *Rostov-on-Don* in the eastern Mediterranean fired four 3M-14K Kalibr missiles into Syria. A diesel-electric submarine, she launched the missiles from her torpedo tubes, as did other Kilo-class submarines in the same area. Torpedo-tube-launched cruise missiles—both anti-ship and land-attack variants—have changed the strike-from-the-sea equation for both the Russian and U.S. Navies.

In the offing for the Russian Navy is the reported 3M-22 *Tsirkon* (zircon) missile, to be launched from the vertical-launch cells in cruisers and submarines. The Tsirkon is a hypersonic missile, reported to have a speed of Mach 5 to 6, achieved with a "scramjet" engine. A scramjet—supersonic combusting ramjet—is a variant of the ramjet air-breathing engine, in which the combustion takes place in the supersonic airflow. This missile achieves hypersonic speeds throughout its flight regime. The range of the missile is estimated at some 250 n.miles. The missile entered sea trials in 2017 and is expected to become operational in the early 2020s.

The post–Soviet era "attack" submarines of Project 885/*Yasen* (ash) design were considered cruise missile submarines from the outset by their designers, who gave them eight large,

The later diesel-electric Project 636/Kilo-class submarines have been armed with the Kalibr land-attack missile launched from torpedo tubes. About 70 submarines of this type have been produced for the Soviet/Russian navies and for several other countries. *Leo van Ginderen Collection*

The *Severodvinsk*, completed in 2014, is the lead submarine of the latest Russian class of nuclear-propelled, torpedo-attack submarines. Amidships she has eight large, vertical-launch cells that can hold 32 of the ubiquitous Kalibr missiles. (This arrangement is similar to the U.S. *Virginia*-class attack submarines beginning with the SSN 802, to be launched in 2021).

vertical missile tubes amidships in addition to a large torpedo battery of eight 21-inch (533-mm) bow tubes.[31] The vertical-launch tubes could accommodate 32 Kalibr-size weapons. And, apparently, cruise missiles also could be launched from the torpedo tubes.

The lead Project 885 submarine, the *Severodvinsk*, was laid down at the massive shipyard of the same name in December 1993, but construction halted soon afterward because of the financial and political chaos in the "new Russia."[32] Construction was eventually resumed, and the lead submarine was placed in commission on 17 June 2014. Although on the building ways for two decades, the submarine was extensively redesigned during that time and the *Severodvinsk* that entered service with the Russian Navy was very different from the ship that was begun two decades earlier. Incorporating a high degree of acoustic and non-acoustic stealth, the *Severodvinsk* is 390 feet long and has a submerged displacement of approximately 13,800 tons. Among her unusual features is a bow sonar dome similar to those in U.S. attack submarines, a first in Russian undersea craft; however, the subsequent submarines of the class are reported to have a different sonar arrangement. The *Severodvinsk*—like other Soviet/Russian nuclear-propelled submarines—has a very high degree of automation: Her crew numbers just over 60 men, less than half the number on board a contemporary U.S. nuclear attack-cruise missile submarine.[33]

Series production of these *Severodvinsk* follow-ons is ongoing. Series production of Kilo-class diesel-electric submarines capable of launching Kalibr cruise missiles from torpedo tubes also continues in Russian shipyards. Those submarines are intended for the Russian Navy and several foreign fleets.

U.S. Cruise Missile Rebirth

AFTER THE REGULUS II MISSILE WAS CANCELLED in December 1958, there were no strategic cruise missiles under development for the U.S. Navy. Almost two decades later, in January 1976, Dr. Henry Kissinger, the U.S. Secretary of State, met with Soviet leaders in Moscow to discuss strategic arms limitations. A key issue was the Soviet plan to produce 300 Tupolev Tu-22M Backfire bombers, a supersonic, variable-sweep-wing aircraft. Although U.S. intelligence officials argued over whether the Backfire was a theater or a strategic (intercontinental) bomber, it unquestionably was a potent nuclear strike vehicle. In response, Kissinger proposed a U.S. force of 375 cruise missiles with nuclear warheads—then called Sea-Launched Cruise Missiles (SLCMs)—that would be carried in surface warships.[1] (Subsequently the term SLCM was used for *submarine-launched cruise missiles.)

Secretary Kissinger's proposal led to interesting controversies in Washington. According to the secretary's memoirs, at a 19 January 1976 meeting General George Brown, the Chairman of the Joint Chiefs of Staff, had given this answer to a direct question posed by President Gerald Ford:[2]

> *Ford:* As a practical matter, how many surface ships do we now have in mind would be deployed with cruise missiles?
> *Brown:* There are more than 200 ships today that could take such cruise missiles.

Forty-eight hours later, according to Kissinger, the Chief of Naval Operations, Admiral James Holloway, acting for the JCS chairman, who was at that moment on travel, "disclaimed any American interest in surface-launched cruise missiles. The Navy, Holloway seemed to be saying, was against any agreement limiting it to 375 surface-launched cruise missiles because it was not planning to build that many, *if any*."[3] [Emphasis added.]

133

A Tomahawk cruise missile in flight. Note the turbofan engine's air scoop under the fuselage. The Tomahawk's wings, fins, and air scoop all extend after the missile begins flight. Thus the missile could be launched directly from the storage tube or canister, as could Soviet cruise missiles. *U.S. Navy*

Sailors and civilian technicians from the submarine tender *Frank Cable* (AS 40) load a Tomahawk missile into the bow vertical-launch cells of the torpedo-attack submarine *Oklahoma City* (SSN 723). In 2020 the U.S. Navy had two submarine tenders in commission, both with composite Navy and civilian crews. *U.S. Navy*

Admiral Holloway, a naval aviator and a former carrier commander, may have been reflecting that community's disdain for land-attack cruise missiles that could threaten the carrier's nuclear strike mission. But a dramatic change of Navy attitudes toward land-attack cruise missiles was in the offing.[4]

Resurrecting the Cruise Missile

A few years earlier—in 1970—a study by the U.S. Center for Naval Analyses (CNA) had suggested that a "revolutionary" underwater-launched cruise missile was feasible. In reality it was hardly that revolutionary: the Soviet Navy had sent to sea the world's first underwater-launched cruise missile in 1967—the P-70 *Ametist* anti-ship missile (U.S.-NATO SS-N-7 Starbright).

Based in part on the CNA study, in January 1972, Secretary of Defense Melvin R. Laird directed that the Navy pursue development of a Strategic Cruise Missile (SCM). The Soviet Navy already had such land-attack cruise missiles while the United States had none. Thus, there was the possibility of getting the Soviet Union to agree to reduce their nuclear cruise missile inventory with a U.S. submarine-launched cruise missile providing a quid pro quo.

Several technology advances came together at the time to facilitate the development of a new land-attack cruise missile in the United States. These included: *guidance, computing power, engines,* and *high-energy fuels.*

In the area of guidance, an early terrain-matching radar navigation system had been installed in the Air Force Mace cruise missile in the late 1950s. Called ATRAN, it had been devised by Goodyear. An advanced ATRAN system was to have been installed in the Navy's Triton supersonic cruise missile, but that missile had been cancelled.

In 1958, Ling-Temco-Vought's subsidiary Electro Systems patented a similar but more capable system called Terrain Contour Matching (TERCOM). This was to have had a key role in Chance Vought's Supersonic Low-Altitude Missile (SLAM). That project, too, was cancelled, in 1959; nevertheless, TERCOM flight testing began that year. The guidance unit was flown in several aircraft: the Beech King Air, Lockheed C-141 Starlifter, Chance Vought A-7 Corsair, and the Boeing B-52 Stratofortress, as well as in unmanned drones.

As for computing power, during this period digital computers were being produced that were smaller, required less electrical power, and had ever increasing data storage capacity.

Meanwhile, relatively small turbojet and turbofan engines existed, having been developed by the Westinghouse Corporation as early as 1945. At that time they had been used in the Navy Gorgon-series air-to-surface missiles. In 1962 the Williams Research Company demonstrated its small WR-2 turbojet, producing 70 pounds of thrust. It was used to power the Canadian USD-501 reconnaissance drone and the American MQM-7 target drone. In 1964 the company proposed a turbofan engine for the "flying belt"—a one-man, strap-on propulsion pack that was to enable an infantryman to move cross-country through the air at a low attitude for a distance of about ten miles. (The flying belt gained a great deal of publicity when it appeared in the James Bond movie

Thunderball, allowing the hero to escape from still another dicey situation.[5]) The Williams WR-19 turbofan emerged from development in 1967. It weighed only 68 pounds and developed 430 pounds of thrust.

In this same period, several firms were developing high-energy fuels. These could provide more power to the advanced engines without major increases in fuel volume.

The upshot of these key technological advances was the emergence during the summer of 1973 of two strategic cruise missile development programs within the U.S. Defense Department:

- Air Force: Air-Launched Cruise Missile (ALCM)
    Boeing AGM-86B
    General Dynamics BGM-109
- Navy: Submarine-Launched Cruise Missile (SLCM)
    General Dynamics BGM-109
    Ling-Tempo-Vought BGM-110

The Defense Department directed that the two services cooperate in developing key components of their missiles. The Air Force contributed the turbofan engine and high-energy fuel, while the Navy provided the TERCOM guidance system. In December 1973, Deputy Secretary of Defense William P. Clements directed the Navy to conduct a fly-off competition between the BGM-109 and BGM-110. The two missiles were similar functionally but differed in several important details. The General Dynamics BGM-109 missile had wings that deployed scissors-fashion through slots in the fuselage after the airframe left the water, as well as four pop-out tail fins. The Ling-Temco-Vought BGM-110 missile had a single fiberglass wing that pivoted out above the missile body after leaving the water and three wrap-around tail fins that rotated to an open, locked position.

Two submerged launch tests were conducted with each missile to determine how well it could transition from underwater launch to flight. In February 1976, the General Dynamics BGM-109 completed two flawless trials. However, the Ling-Temco-Vought BGM-110 trials did not go as well. The first attempt failed due to a torpedo tube malfunction, for which the Navy accepted responsibility. During the second trial the one-piece wing failed to deploy. On 8 March 1976, the Navy ended the trials for the BGM-110, because of the wing failure and development cost overruns. On 17 March 1976, General Dynamics was awarded a contract to produce the BGM-109 Tomahawk land-attack cruise missile, and the Williams Company was awarded a contract to supply the F107-WR-100 turbofan engine.

Later that month the first air launch and free flight of a Tomahawk missile took place from an Air Force B-52 Stratofortress bomber. The air-launched Tomahawk was in competition with the Boeing AGM-86B for Air Force service. In March 1980, the Air Force awarded Boeing a contract for 3,418 AGM-86B air-launched cruise missiles to be carried by B-52 bombers. The ALCM would become operational in December 1982.

A Navy A-6 Intruder carries an air-launched Tomahawk missile under its right wing. The Tomahawk was proposed to the Air Force as an air-launched weapon, but was rejected, primarily because it was "not invented here." "PMTC" on the aircraft indicates Pacific Missile Test Center. *U.S. Navy*

But as late as 1982 there still were discussions in the Navy of the possibility of adapting air-launched Tomahawk missiles; A-6 Intruder aircraft had test launched them successfully. The naval aviation community—again—was adamantly against the air-launched Tomahawk, as they had been against the ship-launched variants. At a naval aviation symposium in San Diego in July 1982, one Navy pilot—commenting on the Navy leadership's support of an air-launched Tomahawk—declared, "When officers go back across the Mississippi [from San Diego to Washington] they seem to have their brains removed."[6] Several of the aviators complained that the Tomahawk was too slow and too vulnerable to air defenses to be an effective weapon. The Navy air-launched variant was not pursued.

A key factor in the U.S. development of sea-based cruise missiles was the appointment of Admiral Elmo R. Zumwalt as Chief of Naval Operations; he took office in July 1970. Earlier, in 1960–1961, he had commanded the guided missile frigate *Dewey* (DLG 14), armed with Terrier anti-aircraft missiles. Taking the *Dewey* into the Baltic and encountering Soviet warships, Zumwalt had complained that he felt "naked" without a surface-to-surface missile.[7]

Admiral Zumwalt had served as head of the Navy's Systems Analysis Division in OpNav from 1966 to 1968, and there he had directed the study that led to the Harpoon.

An anti-ship cruise missile that would become operational in 1977, Harpoon was intended to be launched from aircraft, submarines, and surface ships. Zumwalt later wrote that the most significant "string" attached to the Harpoon study "was the verbal message relayed to me . . . [that the missile] was to have a range of no more than fifty miles if it was to be acceptable to the CNO. Evidently the naval aviation community still was nervous about its prerogatives."[8] The Harpoon had a range of 60 miles.

★   ★   ★

In April 1971, the Naval Air Systems Command (NavAir)—responsible for aircraft development—proposed a 30-inch-diameter, 300- to 500-n.mile-range cruise missile, to be launched by a new class of cruise missile submarines, each with 20 launch tubes. The concept, referred to as the Submarine Tactical Anti-ship Weapon System, would be based on anti-ship missiles. The NavAir report recommended a vertical launch system for the new cruise missile, leaving the submarine's standard torpedo tubes for ASW torpedoes and other weapons.

Secretary of Defense Laird said publicly that the missiles would have a range of about 100 miles to hit enemy ships or targets along the shore.[9] By late 1971, the Navy was considering two parallel, submarine-launched cruise missile programs: the short-range, encapsulated Harpoon, and the long-range Advanced Cruise Missile (ACM). Both missiles were intended for the anti-ship role. The latter was also called the Submarine Tactical Missile (STAM).

In the late 1960s the Navy and some members of Congress—at the urging of then–Vice Admiral H. G. Rickover—advocated a large "tactical cruise missile submarine." This would be a large, nuclear-propelled submarine armed primarily with long-range anti-ship missiles. Although specifically intended for the anti-ship role, obviously the submarine could be armed with land-attack missiles.

In reality, Admiral Rickover supported the new cruise missile submarine—soon given the label "AHPNAS," for Advanced High-Performance Nuclear Attack Submarine—as a vehicle for developing a new, large (60,000-horsepower) nuclear reactor plant. Carrying 20 weapons in vertical-launch tubes plus torpedo tubes, the proposed SSGN would have about twice the displacement of the *Los Angeles* (SSN 688) attack submarines (which had 30,000-horsepower nuclear plants) then under construction and would cost about 50 percent more than the $300 million for the SSN. The AHPNAS reactor plant would drive the submarine at 30-plus knots. Design of the submarine began in 1970, and the preliminary design was completed by 1972.

Admiral Rickover told Congress that the AHPNAS program was the "single most important tactical development effort the Navy must undertake."[10] He also argued that

> the cruise missile would provide a totally new dimension in submarine offensive capability. In essence, the U.S. submarine would have the ability to react quickly, to engage the enemy on the submarine's own terms, and to press this initiative until each

unit had been successfully attacked, regardless of the speed and tactics of the enemy. The very existence of this advanced high-performance nuclear attack submarine would constitute a threat to both the naval and merchant arms of any maritime force. . . .

The submarine could act as an escort operating well ahead of a high-speed carrier task force, clearing an ocean area of enemy missile ships. . . . Employed in the role of an escort for combatants or merchant ships, the advanced high-performance submarine could operate independently or in conjunction with other escort vessels.

Admiral Zumwalt, who had become Chief of Naval Operations (CNO) in July 1970, opposed the AHPNAS concept. First, Zumwalt feared that the large SSGN if produced in significant numbers would ravage the shipbuilding budget. Second, as a surface warfare specialist (the first to serve as CNO since Arleigh Burke in 1955–1962), Zumwalt wanted to place offensive strike capability in cruisers and destroyers as well as in submarines. At the time, the Navy's only long-range strike force—beyond the range of naval guns—consisted of the strike aircraft on 15 large aircraft carriers. He promoted placing the Harpoon anti-ship missile and the new SLCM in surface ships.

Despite Rickover's almost unprecedented skill in garnering congressional support for his programs, by the early 1970s his power base had eroded to the extent that he was unable to initiate the new reactor program—his most ambitious to date. In 1972, at Admiral Zumwalt's direction, the Navy dropped the concept but continued its separate strategic (Tomahawk) and tactical (Harpoon) cruise missile programs. This decision ended all thought at the time for a new class of SSGNs. Both types of cruise missiles would be launched from the torpedo tubes of attack submarines (SSN). The first flights of the Harpoon occurred that December, and the missile became operational in surface ships, submarines, and aircraft beginning in 1977.[11]

In November 1972, the Navy rejected other long-range missile options in favor of the Tomahawk SLCM, which would be launched from surface ships and—at Admiral Zumwalt's personal insistence—from existing submarine torpedo tubes (and could be handled by existing torpedo loading equipment). This limited the missile to a 21-inch diameter, a length of less than 20½ feet, and a weight under 4,200 pounds.

The *Los Angeles* SSNs then in production had four 21-inch torpedo tubes and space for 21 reloads. Carrying, for example, eight Tomahawk cruise missiles would leave 17 spaces for torpedoes, SUBROC anti-submarine (nuclear) rockets, and Harpoon short-range missiles. Of the only four launch tubes, probably two would always be loaded with torpedoes in case a Soviet submarine was encountered, leaving at most two tubes for launching missiles. Could these limitations be overcome?

In one of the most innovative submarine design schemes of the era, engineers at the Electric Boat shipyard in Groton, Connecticut, proposed reducing some of the forward

A submarine-launched Tomahawk cruise missile scores a direct hit on a target structure on San Clemente Island off the California coast during a test flight. The missile was launched from a submarine more than 400 miles off the coast. The conventional-warhead TLAM has proven to be extremely accurate in tests as well as in combat. *U.S. Department of Defense*

ballast tank volume in *Los Angeles* SSNs and fitting 12 vertical-launch tubes for Tomahawk missiles, for a 50 percent increase in total weapons in the submarines. Admiral Rickover had rejected this proposal, preferring his AHPNAS cruise missile submarine. But the AHPNAS program ended in 1974 and with it died his large reactor project. (A smaller version became the S8G reactor plant in the Trident ballistic missile submarines.)

With Tomahawk in development for large-scale production and the AHPNAS program ended, the decision was made in the late 1970s—shortly before Rickover's own removal on 31 January 1982—to pursue the vertical-launch configuration for submarines. Beginning with the USS *Providence* (SSN 719), commissioned in 1985, 12 vertical-launch tubes for Tomahawk were installed in each *Los Angeles*–class submarine. They were fitted in the forward, non-pressure hull, between the sonar dome and the pressure hull.[12] There were modifications to the submarines' mechanical and electrical systems, as well as to their combat control system; however, in perspective the modifications were relatively minor. The second submarine with vertical-launch tubes, the USS *Pittsburgh* (SSN 720), made the first vertical launch of a Tomahawk—an anti-ship variant—on 26 November 1986, on the Navy's Atlantic weapons training range.

The torpedo-attack submarine *Santa Fe* (SSN 763) with the hatches for six of her 12 Tomahawk vertical-launch cells open. These later *Los Angeles*–class submarines had the launch cells installed in their forward ballast tank area, aft of their bow sonar dome, with minimal impact on the submarines. *U.S. Navy*

Twenty-three submarines of the 62 ships of the *Los Angeles* design were constructed with vertical-launch tubes; these were followed by the *Virginia* (SSN 774) class, also fitted with 12 vertical-launch tubes for Tomahawk in addition to four 21-inch torpedo tubes. The latter class remained in production when this volume went to press.

The Tomahawk Missile

Although Tomahawk had begun life as a nuclear land-attack weapon, the first cruise missile in the Tomahawk "family" was the Tomahawk Anti-Ship Missile (TASM). With a range of some 250 n.miles and a 1,000-pound conventional warhead, TASM used an inertial navigation system and a terminal radar seeker for attacking surface ships. It became operational on surface ships in 1982 and on submarines in 1983.[13]

The destroyer *Merrill* (DD 976) was fitted with the first Tomahawk installation in October 1982, for at sea evaluation; the battleship *New Jersey* (BB 62) was the second ship receiving the Tomahawk, in March 1983. These Tomahawk missiles were deployed in Armored Box Launchers (ABLs) on the *New Jersey* and the three other *Iowa* (BB 61)–class battleships, which were reactivated from the reserve fleet in the 1980s by

A Tomahawk is fired from an Armored Box Launcher (ABL) on the anti-submarine destroyer *Merrill* (DD 976). These launchers were installed in a large number of U.S. battleships, cruisers, and destroyers, with minimal impact on the ships' configuration. *U.S. Navy*

An *Iowa* (BB 61)-class battleship launches a Tomahawk cruise missile during an exercise, demonstrating the warship's long-range strike capability. In comparison, her main battery of nine 16-inch/50-caliber (406-mm) guns has a range of about 24 nautical miles. The four *Iowa*-class battleships were reactivated during the Reagan administration (1981–1988) and deactivated in 1990–1992. *U.S. Navy*

John Lehman, then Secretary of the Navy; the ABLs also were fitted in five cruisers and in seven destroyers. Each ABL held four Tomahawks, providing 32 missiles per battleship (plus 16 Harpoons) and eight Tomahawks per cruiser and destroyer (plus eight Harpoons on those ships).

A major breakthrough in the Tomahawk cruise missile program occurred when the Navy developed the Vertical Launch System (VLS) for surface ships and, later, as described above, for submarines. The surface ship VLS "cells" could hold Tomahawk missiles as well as the various Standard surface-to-air and other missiles. Designated Mark 41, the VLS cells soon were being installed in 22 of the new-construction cruisers of the *Ticonderoga* (CG 47) class and all destroyers of the *Arleigh Burke* (DDG 51) class—122 and 96 cells, respectively. These cruisers and destroyers, fitted with the advanced Aegis air defense system, carry both anti-air and anti-ballistic missile weapons in the VLS, with only a fraction of their "loadout" devoted to Tomahawks.

The vertical-launch system for U.S. Navy surface ships consists of eight-cell modules. These two modules were being installed in a *Spruance* (DD 963)–class destroyer at the Ingalls shipyard in Pascagoula, Mississippi. The first VLS modules were installed in the Aegis test ship *Norton Sound* (AVM 1). *Litton Ingalls Shipbuilding*

A canister containing a Tomahawk missile being lowered from the submarine tender *Emory S. Land* (AS 38) is mated to an amidships vertical-launch cell on the guided missile destroyer *Benfold* (DDG 65). The loading took place at Guam. Note the destroyer's quad-mounted Harpoon missile launchers and the Phalanx gun system *(far right)*. *U.S. Navy*

A sailor checks the vertical-launch cells on the Aegis cruiser *Hue City* (CG 66). The VLS cells are fitted in eight-unit modules in cruisers and destroyers. The Aegis system in these ships is the world's most advanced air defense system; it also has been installed ashore in Europe. *U.S. Navy*

The missiles that the Mark 41 launcher could accommodate in addition to the various Tomahawk variants were:

ASROC anti-submarine rocket
Evolved Sea Sparrow surface-to-air (quad pack)
Sea Sparrow surface-to-air
Standard Strike land attack
Standard surface-to-air/anti-ballistic

Also, the "modular" nature of the VLS permitted the removal of the ASROC anti-submarine rocket launcher and magazine from 26 *Spruance* (DD 963)–class ASW destroyers and the installation in their place of a 61-cell VLS. Not having the Aegis anti-air system, these ships carried only Tomahawk missiles.

The advantages of VLS over previous, above-deck launchers were significant. The VLS alleviated the need to move the missile from a magazine onto a launcher and to then train the launcher; a missile that failed to launch did not have to be jettisoned overboard; and essentially all missiles in the VLS magazine were available for launching without having to move them.

In addition, the reactivated battleships were considered for VLS magazines for Tomahawk missiles. It was envisioned that in a "second phase" modernization of the dreadnoughts the after turret of three 16-inch (406-mm) guns would be removed and VLS for Tomahawks installed in its place.[14] (The ships would retain their two forward, three-gun 16-inch turrets.)

Such a modification would be complex and expensive: removing the massive after turret meant major work, including reballasting the ships to compensate for removal of the 1,700-ton turret and its ammunition. In any case, the second phase modernization was never undertaken. Secretary Lehman stepped down in 1987, and the *Iowas*—expensive to man and to operate—were decommissioned in 1990–1992 and turned into museums.

. . . and Under the Sea

Meanwhile, submarines were being armed with Tomahawk TASMs. A missile was successfully launched from the torpedo tubes of the nuclear-propelled attack submarine *Barb* (SSN 596) on 1 February 1978; the *Guitarro* (SSN 665) became the first submarine to go to sea armed with Tomahawks in 1983. A total of 23 Improved *Los Angeles*–class submarines went to sea with 12 Tomahawks in their forward VLS cells plus, at times, additional Tomahawks in their torpedo rooms for tube launching. For example, in November 1998, the *Miami* (SSN 755), operating in the Persian Gulf, launched 20 Tomahawks from her VLS cells and torpedo tubes at targets in Iraq during the four-day bombing campaign of Operation Desert Fox.

Also, when the first four Trident ballistic missile submarines of the *Ohio* (SSBN 726) class were removed from service because of U.S.-Soviet strategic arms agreements, they were modified between 2003 and 2007 to become cruise missile craft. Each of the four converted submarines was able to carry a maximum of 154 Tomahawk missiles in VLS cells in place of her 24 Trident SLBM tubes.[15] In addition, each submarine was fitted with berthing, messing, and equipment spaces for 66 special operations personnel plus their gear. As SSGNs the submarine could be reconfigured as required by operational requirements at the time to provide:

- Maximum strike—launch tubes No. 3 through 24 could each have "seven-pack" missile canisters; all 154 missiles could be fired in six minutes.
- Strike/special operations—launch tubes No. 5 through 24 could be loaded with 140 missiles; launch tubes No. 3 and 4 could be loaded with special operations stowage canisters; two swimmer delivery vehicles could be carried.
- Strike/special operations—same as above, with launch tubes No. 5 and 6 empty or loaded with additional special operations equipment (these tubes would be blocked by the hangar-like dry deck shelters mounted on the after deck); launch tubes No. 7 through 24 could be loaded with 126 missiles.

With additional, temporary bunks and by bunk sharing ("hot bunking") up to 100 special operations personnel could be accommodated for short periods.

The four oldest *Ohio* (SSBN 726)–class ballistic missile submarines were converted to the SSGN configuration. Each could carry two dry deck shelters aft of their sail structure to accommodate swimmers or a "wet" swimmer delivery vehicle. Vertical-launch Tomahawk cells replaced their ballistic missiles. This is the *Ohio* pulling away from the tender *Emory S. Land* (AS 39), then moored in Malaysian waters, with two shelters fitted. *U.S. Navy*

Navy SEALs huddle together inside a flooded dry deck shelter mounted on the back of the *Los Angeles*–class attack submarine *Philadelphia* (SSN 690). The shelter has a built-in decompression chamber with a hatch providing direct access to the carrying submarine. Only a few of these shelters exist and are carried by converted *Ohio*-class SSGNs as well as a few SSNs. *U.S. Navy*

The four Trident SSBN/SSGN conversions were:

Submarine	Comm. as SSBN	Converted to SSGN
SSBN 726 *Ohio*	1981	2003–2006
SSBN 727 *Michigan*	1982	2003–2006
SSBN 728 *Florida*	1983	2003–2006
SSBN 729 *Georgia*	1984	2004–2007

(An alternative to converting the ex-Trident submarines to the SSGN configuration proposed modifying the *Virginia*/SSN 774 class with the installation of an amidships section containing Tomahawk vertical-launch tubes. While this concept was endorsed by Admiral J. M. Boorda, the Chief of Naval Operations from 1994 to 1996, the nuclear submarine community pushed for the Trident conversions—larger submarines with two crews per submarine.[16] The fitting of VLS cells in attack submarines would have distributed the missile "firepower," made enemy ASW against missile submarines more difficult, and offered other advantages as well. In the event, this SSN missile concept was belatedly adopted with the retirement of the ex-Trident SSGNs; see below.)

A Royal Navy Tomahawk in flight. Great Britain is the only other nation to acquire Tomahawk missiles, although Israel had shown interest in the land-launched or GLCM version of the TLAM. The Royal Navy TLAMs are carried by nuclear-propelled attack submarines. *U.S. Navy*

The Royal Navy initially procured 65 TLAMs from the United States in 1968 and was fitting several nuclear-propelled, torpedo-attack submarines for launching them from their 21-inch torpedo tubes. Subsequently, Britain procured additional TLAMs. In November 1998, HMS *Splendid* attained operational capability with Tomahawk for the Royal Navy, and in March 1999 she launched Tomahawks against Serbian targets during the Kosovo War. She fired 20 Tomahawks during that conflict. She again fired TLAMs in 2003, this time against Iraqi targets in the invasion of Iraq.

As noted above, the *Los Angeles*–class attack submarines were followed into service by the *Virginia* class. The first ten *Virginia* submarines—like their predecessors—had 12 vertical-lunch tubes forward for Tomahawk missiles plus four torpedo tubes. The next 18 (SSN 784–801) have two large, bow "multi-purpose" vertical tubes replacing the 12 Tomahawk tubes in the bow of previous submarines. Each of these two large (87-inch-diameter) tubes can be used for unmanned vehicles or other systems, or with an insert each of the two large tubes can launch six Tomahawks.[17]

The later Block V submarines, built from 2019 onward, have the additional *Virginia* Payload Module (VPM), an 84-foot-long mid-body section.[18] The VPM adds four

This artist's concept shows the amidships missile tubes fitted in later *Virginia*-class submarines. The four launch cells of the *Virginia* Payload Module (VPM) can each accommodate seven Tomahawk or similar-size missiles. This configuration provides flexibility for future missile sizes or unmanned underwater vehicles. *General Dynamics/Electric Boat*

additional, large (87-inch-diameter) tubes amidships, providing the option for 28 additional Tomahawk missiles (seven per tube), thus giving each *Virginia* SSN a potential loadout of 40 Tomahawk missiles in vertical-launch tubes. This would be in addition to weapons in the submarine's four 21-inch (533-mm) torpedo tubes and those stowed in the torpedo room—a total of 25 torpedoes, although Tomahawks could be carried internally and launched from the torpedo tubes. The VPM configuration results in an overall increase in submarine length to approximately 460 feet and also of displacement, with a submerged displacement of 10,200 tons (compared to the basic configuration of 377 feet and 7,800 tons).

Significantly, the large-diameter, multi-Tomahawk launch tubes in the bow and amidships in these later *Virginia*-class submarines also make it possible to carry larger missiles and other payloads. The latter could include a variety of unmanned underwater vehicles.

Building *Virginia*-class submarines with the VPM would compensate for the sharp loss in the submarine force's weapon-carrying capacity projected for the mid-2020s with the retirement of the Navy's four *Ohio*-class cruise missile/special operations support submarines. The proposed program of 22 *Virginia*-class submarines built with VPMs plus their bow vertical-launch tubes would be able to carry 880 Tomahawks in vertical-launch tubes.

★   ★   ★

The TASM variant of Tomahawk was relatively short-lived. The problems of identifying and targeting ships at distances of several hundred miles were—at the time—beyond fleet capabilities. Also, Tomahawk being a subsonic (Mach 0.75) weapon, a high-speed target ship could move a significant distance during a long-range attack. There were several fleet experiments in this context.

The TASM soon was followed into U.S. service by the TLAM—Tomahawk Land-Attack Missile—which became operational in 1984. The conventional TLAM quickly became the "weapon of choice" for U.S. political leaders and military commanders. The land-attack missiles—first used in the 1991 assault against Saddam Hussein's Iraq—heralded a new

Table 13-1. U.S. Navy Ships Fitted to Carry Tomahawk Missiles

Type	Class	Number of Ships	Launchers	Tomahawk Missiles per Ship
BB 61	*Iowa*	4	8 ABL	32
CGN 38	*Virginia*	4	2 ABL	8
CGN 9	*Long Beach*	1	2 ABL	8
CGN 25	*Bainbridge*	1	2 ABL	8
CG 47	*Ticonderoga*	22	122 VLS cells	Varies★
DDG 51	*Arleigh Burke*	60+ ★★	90 or 96 VLS cells	Varies★
DD 963	*Spruance*	24	61 VLS cells	61
DD 963	*Spruance*	7	2 ABL	8
SSBN/SSGN 736	*Ohio*	4	154 VLS cells	154
SSN 688	*Los Angeles*	23	12 VLS cells	12★★★
SSN 774	*Virginia*	12+★★	12 VLS cells	12★★★
SSN 803	*Virginia* Block V	22★★ planned	40 VLS cells	40★★★

★ These ships also carry surface-to-air, anti-ballistic missile, and ASW missiles.
★★ Additional ships under construction.
★★★ Additional Tomahawks can be launched through torpedo tubes.

era in naval warfare, bringing unprecedented range and accuracy for warships attacking land targets. The TLAM of 1991, after being launched from a surface ship or submerged submarine, initially was directed toward its target by an inertial-guidance system that used the Tomahawk's sensors and gyroscopes to measure acceleration and changes in direction. Once the missile crossed the shoreline the more precise TERCOM took control, drawing information from the weapon's computerized contour maps and comparing them with what the missile "saw" as it flew toward its target.

As it neared its target, skimming at altitudes of 100 to 300 feet, the Tomahawk turned to a third guidance system: DSMAC (Digital Scene Matching Area Correlator), which compared the target it "saw" to a "picture" in its computer memory and made final course changes for a precise hit. Published accounts credit the TLAM with an accuracy of *about twelve feet* at a range of several hundred miles.

The TLAM—like the TASM—has a conventional "unitary" warhead of approximately 1,000 pounds of high explosives. There also was a TLAM-D warhead that dispensed

166 BLU-97 bomblets, each weighing 3.4 pounds, in packets of 24. These sub-munitions combined armor-piercing, fragmentation, and incendiary effects and could attack multiple targets. In 1991 in Iraq, for example, a submarine-launched TLAM-D released bomblets against three separate targets and then performed a terminal dive to strike a fourth itself.

During the Gulf War (1991–1992) modified TLAM-Ds were used to cast very fine carbon fiber wire over outdoor switching and transformer facilities that supplied electrical power to Iraqi command and control centers and radar installations. The resulting short-circuits disrupted air defense networks, other military facilities, and civilian activities. After the conflict, occupying forces could remove the carbon fiber wires, which, albeit a tedious process, allowed the electrical grid to be re-established without having to replace destroyed electrical components.

Cruise Missiles at War

Early on the morning of 17 January 1991, a booster rocket launched a missile from the U.S. guided missile cruiser *San Jacinto* (CG 56), operating in the Red Sea. Immediately after launch, the missile's tail fins deployed and wings extended. The turbofan engine started as the missile began its flight over the sea. When land appeared beneath the missile, its microcomputers took control, setting a course leading several hundred miles across the Arabian Peninsula and over Iraq. That Tomahawk land-attack missile was the first weapon to strike Baghdad in the Gulf War's Operation Desert Storm—and the first U.S. cruise missile ever launched in combat.

The first missile salvos reportedly struck the presidential palace, Ministry of Defense headquarters, and the central communications center in Baghdad. Some of the weapons were targeted against fixed air-defense installations.

The *San Jacinto* fired 16 Tomahawks during the 42-day conflict. In that opening salvo the *San Jacinto* and eight other U.S. warships, including the battleships *Missouri* (BB 63) and *Wisconsin* (BB 64), fired 52 TLAM-C Tomahawks. Reportedly, all but one of those 52 missiles struck their designated targets.[19] During that conflict 297 Tomahawks were launched, of which 282 successfully transitioned to flight (95 percent), a remarkable record for a swiftly planned attack. Two Tomahawks were shot down by Iraqi forces, although some sources put that toll at six missiles, and, reportedly, the Iraqis recovered one missile intact.

Televised images of Tomahawks—sometimes flying high, sometimes low over Baghdad—became one of the spectacles of that televised war, which put real-time scenes of battlefields and battle skies into homes and bars throughout the world. "The skies over Baghdad have been illuminated," Bernard Shaw reported on CNN television as viewers saw on their screens "bright flashes going off all over the sky." Video images originating from high-tech weapons gave viewers startling views of targets being detected and then instantly wiped out. (The few images of Tomahawks were taken from the ground as they flew overhead at high subsonic speeds.)

The Department of Defense summary report of the 1991 Gulf War stated: "The TLAM played an important role in the air campaign as the only weapon system used

The guided missile cruiser *Shiloh* (CG 67) in the Arabian Gulf launches Tomahawks at an Iraqi target from her forward Vertical Launch System (VLS) on 3 September 1996. Those TLAMs were launched in reaction to Saddam Hussein's offensive actions in Kurdish territory. The VLS can accommodate a variety of missile types. *U.S. Navy*

to attack central Baghdad in daylight. The cruise missile concept—incorporating an unmanned, low-observable platform able to strike accurately at long distances—was validated as a significant new instrument for future concepts."[20]

The Tomahawks that were launched during the Gulf War were pre-programmed. Target information was provided to the launching ship and input to the missile before firing. The ship could not change the targeting data: the missile would fly the assigned profile. Most of the missiles, as noted, struck their targets as intended. There were some problems with DSMAC guidance when earlier attacks had damaged buildings near the target, thus changing the picture that the missile sensors were expected to identify.

Sea-launched Tomahawk land-attack missiles have been employed extensively since Desert Storm:

- 17 January 1993: 45 Tomahawks were launched at what American officials described as a nuclear fabrication plant near Baghdad; the strike was in response to Iraq's defiance of a no-fly zone established by the United States and its allies.
- 26 June 1993: 23 Tomahawks fired at the Iraqi intelligence command and control center.
- 10 September 1995: 13 Tomahawks fired at a key air defense facility outside of Banja Luka in Bosnian Serb territory during Operation Deliberate Force.
- 3 September 1996: 44 Tomahawks and Air Force AGM-86 air-launched cruise missiles fired at air defense targets in southern Iraq.

- 20 August 1998: About 75 Tomahawks fired at targets in Afghanistan and Sudan in retaliation for the bombing of American embassies in Africa by Al-Qaeda.
- 16 December 1998: Tomahawks fired at key Iraqi targets during Operation Desert Fox. CNN reported that more than 200 Tomahawks were used in the four-day operation.
- March 1999: 218 Tomahawks fired by U.S. ships and the British submarine *Splendid* against targets in Yugoslavia during Operation Allied Force.
- October 2001: About 50 Tomahawks fired at targets in Afghanistan during the start of Operation Enduring Freedom.
- March–May 2003: During the invasion of Iraq—Operation Iraqi Freedom more than 725 Tomahawks fired at Iraqi targets.
- 17 December 2009: Two Tomahawks were fired at targets in Yemen.
- March 2011: 159 Tomahawks fired by U.S. and British ships and submarines against targets in Libya.

No TLAMs were launched during the next six years by U.S. or British surface ships or submarines as the Obama administration (2009–2016) sought to avoid entanglements in the continuing and expanding Middle East conflicts, especially the bloody civil war in Syria. In the early hours of 7 April 2017, three days after the Syrian regime of Bashar al-Assad *again* used poison gas (sarin) against its own people, two U.S. destroyers launched, on the direct orders of President Donald Trump, 60 Tomahawk missiles into Syria.

The target was the Al-Shayrat air base near the city of Homs, identified as the base from which Syrian aircraft had flown to drop the sarin canisters, which had killed almost 100 people and injured many more.[21] The 59 missiles (one missile suffered an apparent guidance failure and was lost en route) struck their targets, damaging airfield facilities and destroying or damaging 23 of the Russian-provided aircraft—that is, about one-fifth of Assad's air force.[22] Russian military personnel had been warned to leave the facility some four hours before the RGM-109E Block IV missiles, launched from the destroyers *Porter* (DDG 78) and *Ross* (DDG 71) in the eastern Mediterranean, arrived.

Of course, this massive number of Tomahawks fired from U.S. surface ships and submarines and Royal Navy submarines since 1991 were launched *without putting a single American or British life at risk.*

Land-Launched Tomahawks

On 12 January 1977, the U.S. government decided to develop a ground-launched variant of the Tomahawk, in part to counter Soviet deployment of the Soviet RSD-10 Pioneer (NATO SS-22 Saber) intermediate-range ballistic missile. The U.S. Air Force had earlier rejected an air-launched Tomahawk in favor of the Boeing ALCM but was willing to adopt the BGM-109G variant of the Navy's Tomahawk as a Ground-Launched Cruise Missile (GLCM)—to be named Gryphon—for deployment at land bases in European NATO countries.

A mockup of the Gryphon cruise missile's Transporter-Erector-Launcher (TEL) vehicle in a forest setting. The TEL vehicle—carrying four missiles—would have provided tactical mobility for the missile, enhancing survivability against potential Soviet attacks. *U.S. Air Force*

The NATO leadership agreed on 12 December 1979 to the deployment of 464 U.S. Air Force–operated GLCMs in Western Europe. (The original Gryphon/GLCM program had called for 565 missiles with 137 launch vehicles.)

The first GLCMs to deploy to Western Europe arrived at the Royal Air Force base at Greenham Common (Berkshire) on 14 November 1983; they became operational on 1 January 1984. The other NATO deployments rapidly followed, and all of the planned GLCMs were in place by 1988. The Air Force's 868th Tactical Missile Training Group at Davis Monthan AFB, Arizona, trained the GLCM crews.

The European deployments were not made without opposition from within NATO countries. There were heated debates in several parliaments; church organizations and several political parties actively opposed the GLCMs. The Belgium and Dutch government stated that they would accept the missiles if there was no progress in agreements to limit nuclear weapons in Europe.

The Air Force's Gryphon variant of the Tomahawk had about 90 percent commonality with the Navy missile. The GLCM firing unit (designated a "flight" by the Air Force) was composed of four Transporter-Erector-Launcher (TEL) vehicles, each with four launch cells. Thus, a flight of four TELs had 16 missiles, plus 2 launch control vehicles (one primary, one backup), 16 support vehicles, and 69 personnel. These vehicles all were

Table 13-2. U.S. Air Force Gryphon Missile Deployments

USAF Tactical Missile Wing	Location	Missiles/Launchers
38th	Wuescheim Air Station, West Germany	96/24
485th	Florennes Air Base, Belgium	48/12
486th	Woensdrecht Air Base, the Netherlands	48/12
487th	Comiso Air Station, Italy	112/28
501st	RAF Greenham Common, England	96/24
550th	RAF Molesworth, England	64/16

air transportable in C-5 Galaxy, C-130 Hercules, and C-141 Starlifter cargo aircraft. Each TEL with four missiles and mated nuclear warheads weighed 77,900 pounds, was 55 $^2/_3$ feet long, and had selfcontained electrical power.

The Gryphon had a range of 1,550 miles, which meant the deployed missiles could reach into the Soviet Union. From some firing locations it could strike the capital, Moscow, making the Gryphon effectively a "strategic" weapon. Each Gryphon carried a W84 nuclear warhead with a variable yield of 0.2 to 150 kilotons. (This was a different warhead from that fitted in the sea-launched Tomahawk missile.)

An alternative payload was considered for the GLCMs—chemical warheads.[23] In the early 1980s the U.S. Army proposed placing chemical warheads on the missiles. At the time there were no operational chemical weapons in the U.S. arsenal except for a small number of outdated weapons stored in West Germany and the United States. In the past the military had aerial bombs and short-range rockets that could deliver poisonous nerve gas and either chemical agents.

In 1981 the administration of Ronald Reagan had lifted the 12-year American moratorium on producing chemical weapons; Congress approved $23 million for building facilities at Pine Bluff, Arkansas, where chemical weapons could be produced. But there were strong indications that most if not all NATO nations would strongly oppose the deployment of chemical-warhead cruise missiles. There is no indication that chemical weapons were in fact ever produced at the Arkansas facilities, and no chemical warheads were fitted to the GLCMs. The Gryphon GLCM deployments in Western Europe were short-lived. The Intermediate-range Nuclear Forces (INF) treaty between the United States and the Soviet Union was signed in Washington, D.C., by President Ronald Reagan and the Soviet leader, Mikhail Gorbachev, on 8 December 1987. The INF treaty, which came into force on 1 June 1988, called for the elimination of an land-launched cruise and ballistic missiles with ranges of 310 to 3,420 miles (i.e., 500 to 5,550 kilometers).

The first GLCMs were withdrawn from Western Europe on 8 September 1988, and the last were shipped out of Comiso, Italy, on 26 March 1991. The GLCMs were destroyed except for a few unarmed examples retained for display/museum purposes.

(The Air Force Gryphon GLCM program was a partner to the U.S. Army's deployment of 108 Pershing II ballistic missiles to Western Europe. The Pershing missiles also were removed under the terms of the INF treaty. [24])

In the early 1990s, Israeli officials sought to acquire Gryphon GLCMs, but their sale to Israel was disapproved by the U.S. government. The Gryphon, of course, was configured for surface-to-surface launch. So far as is known the Israelis did not request submarine-launched TLAMs.

In 2000 there were reports that one or two of the German-built, Israeli *Dolphin*-class diesel-electric submarines had carried out cruise-missile test launches. The missiles, launched off Sri Lanka in the Indian Ocean, were said to have struck a target at a range of about 930 miles.[25] The missiles were described as capable of carrying nuclear warheads. As was their usual policy, Israeli officials would not comment on these reports.

Their submarine-launched missile is believed to have been a variant of the Israeli-developed Popeye Turbo weapon, originally an air-launched cruise missile.[26] Few details of the submarine-launched weapon were available when this volume went to press. The six submarines of the *Dolphin* class, completed from 1999 to 2018, each has six 21-inch (533-mm) and four 26½-inch (650-mm) torpedo tubes, for a total of 16 tube-launched weapons. (Israeli submarines did have the shorter-range, Harpoon anti-ship missile, provided by the United States.)

The U.S. Navy's Tomahawk Block III included an advanced GPS receiver to update the inertial navigation system, as well as other features. In 1999 the Raytheon Company began the "remanufacture," or updating, of 424 existing Block II missiles and the conversion of 200 "beached" TASM anti-ship missiles to the TLAM Block III configuration.

The subsequent version of the missile was the Tactical Tomahawk TLAM-E, a labeled the "Block IV" weapon, which became operational in 2004. It carried a smaller warhead that permitted the missile to carry extra fuel to increase its range, to a reported 900 n.miles. Also, the missile had improved inertial guidance, a radar altimeter, a GPS receiver, and a forward-looking, passive infra-red sensor. A data link allows controllers to reprogram the missile in flight.

Thus, thanks to a strategic arms initiative of Dr. Henry Kissinger and the desire of Admiral Elmo Zumwalt to enhance the Navy's warfighting effectiveness beyond the relatively few large-deck aircraft carriers, the U.S. Navy has generated a massive sea-based cruise missile strike capability.

Nuclear Options

The original incentive for the Tomahawk cruise missile was to provide the fleet with a nuclear strike weapon. The Tomahawk Land-Attack Missile (Nuclear)—the TLAM(N)—entered the U.S. inventory in 1987.[27] Like carrier-based nuclear strike aircraft, the TLAM(N) generally was looked upon as a strategic weapon. The link between the Tomahawk *land-attack missile* and the potential of conflict at sea between the Soviet Union and the United States was largely unnoticed. However, in 1985, addressing the Senate Armed Services Committee, then-Commodore Roger Bacon stated:

> This missile provides a key deterrent to Soviet plans to use nuclear anti-ship missiles aboard Soviet naval aviation Backfires and Badgers to attack our naval combatants, especially our aircraft carriers. [Soviet Naval Aviation] Backfires and Badgers regularly train, and plan for[,] such missions. By removing any Soviet perceptions that Soviet naval aviation could initiate nuclear war at sea, unharmed, from land-based sanctuaries, TLAM(N) makes it clear that nuclear strikes against the U.S. Navy could have widespread consequences. It thereby increases our ability to deter such attacks.[28]

Thus, planning envisioned ship/submarine-launched nuclear Tomahawks used to strike bomber bases within Soviet territory without the employment of "strategic" weapons—that is, submarine- and land-based ballistic missiles and strategic bombers. At that time the United States planned to deploy TLAM(N)s on 82 surface ships and 101 submarines. However, the service life of the TLAM(N) was brief—it was removed from the fleet in 1992, with the end of the Cold War with nuclear weapons removed from all U.S. warships except for strategic (ballistic) missile submarines.

The U.S. government has not revealed how many nuclear-armed Tomahawks were deployed. In testimony before Congress in 1981, Secretary of Defense Caspar W. Weinberger said that the administration planned to deploy "several hundred" TLAM(N)s. It was reported in the press that the Navy had said the exact figure was 384.

The Ballistic Missile Option

Significantly, the *Virginia*-VPM configuration led to a proposal to arm those submarines with *non-nuclear* ballistic missiles. In January 2012, Secretary of Defense Leon Panetta unveiled the concept of arming those submarines with a "conventional prompt-strike option."[29] The military requirement for this type of weapon was based on the perceived need to strike a target anywhere on the globe—with a conventional warhead—within 60 minutes of a regional commander's order.

Defense officials envisioned so-called prompt-strike weapons as potential substitutes for nuclear-armed ballistic missiles on submarines and land-based ICBMs when confronted with time-urgent situations, such as indications that North Korea was preparing nuclear weapons for launch or an important terrorist leader had been sighted at a temporary location.

Under this proposal the *Virginia* payload models would be modified to carry up to 12 "medium-range" ballistic missiles with conventional warheads. Earlier the U.S. Congress had halted proposed development of a non-nuclear version of the Trident D-5 SLBM for basing on the *Ohio*-class SSBNs, citing concerns about strategic "ambiguity" or miscues. This concern envisioned Russia or possibly another nation detecting an SLBM launch from an *Ohio* (or successor) SSBN and, believing that it could be a nuclear strike, immediately initiating a major nuclear retaliatory attack.

In 2012, shortly after Secretary Panetta had revealed the conventional SLBM concept, Defense officials decided to restrict the *Virginia* VPM to launching cruise missiles. Accordingly, in July 2013, Congress moved to cancel development of the non-nuclear ballistic missile program. Thus, the U.S. Navy would deploy conventional cruise missiles and nuclear ballistic missiles at sea—at least for the near term.

Is There a Better Cruise Missile in Your Future?

BUILDING IN LARGE PART ON GERMAN MISSILE TECHNOLOGY developed in World War II, both the United States and the Soviet Union sent to sea land-attack cruise missiles to strike the enemy's homeland with nuclear warheads. The U.S. effort—which initially deployed the Regulus cruise missile at sea as a strategic strike weapon—was terminated after a few years in favor of submarine-launched ballistic missiles.

The similar Soviet sea-based strategic missile programs—both cruise missile and ballistic missile—suffered a "holiday" for several years following the December 1959 establishment of Strategic Rocket Forces as a separate military service. But the large, ongoing Soviet anti-ship cruise missile effort provided a viable basis for a rapid return to the land-attack role. The continued design and production of shorter-range, anti-ship missiles and the construction of cruise missile-carrying submarines meant that the Soviet Union could rapidly reconstitute a sea-based, land-attack cruise missile program.

In the 1960s the U.S. Navy could afford to dismiss proposals for strategic SLCMs because of its nuclear-capable, carrier-based strike aircraft and the rapid deployment of the Polaris SLBM force with 656 ballistic missiles sent to sea in 41 nuclear-propelled submarines in less than a decade. But *theater* nuclear strike considerations eventually led the United States to reinstitute a strategic SLCM program based on the versatile, multi-mission Tomahawk missile. Unfortunately, that highly successful program—which saw the first SLCMs at sea in the late 1970s—has continued into the 21st century with minimal advances in missile technology beyond limited improvements to that weapon.

★   ★   ★

In the Soviet Union, following the hiatus caused by the establishment of Strategic Rocket Forces at the end of 1959, there was new impetus for the development of naval forces—including sea-based strategic weapons—in large part because of the Soviet chagrin over

160

A Tomahawk missile launched from the submarine *Florida* (SSGN 728) breaks the surface and begins its transition to cruise flight during an exercise off the Bahamas. The missile was designed from the outset for launching from standard 21-inch (533-mm) torpedo tubes as well as from various other missile launching systems. *U.S. Navy*

the Cuban missile crisis of 1962. This effort was accelerated by the subsequent fall, in October 1964, of Nikita Khrushchev, who had disdained conventional naval forces. Led by Admiral Sergei G. Gorshkov, who served as Commander-in-Chief of the Soviet Navy from 1956 to 1985, the Soviets led the world in several aspects of submarine and related missile developments, among them the first submarine-launched ballistic missile, the first submerge-launched cruise missile, and the world's largest, fastest, deepest-diving, and most automated combat submarines.[1] Anti-ship cruise missile development continued, with implications for later efforts in land-attack cruise missiles.

The Soviet Union's impressive advances in the quality and quantity of naval weapons and platforms essentially halted with the collapse of the Soviet regime in December 1991. Soon missile production and submarine construction ceased, and defense-related funding was cut precipitously. However, the various submarine and missile design bureaus continued their work, albeit at a slower pace, many of their engineers and scientists "furloughed" or forced to take part-time jobs to support their families. Only after some two decades was the "new Russia" again producing highly innovative cruise missiles and missile-launching submarines. The latter include the Kilo (Projects 636 and 877) diesel-electric craft that can launch the Kalibr land-attack missiles from their torpedo tubes. These submarines are in the Russian fleet and those of several other nations. Also, nine older missile submarines of the massive Oscar (Project 949) series were being modified to carry a variety of advanced missiles. The development continues of more advanced cruise missiles for both the anti-ship and land-attack roles.

★   ★   ★

In the U.S. Navy the Tomahawk—an "old" weapon in terms of modern technologies—has served into the first decades of the 21st century. The Block VI version of the conventional land-attack Tomahawk, which went to sea in 2004, does incorporate several advanced features. Further, both the Navy and the Defense Advanced Research Projects Agency (DARPA) have expended resources in developing cruise missile technologies, while the Boeing, Lockheed Martin, and Raytheon firms (as well as several non-American companies) are "maturing" advanced missile concepts for the so-called Next Generation Land-Attack Weapon program.[2] But as this volume went to press the venerable Tomahawk remains the weapon of choice for U.S. presidents when a military response is needed in a crisis situation. At the beginning of the 21st century the American president's choices of military action had been significantly limited. While advanced-technology missiles were being discussed and proposed, the Tomahawk remained the only sea-launched, land-attack cruise missile in U.S. inventory well into the century (and that weapon without a nuclear variant).

The U.S. Navy also lacked a modern anti-ship cruise missile; the Harpoon, a relatively short-range, anti-ship weapon, and the Tomahawk anti-ship missile with far greater range, have been removed from the inventory of U.S. submarine weapons. Only the conventional land-attack Tomahawk remains in U.S. submarines as this book went to press, surface ships having the conventional TLAM in addition to the outdated Harpoon anti-ship missile. The very-long-awaited surface-launched, anti-ship missile for the controversial littoral combat ship (LCS) program was the Norwegian-developed Naval Strike Missile (NSM). This missile, with a range of some 100 n.miles and a 276-pound warhead, is suitable neither for submarines nor for the land-attack role.

★   ★   ★

The Russian Navy, despite severe financial, personnel, and other problems, continued a robust program of cruise missile development for surface ships, submarines, and coastal defense—both anti-ship and land-attack weapons. Also, land-launched "air-breathing" and "boost-glide" hypersonic vehicles were in the offing. The Russian efforts were articulated by President Vladimir Putin in March 2018.[3]

These weapons were identified as (1) a nuclear-powered cruise missile with global range and (2) the Avangard boost-glide vehicle. Little is known about the new cruise missile; it was said in 2017 that it had been successfully tested and would soon be ready for production. The Avangard's boost-glide design provides maneuverability to permit its payload—the RS-28 Sarmat ICBM—to evade potential ballistic missile defenses. It was reported to have a speed in excess of Mach 20. President Putin stated that the weapon could change its course and altitude en route to the target, making it "absolutely invulnerable to any air or missile defense means."[4]

The ten-metric-ton Avangard was believed to have been flight tested twice in 2016, followed by additional flight tests. In one test the (unarmed) boost-glide vehicle was launched from the Dombarobsky missile test site in southern Orenburg Province toward a target at the Kura missile test range, a distance of 3,760 miles. Russian sources indicated that the missile would become operational by 2020.

(In addition, Putin in 2018 announced the development of a land-based RS-28 Sarmat ICBM/NATO designation Satan 2; a nuclear-armed underwater, submarine-launched drone, named Poseidon; and a hypersonic, air-launched nuclear missile, called Kinzal.)

Dishonoring a Treaty

The Reagan-Gorbachev Intermediate-range Nuclear Forces (INF) treaty of 1987 was the only agreement of the Cold War era that eliminated an entire class of nuclear weapons—land-based ballistic and cruise missiles, with nuclear or conventional warheads, with ranges between 310 to 3,400 miles (500 to 5,500 kilometers, in the treaty wording). The bilateral treaty appears to have been effective for almost three decades. Significantly, the treaty did not affect intermediate-range missile development by other nations, especially by China, North Korea, or Iran, all of which had robust missile programs.

In early 2008, the Russians began testing a nuclear-capable cruise missile, designated SSC-8 by Western intelligence (Russian designation 9M729). In 2014, after observing continued testing of the missile, the Obama administration announced that Russia had violated the INF treaty. However, U.S. administration officials later said that although the missile had a range prohibited by the treaty, as of 2015 test flights apparently had not exceeded the 310-mile mark. Subsequently, Russia began a limited deployment of the missile, which has an estimated range of more than 3,400 miles, with various warhead options, some of which reduce its maximum range.[5]

In late October 2018, President Donald Trump announced that the United States would withdraw from the landmark treaty because of the alleged Russian violations; the withdrawal became formal on 2 August 2019. The Secretary of Defense at the time, James Mattis, a retired Marine general, had consulted with officials from the 28 other members of NATO, seeking their ideas on how to react to the Russian violations of the INF treaty. He told the press that no ideas had been forthcoming from the allies.[6] Also, Mattis did not rule out the possibility of the United States again deploying intermediate-range missiles in Europe.

The Russian government denied violating the INF treaty and said that U.S. withdrawal would be dangerous and could spark a new nuclear arms race. President Putin declared that the United States had already violated the treaty with the deployment in Romania of the Navy's Aegis ballistic missile defense system because it could launch intermediate-range missiles. The U.S. government rejected the allegation, stating that the system could only launch interceptor missiles. (Apparently Putin made no reference to the similar U.S. Aegis system being installed in Poland.) The Russian leader also said, on 24 October 2018, that if the United States responded to the alleged Russian violations by deploying intermediate-range missiles in Europe, the host nations would be targeted by Russian weapons.[7]

By 2018 the Russians had several battalions of the 9M729 missile (NATO SSC-8), which had precipitated the controversy; each battalion has four launch vehicles with four missiles available for each launcher. Russian officials cited a missile range of only 300 miles. U.S. sources claimed that the 2M729's range was 1,460 miles.[8] The missiles could carry conventional or nuclear warheads. (The SSC-8/9M729 appears to be a longer-range, improved version of the 9M720 ballistic missile, given the NATO designation SS-26 Stone; both of the missiles are mounted on wheeled launchers.)

Possibly more threatening was Russia's development of a nuclear-powered cruise missile said to have unlimited range while carrying a nuclear warhead. Named *Burevestnik*, that weapon made international headlines when there was a nuclear explosion reported at the Nyonoksa test site on the White Sea on 8 August 2019, causing nearby towns to be evacuated. Seven scientists were reported to have been killed in the incident. (The United States had earlier abandoned research on such a weapon, dubbed Project Pluto.)

Beyond the Russian violation, the U.S. government's objection to the INF treaty was that it was a bilateral agreement between only the United States and the Soviet Union/Russia. Thus, the treaty did not affect other nations' missile developments, whereas the Iranian missile program at the time was already in violation of United Nations resolutions to restrict such development. During the machinations over the United States withdrawal from the INF agreement, President Putin made a surprise "offer" on 5 September 2019, stating to President Trump that the United States could "buy" Russian hypersonic missiles! "If you want, we can sell you some and this way we will balance everything out," he told Trump, according to TASS. Subsequently, Reuters confirmed Trump's refusal. While it could not be determined if the Russian leader's "offer" wasn't just a propaganda statement, the basic concept articulated by Putin was historically significant.

★   ★   ★

At that time of withdrawal from the INF agreement the United States had no ground-launched nuclear weapons that could be deployed to Europe; there were numerous land-based tactical aircraft that could carry nuclear bombs. The most realistic and timely responses could be an increase in air-dropped nuclear weapons for U.S. and NATO tactical aircraft based in Europe and—more practically—the deployment of nuclear-armed TLAMs on U.S. submarines operating in European waters. No nuclear-armed TLAMs existed at the time.

American Responses

The Russian developments in hypersonic air-breathing and boost-glide strike vehicles led American defense officials to articulate the need to accelerate equivalent efforts. To "catch up" with the presumed Russian lead in hypersonic weapons, the Department of Defense has made such weapons, as an American official remarked, its "first, second, and third" weapon development priorities.[9] Beyond earlier efforts sponsored by DARPA, contracts were awarded in this field to Northrop Grumman, Boeing, Lockheed Martin, and Raytheon, the nation's leaders in advanced weapon development.

Loren Thompson, a leading American defense analyst, has said that the hypersonic weapons market should be worth "many billions of dollars. . . . We're talking about an entirely new class of weapons and the operating concepts to go with it."[10]

On 21 November 2018, the U.S. Navy announced that it would award Lockheed Martin a sole-source contract to build the rocket motors and missile bodies that will be used in test flights of a submarine-launched, hypersonic weapons program. Earlier that month the Department of Defense directed the Navy to establish a formal project office for the hypersonic weapons effort. (Also, in late 2018, the U.S. Missile Defense Agency awarded contracts to more than a score of firms to further research into hypersonic missile defense systems, while the U.S. Army announced that it was developing a "battlefield" hypersonic missile, with Navy participation, to be operational by 2023.)

Meanwhile, the Navy used a land-based VLS at a site on San Nicholas Island, California, to test-launch a Tomahawk on 15 August 2019. The missile flew 310 miles to accurately strike a target. A Department of Defense statement declared, "Data collected and lessons learned from this test will inform the Department of Defense's development of future intermediate-range capabilities."[11]

Considering the many hundreds of Tomahawk and Gryphon land-attack missiles fired in combat and in tests and training, it is difficult to understand the contributions of this launch to future weapons development. Still, Russia's deputy foreign minister, Sergei Ryabkov, immediately criticized the Tomahawk test and accused the United States of "stoking military tensions," according to the U.S. Department of Defense.[12]

Thus, the Tomahawk, in the U.S. arsenal for some four decades, became the harbinger of futuristic missiles that could strike from land and from the sea.

Appendix A

U.S. Navy Land-Attack Cruise Missiles

Loon LTV-N-2

The Loon was the U.S. Navy's version of the German-developed V-1 "buzz bomb." It was called Loon by the Navy and designated as a launch test vehicle—LTV-N-2. The U.S. Navy briefly considered a nuclear-armed version of the Loon for submarine launching as an interim land-attack weapon. An American copy of the V-1—dubbed JB-2, for Jet Bomb No. 2, by the Army—was rushed into production. After the war, in 1947, the Navy fitted the submarine *Cusk* (SS 348) with a launching ramp and equipment to launch the missile in support of the development of the Regulus missile; subsequently a small missile hangar was fitted to the submarine.

The *Cusk* became the world's first submarine to launch a guided missile—a Loon—on 18 February 1947. (That missile crashed after traveling 6,000 yards, the failure apparently due to a control malfunction.)

The potential of the Loon as a land-attack weapon was immediately considered, especially since the first American submarine-launched missile, the Regulus, would not be available with a nuclear warhead before 1954. The warhead proposed was the "Elsie," the Mark 8 nuclear weapon developed by Los Alamos specifically for use by naval aircraft against hardened land targets—such as submarine "pens" (bunkers)—and was the first U.S. nuclear weapon fused to detonate after striking the ground as opposed to an air burst. It was an improved Little Boy design with an explosive yield of about three kilotons.

Providing a nuclear warhead in the Loon would have produced the world's first nuclear-armed missile. However, the project died in 1950, primarily because of the limited range and accuracy of the missile. The latter was estimated as a 40 percent probability of striking within a mile of the target and 70 percent of hitting within five miles. Even with a three-kiloton warhead this was considered too poor for practical use.

The submarine *Carbonero* (SS/SSG 337) also was employed in Loon launch trials.

Operational:	cancelled as naval land-attack weapon
Design:	Willys-Aero
Weight:	empty 2,245 lbs
	payload 1,875 lbs
	gross 5,200 lbs
Length:	27 feet 1 inches
Wingspan:	17 feet 8½ inches

Wing area: 60.7 feet²
Height: 5 feet (bottom of fuselage to top of engine)
Propulsion: 1 PJ31–1 pulse-jet engine (Ford); 900 lbst
                  1 solid-propellant rocket booster
Speed: 440 mph
Range: 150 miles
Guidance: preset and radio command
Warhead: 1,875 lbs conventional
Launch Mode: submarine

Regulus I SSM–N–8/RGM–6

The Regulus I was the U.S. Navy's first missile to carry a nuclear warhead and its first operational submarine-launched missile. Known as the Regulus Attack Missile (RAM), the weapon was fitted in five U.S. Navy submarines that conducted deterrent patrols in the Western Pacific. It was also carried briefly in aircraft carriers and heavy cruisers.

The Regulus I was to have been succeeded by the more-capable Regulus II. However, the Regulus I was retained in service after the later weapon was cancelled. The retirement of the Regulus I in 1964 marked the end of long-range cruise missiles in the U.S. Navy until introduction of the Tomahawk SLCMs in the early 1980s.

Originally the Regulus was to have been armed with a conventional warhead (4,000 pounds), in part because of the limited nature of the data on nuclear warheads made available to the Navy. In 1949 a nuclear warhead was proposed for the missile and operational Regulus missiles were fitted with nuclear warheads only, initially the Mark 5 and, from 1958, the W27.

Regulus guidance consisted of an autopilot with radio or radar commands from the launching submarine, other submarines, surface ships, or aircraft. Radar commands were transmitted using the Trounce system. Several attack routes could be flown, and approaches to the target could be at altitudes from up to 40,000 feet down to tree-top level. The normal profile used during Regulus submarine deterrent patrols was a high altitude of about 30,000 feet. When diving on its target the Regulus could attain a speed of Mach 1.1.

The missile had folding wings and tail fin for shipboard stowage.

Designation. The Regulus I was originally designated SSM–N–8 in the multi-service designation system; the designation changed to RGM–6 in 1963. The recoverable training versions were designated KDU-1 and, after 1963, BQM-6C.

Operational. The first XSSM–N–8 test vehicle flew on 29 March 1951, under the control of an airborne controller. Fitted with wheels, the Regulus took off under its own power, circled the airfield, and landed safely.

The first shipboard launch was made from the missile test ship *Norton Sound* (AVM 1, ex-AV 11) on 3 November 1952, and the aircraft carrier *Princeton* (CVA 37) launched a Regulus missile on 16 December 1952. The first submarine launch of a Regulus I occurred on 15 July 1953, from the surfaced submarine *Tunny* (SSG 282).

The Regulus I became operational in May 1954, on board the *Tunny* in the Pacific Fleet. In the Pacific the first operational missiles went to sea on the cruiser *Los Angeles* (CA 135) in 1955. Several heavy cruisers, as well as *Essex* (CVA 9)–class carriers, launched the missile in trials.

From 23 October 1959, to 14 July 1964, submarines carrying Regulus I missiles were continuously on patrol in the North Pacific area. A total of 41 Regulus deterrent patrols were conducted in that period, with one or two submarines with a total of four or five missiles normally "on station," their missiles aimed at targets in the Soviet Far East.

A total of five Regulus-armed submarines entered service. Additional nuclear submarines were planned, but with the cancellation of the Regulus II those submarines were reordered as torpedo-attack submarines of the *Thresher* (SSN 593) class.

The first operational flight of the KDU-1 drone version of the Regulus I occurred on 31 March 1955. More than 900 Regulus/KDU-1 launches were recorded; one of the reusable training missiles was flown 18 times.

Production. Chance Vought produced 514 Regulus missiles through December 1958: 228 tactical missiles, 209 flight test and training missiles, and 77 target drones (KDU-1).

Operational:	23 Oct 1959–14 July 1964
Design:	Chance Vought
Weight:	13,485 lbs
Length:	34 feet, 3¾ inches (over tail fin)
Diameter:	4 feet, 8 ½ inches
Wingspan:	21 feet
Height:	8 feet, 10 inches
Propulsion:	1 turbojet; 4,600 lbst (Allison J33-A-14/-18A)
	2 booster rockets; 16,500 lbst each (Aerojet General)
Speed:	high subsonic (Mach 0.85–0.95)
Range:	575 miles
Guidance:	preset or radio/radar control (Trounce)
Warhead:	1 Mark 5 nuclear (40–50 KT) or 1 W27 nuclear (1.9 MT)
Launch Mode:	surface ship and submarine

Regulus II SSM-N-9/RGM-15A

The Regulus II was an advanced land-attack missile designed for launching from surfaced submarines and surface warships. Early successes of Regulus I program led to the development of an improved follow-on; the Regulus II was initiated in July 1953, by Chance Vought. A major factor in the decision to proceed with Regulus II was the difficulty being encountered with the development of the Rigel missile.

Despite a highly successful development and test program, on 12 December 1958 Secretary of the Navy Thomas S. Gates ordered termination of the Regulus II program, because of the decision to accelerate development and deployment of the Polaris SLBM. At the time the project ended 12 cruisers and 12 nuclear-propelled submarines were planned for Regulus II installations, in addition to two diesel-electric submarines already in service. As part of the termination, the new-construction submarines of the *Permit* (tentatively SSGN 594) class intended to carry the Regulus II were reordered as torpedo-attack submarines of the *Thresher* (SSN 593) class. The two diesel-electric submarines d and one nuclear-propelled submarine went to sea with the Regulus I.

A tank landing ship was converted to house the missile-launching system for the *Permit* SSGN design, the USS *King County* (LST 587; redesignated AG 157).

Design. A more-streamlined and efficient design than the Regulus I, this missile had a pointed nose, small canards, swept-back wings.

The turbojet engine was mounted under the after portion of the fuselage; the missile was launched with a single solid-propellant rocket booster fitted under the fuselage. Speed was approximately Mach 2. The missile could reach an altitude of more than 58,000 feet or fly at tree-top level to avoid radar detection.

There were proposals to extend the range beyond that indicated below through the use of external wing tanks.

The Regulus II was to carry the W27 warhead (initial planning provided for the Mark 8). No conventional warhead was envisioned.

Like the Regulus I, the missile was fitted with a fully retractable landing gear for training flights. The missile had folding wings and tail fin for shipboard stowage.

Designation. The Regulus II, originally designated SSM-N-9, was given the all-service designation RGM-15A in the post-1963 scheme. The training/target version originally was designated KDU-2.

Operational. The first Regulus II test flight was conducted on 29 May 1956. The only submarine launch occurred on 16 September 1958, from the surfaced submarine *Grayback* (SSG 574); one additional shipboard launch was made on 11 December 1958, from the Regulus test ship *King County* (AG 157, ex–LST 857).

A total of 48 missile test flights were conducted prior to cancellation of the project, of which 30 were considered successful—that is, achieving all primary objectives; 14 partially successful; and 4 failures.

At the time of cancellation the missile was scheduled to have become operational in January 1960.

Production. The missile production run was from March 1956 through 1958. More than 100 missiles were used for training or expended as targets.

Operational:	cancelled
Design:	Chance Vought
Weight:	22,564 lbs missile
	4,653 lbs rocket boosters
Length:	57 feet + nose boom 10 feet, 2 inches
Wingspan:	20 feet, ½ inch
Wing area:	145 feet²
Height:	12 feet, 6 inches
Propulsion:	1 turbojet; 15,000 lbst in afterburner (General Electric J79-GE-3)
	1 rocket booster; 115,000 lbst for 4 seconds (Aerojet General)
Speed:	maximum 1,320 mph (Mach 2)
	cruise 630 mph (Mach 0.94)
Range:	655 miles with 515 miles at Mach 2
	920 miles with 115 miles at Mach 2
	1,200 miles below Mach 2
Guidance:	inertial
Warhead:	1 W27Y1 nuclear (1.9 MT)
Launch mode:	surface ship and submarine

Rigel SSM-N-6

The Rigel was highly advanced concept for its time, a high-speed (Mach 2) land-attack missile to be launched from surfaced submarines. The program was initiated by the Navy in 1946 and in 1948 was designated as the follow-on to the Regulus I.

Difficulties with the launching requirements—a large ramp was necessitated by the ramjet propulsion—led to cancellation of the project on 5 August 1953.

Design. The Rigel had an aircraft-type configuration with canards forward, twin ramjets mounted on small tail wings, and four solid-propellant rocket boosters mounted between the four tail surfaces. Despite the power of its ramjet and boosters, the Rigel would have required a catapult some 400 feet long, making it impossible to operate from a submarine. Subsequent efforts to develop a scheme for launching the missile directly from its stowage canister were not successful prior to cancellation.

Early planning called for a Mach 2 missile with a range of 575 miles and a cruise altitude of 50,000 feet, with a 3,000-pound warhead and a CEP of 600 yards.

Operational. The first Rigel test vehicle flight on 4 May 1950, reached a speed of Mach 1.9 and a range of 20.7 miles; a later vehicle attained Mach 2 and travelled 73.7 miles. No tactical missiles were produced.

All flight tests employed a 6/10th model of the proposed tactical missile. No full-scale missiles were produced, because of the limitations of ramjet engines available during the test phase.

Operational:	cancelled
Design:	Grumman
Weight:	approx. 23,800 lbs
Propulsion:	2 ramjet engines + 4 rocket boosters
Range:	approx. 690 miles
Guidance:	radio control + preprogram or terminal homing
Warhead:	1 Mark 5 nuclear (variable yield; see text)
Launch mode:	submarine

Tomahawk BGM-109/UGM-109

The Tomahawk is a longrange cruise missile developed for both surface and submarine launch against both surface ships and land targets. It initially was known as the SeaLaunched Cruise Missile (SLCM), for nuclear strike against Soviet land targets.

The missile evolved into a multi-role weapon, and in 1979 the Navy began using the terms Tomahawk Land-Attack Missile (TLAM) and Tomahawk Anti-Ship Missile (TASM) to distinguish the principal variants, the TLAMs having nuclear and several possible conventional warheads. Chemical warheads were briefly considered in the early 1980s but not pursued.

The TASM was to have been phased out of the fleet in favor of the Block IV Tomahawk Multi-Mission Missile—Tactical Tomahawk (TACTOM)—with a common terminal sensor capable of attacking targets on both land and at sea. The anti-ship variant is no longer in service; all TLAM nuclear missiles have also been retired.

The Tomahawk first was deployed in Armored Box Launchers (ABL) on four battleships, five cruisers, and seven *Spruance* (DD 963)–class destroyers; it subsequently was carried in the vertical launchers (Mark 41) of *Spruance*-class destroyers and continues to be carried by *Ticonderoga* (CG 47)–class cruisers, and the *Arleigh Burke* (DDG 51)–class and *Zumwalt* (DDG 1000)–class destroyers.

It can be fired from 21-inch submarine torpedo tubes and, in the Improved *Los Angeles* (SSN 688) and *Virginia* (SSN 774) classes, from vertical launch tubes. The four converted cruise missile submarines of the *Ohio* (SSBN/SSGN 726) class each can carry up to 154 missiles in their vertical launchers.

The Royal Navy has also purchased Tomahawks for the role of land attack from submarines.

Design. The Block III features a smaller but more lethal, insensitive warhead with extended range permitted by additional fuel. These missiles also have a GPS receiver and an improved Digital Scene Matching Area Correlator (DSMAC) for better accuracy and time-of-arrival control to permit coordinated-missile or aircraft-and-missile strikes. That variant also has a Williams 402 turbofan engine, with a 19 percent increase in thrust and a 2 percent decrease in fuel consumption.

About 100 Block IID missiles were converted to a sub-munition variant called Block IIID; the remaining 525 Tomahawks were upgraded to Block IIIC, with a unitary warhead.

The Navy variants were:

Model	Launch Mode	Type	Warhead
BGM-109A	ship/submarine	TLAM(N)	nuclear (W80 warhead)
BGM-109B	ship/submarine	TASM	conventional (1,000lb Bullpup)
BGM-109C	ship/submarine	TLAM-C	conventional (1,000lb Bullpup)
BGM-109D	ship/submarine	TLAM-D	conventional (bomblets)
BGM-109E	ship/submarine	TLAM/TASM	conventional (unitary)
BGM-109F	ship/submarine	TLAM-F	conventional (bomblets)

The Block IV Tomahawk—Tactical Tomahawk (TLAM-E)—is an improved missile for the land-attack role with enhanced attack characteristics and in-flight retargeting. Also, the missile carries a camera to provide a "snapshot" of the battlefield via a satellite data link. Called TACTOM, it provides:

- In-flight retargeting via two-way satellite data link
- Loiter capability in the area of emerging targets
- Monitoring of missile "health" and status in flight via satellite data link
- Improved anti-jam GPS
- Ability to provide single-frame images of the target or point en route

TACTOM originally was to have been propelled by the Teledyne Continental Motors J402-CA-402 engine, which also is being used in the JASSM missile. However, on 9 December 1999, Raytheon announced a stop-work order on the engine as part of a risk-reduction effort for TACTOM. Williams International had proposed the smaller version of the firm's F-122 engine, being used in the German-Swedish Taurus missile. (Williams had lost to Teledyne in the original TACTOM engine competition.)

The TACTOM carries either a unitary warhead (109C) or sub-munitions (109D). In October 2010, the first live firing of a new warhead, the Joint Multi-Effects Warhead System (JMEWS), was conducted. JMEWS will give the Tactical Tomahawk enhanced penetration capabilities in addition to blast fragmentation.

The accuracy of the early TLAM missiles was on the order of 33 feet (ten meters); later missiles, employing GPS, have considerably more accuracy—some published reports citing an accuracy of just over 12 feet (3.65 meters). Speed is approximately 550 mph.

General Dynamics proposed an ASW variant of the Tomahawk as an alternative to the Sea Lance project (for both surface ship and submarine launch). An airlaunched Tomahawk competed unsuccessfully with the Boeing AirLaunched Cruise Missile (ALCM) for use on B-52 strategic bombers. The BGM-199G Ground-Launched Cruise Missile (GLCM) variant was selected as a theater nuclear weapon for deployment in Western Europe under Air Force control, but those weapons were disposed of under the Intermediate-range Nuclear Forces (INF) treaty. The TLAM(N) fitted with the W80 nuclear warhead has been retired. The Air Force–operated

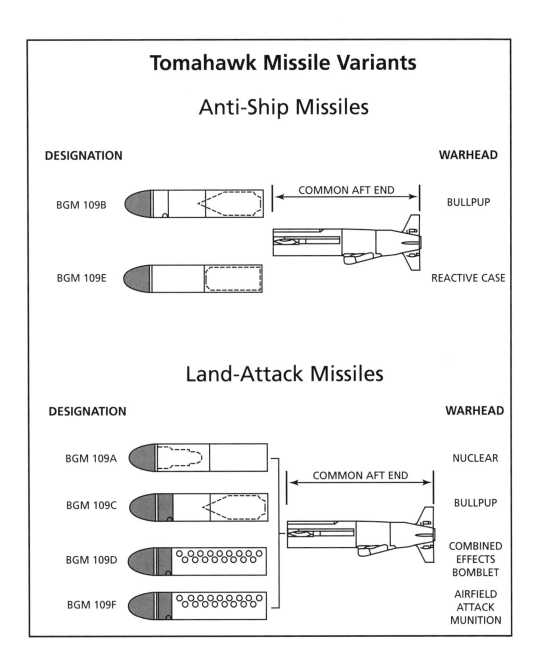

Gryphon Ground-Launched Cruise Missile (GLCM) carried the W84 nuclear warhead with a variable yield of 0.2 to 150 kilotons.

Operational. The first operational use of the Tomahawk was in the 1991 Gulf War (Operation Desert Storm), when the Navy launched 288 Tomahawks—276 from surface combatants and 12 from submarines (SSNs). Subsequently TLAMs have been employed on numerous occasions from U.S. surface ships and submarines as well as British submarines.

Status. Operational and in production. Only TLAM (conventional) and TACTOM variants are operational. IOC TASM in surface ships in 1982; TASM in submarines in 1983; TLAM in surface ships in 1984; TLAM(N) in 1987; IOC TLAM Block III in 1994; TACTOM IOC in 2004.

The first TACTOM launch was from the guided missile destroyer *Stethem* (DDG 63) in October 2002. A Tomahawk cruise missile was successfully launched from the submarine *Barb* (SSN 596) on 1 February 1978; the *Guitarro* (SSN 665) was the first submarine armed with Tomahawk. The destroyer *Merrill* (DD 976) was fitted with the first Tomahawk installation in October 1982, for at sea evaluation; the battleship *New Jersey* (BB 62) was the second ship, receiving the Tomahawk in March 1983.

The Royal Navy originally procured 65 TLAMs in 1988, with the submarine *Splendid* launching the first British missile on 18 November 1998. Subsequently additional TLAMs were procured.

Operational:	1982
Prime Contractor:	Raytheon (formerly McDonnell Douglas)
Weight:	2,650 lbs + 550-lb booster + 1,000-lb capsule for submarine launch
Length:	18 feet 3 inches + 2 foot booster
Span:	8 feet, 9 inches
Diameter:	20½ inches
Propulsion:	Block III: turbofan (Williams F107-WR-402) + solidpropellant booster (CSD/ARC Mark 106)
Block IV:	turbofan (Williams International F415-WR-400) + solid-propellant booster (ARC Mark 135)
Range:	TLAM-C approx. 1,035 miles
	TLAM-D/E approx. 800 miles
Guidance:	inertial and TERCOM (Terrain Contour Matching); GPS in Block III
Warhead:	TLAM-C/E 1,000-lb high explosive
	TLAM-D BLU-97 sub-munitions
	TLAM(N) W80 nuclear warhead (variable 5 to 150 KT)
Launch Mode:	surface ship and submarine

Gryphon BGM-109G

The Gryphon Ground-Launched Cruise Missile (GLCM) was a land-launched version of the highly successful Navy Tomahawk-series cruise missile. Gryphon was a long-range, subsonic, strategic cruise missile specifically developed for use in the European theater. On 12 January 1977, the U.S. government made the decision to develop a ground-launched variant of the Tomahawk, in part to counter Soviet deployment of the SS-22 Saber (Soviet RSD-10 Pioneer) intermediate-range ballistic missile beginning that year.

The NATO leadership agreed on 12 December 1979, to the deployment of 464 U.S. Air Force–operated GLCMs in Western Europe. The first GLCMs arrived in Britain in 1983, and deployments followed rapidly in four other NATO nations. The missiles and 116 launch vehicles were deployed, all of which were in place by late 1988.

The Gryphon/GLCM's operational service was brief; it was banned under the INF treaty that was signed on 8 December 1987, and entered into force on 1 June 1988. The missiles were withdrawn from service between 1988 and 1991 and destroyed.

Design. The GLCM was virtually identical to contemporary Navy Tomahawk land-attack missiles.

The GLCM firing unit ("flight") was composed of four Transporter Erector-Launcher (TEL) vehicles, each of which was fitted with four missiles. Thus, a flight of four TELs had 16 missiles, as well as two launch control vehicles (one primary, one backup), 16 support vehicles, and 69 personnel. The vehicles were air transportable in C-5, C-130, and C-141 cargo aircraft. Each TEL with four missiles and mated nuclear warheads weighed 77,900 pounds, was 55 feet long, and had selfcontained electrical power.

Designation. The name "Gryphon," though officially adopted for the GLCM, was not widely used.

Operational. First flight of prototype GLCM in December 1979. The first GLCMs to deploy arrived in Britain on 14 November 1983, transported across the Atlantic in a C-141 Starlifter transport; the missiles attained IOC on 1 January 1984. The other NATO deployments followed.

The first GLCMs were withdrawn from Western Europe on 8 September 1988. The last deployed GLCMs were shipped back to the United States on 26 March 1991.

Operational:	January 1984–1991
Prime Contractor:	General Dynamics/McDonnell Douglas
Weight:	3,770 lbs fueled
	3,240 lbs without fuel
Length:	21 feet
Diameter:	20¾ inches
Wingspan:	8 feet, 2 inches
Propulsion:	1 turbofan (Williams F107-WR-400)
Range:	1,550 miles
Guidance:	inertial navigation with Terrain Contour Matching (TERCOM); radar altimeter
Warhead:	1 W84 nuclear (variable 0.2–150 KT)
Launch Mode:	ground vehicle

Appendix B

U.S. Navy Land-Attack Cruise Missile Warheads*

Mark 5

This variation of the B5 nuclear bomb was developed as a lightweight warhead for the ship/submarine-launched Regulus I, Rigel, and Triton land-attack missiles and for the land-launched Matador cruise missile. The Regulus I warhead was retired in 1958, replaced by the W27.

The Mark 5 was an implosion weapon with several yield selections, depending upon which nuclear capsule was placed in the in-flight insertion mechanism. During missile flight a signal was sent from the launching cruiser or submarine to arm the warhead. That signal caused the screw mechanism to move the nuclear capsule into the center of the weapon pit; that action in turn determined the warhead yield and armed the warhead.

Inventory:	1954–1958
Yield:	variable to 45 KT
Weight:	2,400–2,650 lbs
Dimensions:	length 6 feet, 4 inches
	diameter 3 feet, 7¾ inches
Weapons:	Matador surface-to-surface missile 1955–1961
	Regulus I surface-to-surface missile 1954–1958
	Rigel surface-to-surface missile (cancelled)
	Triton surface-to-surface missile (cancelled)

W27

The W27 was a replacement for the Mark 5 warhead in the Navy's Regulus I land-attack cruise missile. The warhead also was considered for the Matador, Snark, Rascal, Redstone, and Triton missiles and for the weapons pod carried by the B-58 Hustler strategic bomber.

---

*Additional and comprehensive information on U.S. nuclear warheads can be found in: Chuck Hansen, *U.S. Nuclear Weapons: The Secret History* (Arlington, Tex.: Aerofax, 1988); James N. Gibson, *Nuclear Weapons of the United States* (Atglen, Pa.: Schiffer Military/Aviation History, 1996); and Norman Polmar and Robert S. Norris, *The U.S. Nuclear Arsenal: A History of Weapons and Delivery Systems since 1945* (Annapolis, Md.: Naval Institute Press, 2009).

The W27 was a tritium-boosted, thermonuclear weapon.

Inventory:	W27 Sep. 1957–June 1963
	W27Y1 Apr. 1963–Oct. 1965
Yield:	1.9 MT
Weight:	2,800 lbs
Dimensions:	length 6 feet, 3 inches
	diameter 30 inches
Weapons:	Regulus I surface-to-surface missile

W80

The W80 is a common warhead used in the Advanced Cruise Missile (ACM), Air-Launched Cruise Missile (ALCM), and Tomahawk Land-Attack Missile (TLAM). The warhead is a modification of the B61 bomb. The W80-1 entered production in January 1982, and the W80-0 in March 1982. The first production W80-1 unit was completed in January 1981; quantity production began in February 1982. An estimated 1,850 warheads were produced. The first production W80-0 unit was completed in December 1983, and quantity production began in March 1984. An estimated 350 warheads were produced before production ended in early 1990.

The Mod 0 uses low neutron/gram/second (ngs) plutonium to produce low intrinsic radiation, for personnel protection on board submarines. Safety features for both variants include insensitive high-explosive material and Permissive Action Links (PALs). The W80-0 and -1 were upgraded, becoming the W80-2 and -3, respectively.

The Tomahawk Land-Attack Missile/Nuclear (TLAM-N) missiles were taken out of service in 1992.

Inventory:	1982–present	
Yield:	variable 5 to 150 KT	
Weight:	290 lbs	
Dimensions:	length 2 feet, 7 inches	
	diameter 11¾ inches	
Weapons:	Mod 0	Tomahawk land-attack missile
	Mod 1	ALCM/ACM air-to-surface

Appendix C

Soviet/Russian Navy Land–Attack Cruise Missiles[1]

SS-N-3c Shaddock (P-5)

The Shaddock was a large, air-breathing cruise missile originally developed for the strategic land-attack role in the SS-N-3c variant and, subsequently, for the antiship role as the SS-N-3a.*

The Shaddock was carried by surface ships and submarines, the submarines launching the Shaddock while on the surface. The SS-N-3c land-attack missile had inertial guidance. The anti-ship missile required mid-course guidance for over-the-horizon use. This was sent as a radar picture via Video Data Link (VDL) from a targeting ship or aircraft to the launching ship and then relayed—with the target indicated—to the missile while in flight.

With the shift from the land-attack SS-N-3c missile to anti-ship variants only, the early Whiskey-class SSGs were discarded; the five Project 659/Echo I SSGNs that originally carried the SS-N-3c missile were converted to torpedo-attack submarines (659T). The later 16 Project 651/Juliett SSGs and 29 Project 675/Echo II SSGNs were rearmed with anti-ship missiles.

The anti-ship variants had the Soviet designation P-6 (NATO SS-N-3a/b). The anti-ship variants had a limited land-attack capability (see chapter 19).

The SSC-1 (P-35) was a land-launched, anti-ship variant assigned the NATO code name Sepal; the missile was assigned to coastal defense forces. As of January 1974, Western intelligence had identified 14 SSC-1 mobile missile sites in all four fleet areas.

Design. All Shaddock missiles were launched from surfaced submarines and surface ships. Both the land-attack and anti-ship variants could carry nuclear or conventional warheads.

Operational:	1959–1965
Design:	V. N. Chelomei
Weight:	11,880 lbs
Length:	38 feet, 6 inches
Wingspan:	16 feet, 5 inches
Diameter:	approx. 38½ inches
Propulsion:	turbojet + 2 solid-fuel boosters
Range:	460+ miles
Guidance:	inertial

★ The NATO assignment of suffixes was based on the order in which variants were identified.

Warhead:	nuclear or conventional high-explosive (2,200 lbs)
Submarines:	SSG Project 613/Whiskey variants (1 to 4 missiles)
	SSG Project 651/Juliett (4 missiles)★
	SSGN Project 659/Echo I (6 missiles)
	SSGN Project 675/Echo II (8 missiles)★

★Rearmed with P-6/SS-N-3 anti-ship missiles

SS-N-21 Sampson (R-55 Granat/Relief)

This is an advanced land-attack cruise missile that can to be launched from standard 21-inch (533-mm) submarine torpedo tubes, much like the U.S. Navy Tomahawk Land-Attack Missile (TLAM). The similarity of the SS-N-21 design to the U.S. weapon has led to the Soviet weapon's being called "Tomahawkski" by Western intelligence.

The air-launched version of this missile is the NATO AS-15 Kent, and there is a ground-launched version designated SSC-X-4 Slingshot by NATO.

Speed is approximately Mach 0.7.

Operational. Launch trials for the SS-N-21 were conducted from a modified Project 671RTM/Victor III–class SSN; that submarine was distinguished by a long cylinder fitted on the deck immediately forward of the sail structure. Subsequent trials were conducted by the first two Project 971/Akula SSNs, apparently without visible modifications.

In 1985 a Yankee SSBN completed conversion to an SS-N-21 missile configuration, being given the Western designation Yankee-Notch (Project 667AT).

Operational:	1987–
Design:	L.V. Lyulev (Novator Design Bureau)
Weight:	3,750 lbs
Length:	26 feet, 7 inches
Wingspan:	10 feet, 10 inches
Diameter:	20 feet, 1 inch
Propulsion:	turbofan + solid-propellant rocket booster
Range:	approx. 1,860 miles
Guidance:	inertial + Terrain Contour Matching (TERCOM)
Warhead:	100-KT nuclear or conventional high-explosive
Submarines:	SSN types
	SSGN Project 667AT/Yankee-Notch

SS-NX-24 Scorpion (Kh-90/P-750 Meteorit-M)

This was a submarine-launched, land-attack missile that did not enter operational service although it was tested successfully in December 1983. The 1991 U.S.-Soviet agreement to remove nuclear SLCMs from surface ships and submarines caused termination of the missile. A single Project 667A/Yankee SSBN—the *K-420*—was converted to carry the missile; redesignated 667M. The NATO designation AS-X-19 Kola was for an air-launched variant.

The missile was designed by the Machine Building Scientific Production Association. It had ramjet propulsion, providing a supersonic speed. Length was approximately 41 feet. Range was estimated at from 1,860 to 2,485 miles (3,000 to 4,000 kilometers).

SS-N-30A Sagaris/Sizzler (3M-14K Kalibr/Klub)

This is the land-attack variant of the Kalibr modular "family" of missiles for the anti-ship, anti-submarine, and land-attack roles that could be launched from aircraft, surface ships, and submarines. "Klub" is the name used for missiles transferred to other nations; these include the submarine-launched 3M-54E1 anti-ship, 3M-14E land-attack, and 91-RE1 anti-submarine variants.

The missile can be launched from standard 21-inch (533-mm) torpedo tubes. The terminal speed is Mach 0.8.

Operational. The first combat use of the land-attack variants occurred on 7 October 2015, when a Russian frigate and three smaller patrol ships launched 26 3M-14T Kalibr land-attack missiles from the Caspian Sea against 11 targets in Syria, a distance of more than 900 miles. These strikes were in support of Syrian dictator Bashar al-Assad, a Russian ally. (There were unconfirmed reports that four of these missiles crashed in Iran.)

Subsequently, additional Kalibr missiles were launched from ships in the Caspian Sea and from surface ships in the eastern Mediterranean. On 14 September 2017, the Kilo-class submarines *Veliky Novgorod* and *Kolpino* fired seven Kalibr missiles from the eastern Mediterranean against Syrian targets. Additional submarine-launched Kalibr strikes followed. In 2019 it was reported by the Russian news agency Tass that a new and improved Kalibr cruise missile for surface ships and submarines was under development. The upgraded missile was reported to have a range of more than 2,800 miles or twice that of the current 3M-54 Kalibr cruise missile. The weapon was reported to be in "scientific research" stage and was scheduled to enter service by 2027.

Operational:	1994–
Design:	Novator Design Bureau
Length:	20 feet, 4 inches
Diameter:	21 inches
Propulsion:	turbofan
Range:	approx. 1,500 miles
Guidance:	inertial
Warhead:	nuclear or conventional high-explosive (990 lbs)
Submarines:	SS/SSN/SSGN types

Appendix D

U.S. Cruise Missile Submarines

Tunny (SSG 282)

Class:	Converted *Gato* (SS 212) class
Builder:	Mare Island Naval Shipyard, Vallejo, California
Completed:	1942
Converted:	to SSG 1952
Displacement:	1,525 tons surface
	2,400 tons submerged
Length:	311 feet, 8 inches
Beam:	27 feet, 3 inches
Draft:	18 feet
Propulsion:	3 diesel engines; 2 electric motors; 2 shafts
Speed:	19 knots surface
	9 knots submerged
Crew:	80 (10 officers + 70 enlisted)
Torpedo tubes:	4 21-inch (533-mm) (bow)
Missiles:	2 Regulus I

Barbero (SSG 317)

Class:	Converted *Balao* (SS 285) class
Builder:	Electric Boat Co., Groton, Connecticut
Completed:	1943
Converted:	to SSG 1955
Displacement:	1,525 tons surface
	2,410 tons submerged
Length:	311 feet, 9 inches
Beam:	27 feet, 3 inches
Draft:	19 feet, 3 inches
Propulsion:	2 diesel engines; 2 electric motors; 2 shafts
Speed:	14 knots surface
	8.75 knots submerged
Crew:	81 (10 officers, 71 enlisted)
Torpedo tubes:	6 21-inch (533-mm) (bow)
Missiles:	2 Regulus I

Grayback (SSG 574)

Builder:	Mare Island Naval Shipyard, Vallejo, California
Completed:	1958
Displacement:	2,671 tons surface
	3,652 tons submerged
Length:	322 feet, 4 inches
Beam:	30 feet
Draft:	19 feet
Propulsion:	3 diesel engines; 2 electric motors; 2 shafts
Speed:	19 knots surface
	9 knots submerged
Crew:	87 (10 officers, 77 enlisted)
Torpedo tubes:	8 21 inch (533-mm) (6 bow, 2 stern)
Missiles:	4 Regulus I
	planned: 2 Regulus II

Growler (SSG 577)

Builder:	Portsmouth Naval Shipyard, Kittery, Maine
Completed:	1958
Displacement:	2,768 tons surface
	3,515 tons submerged
Length:	317 feet, 7 inches
Beam:	27 feet, 2 inches
Draft:	19 feet
Propulsion:	3 diesel engines; 2 electric motors; 2 shafts
Speed:	19 knots surface
	9 knots submerged
Crew:	84 (10 officers, 74 enlisted)
Torpedo tubes:	8 21-inch (533-mm) (6 bow, 2 stern)
Missiles:	4 Regulus I
	planned: 2 Regulus II

Halibut (SSGN 587)

Builder:	Mare Island Naval Shipyard, Vallejo, California
Completed:	1960
Displacement:	3,655 tons surface
	5,000 tons submerged
Length:	350 feet
Beam:	29 feet
Draft:	28 feet
Propulsion:	2 steam turbines; approx. 13,000 shp; 2 shafts
Reactor:	1 S3W pressurized-water
Speed:	20 knots surface
	20 knots submerged

Crew: 123 (10 officers, 113 enlisted)
Torpedo tubes: 6 21-inch (533-mm) (4 bow, 2 stern)
Missiles: 5 Regulus I
                 planned: 4 Regulus II

Improved *Los Angeles* Class (SSN 751)

Number: 23
Builder: Newport News Shipbuilding, Virginia (13 units)
                 General Dynamics, Groton, Connecticut (10 units)
Completed: 1988–1996
Displacement: 6,300 tons surface except SSN 771–773 6,330 tons
                 7,147 tons submerged except SSN 771–773 7,177 tons
Length: 360 feet
Beam: 33 feet
Draft: 32 feet
Propulsion: 2 steam turbines; approx. 30,000 shp; 1 shaft
Reactor: 1 S6G pressurized-water
Speed: approx. 15 knots surface
                 approx. 30 knots submerged
Crew: 143 (16 officers + 127 enlisted)
Torpedo tubes: 4 21-inch (533-mm) (angled)
Missiles: 12 Tomahawk★

★12 vertical-launch cells; additional Tomahawks could be launched from torpedo tubes.

Converted *Ohio* Class (SSGN 726)

Number: 4
Builder: General Dynamics/Electric Boat, Groton,
                 Connecticut
Completed: 2002–2004
Converted: from SSBN to SSGN 2006–2007
Displacement: 16,750 tons surface
                 18,750 tons submerged
Length: 560 feet
Beam: 42 feet
Draft: 36 feet, 3 inches
Propulsion: 2 steam turbines; approx. 35,000 shp;
                 1 shaft
Reactor: 1 S8G pressurized-water
Speed: approx. 25 knots surface
                 approx. 25 knots submerged
Crew: 159 (15 officers, 144 enlisted)
Torpedo tubes: 4 21-inch (533-mm) (angled)
Missiles: 154 Tomahawk

***Virginia* Class (SSN 774)**

Number:	14★
Completed:	2004–
Builder:★★	Newport News Shipbuilding, Virginia
	General Dynamics/Electric Boat, Groton, Connecticut
Displacement:	6,950 tons surface
	7,833 tons submerged
Length:	377 feet
Beam:	34 feet
Draft:	32 feet
Propulsion:	2 steam turbines; approx. 25,000 shp; 1 shaft
Reactor:	1 S9G pressurized-water
Speed:	25+ knots submerged
Crew:	132 (15 officers + 117 enlisted)
Torpedo tubes:	4 21-inch (533-mm) (angled)
Missiles:	12 Tomahawks

★ Additional units under construction.

★★ Newport News builds the bow, stern, sail, habitability, auxiliary machinery, and weapons handling sections of all units; Electric Boat builds the pressure hull, command and control spaces, engine room, and main propulsion for all units. Each yard builds a reactor plant module and performs final outfitting, testing, and delivery for alternate submarines.

Appendix E

Soviet/Russian Cruise Missile Submarines

In the post–World War II period the United States and NATO assigned letter designations to Soviet submarines according to the military phonetic system in common use; the letters were assigned in random order. Thus, the first submarine identified under this scheme—Project 613— was given the U.S.-NATO designation *W*—thus, invariably "Whiskey," the phonetic word in military communications for that letter. The Project 627, designated *N,* or "November," was the first nuclear-propelled submarine to be identified.

Project 644 (*NATO:* Whiskey Twin-Cylinder)

One Project 613/Whiskey submarine was converted to a missile test platform with a single hangar/launch canister for Shaddock-type missiles; in some Western intelligence documents this submarine was identified as the Whiskey "Single-Cylinder."

Number:	4
Builder:	Krasnoe Sormovo, Gor'kiy
Completed:	1951–1955
Converted:	to SSG 1960, except *S-162* in 1962
Displacement:	1,156.8 tons surface
	1,466.8 tons submerged
Length:	249 feet, 3 inches
Beam:	21 feet, 8 inches
Draft:	17 feet, 9 inches
Propulsion:	2 diesel engines; 2 electric motors; 2 shafts
Speed:	16 knots surface
	10 knots submerged
Crew:	55
Torpedo tubes:	4 21-inch (533-mm) (bow)
Missiles:	2 P-5 (SS-N-3c Shaddock)
	after 1960: 2 P-5D (SS-N-3a Shaddock) in some units

Project 665 (*NATO*: Whiskey Long-Bin)

Western intelligence sources vary on the precise number of Whiskey Long-Bin submarines; see text.

Number:	6
Builder:	Krasnoe Sormovo, Gor'kiy (4)
	Andre Marti (south), Nikolayev (2)
Completed:	1952–1954
Converted:	to SSG 1958–1963
Displacement:	1,480 tons surface
	1,924 tons submerged
Length:	278 feet, 10 inches
Beam:	22 feet
Draft:	15 feet, 7 inches
Propulsion:	2 diesel engines; 2 electric motors; 2 shafts
Speed:	16 knots surface
	10 knots submerged
Crew:	58
Torpedo tubes:	4 21-inch (533-mm) (bow)
Missiles:	4 P-5 (SS-N-3c Shaddock)
	after 1960: 4 P-5D (SS-N-3a Shaddock) in some units

Project 659 (*NATO*: Echo I)

Number:	5
Builder:	Komsomolsk-on-Amur
Completed:	1961–1963
Displacement:	3,731 tons surface
	4,920 tons submerged
Length:	364 feet, 9 inches
Beam:	30 feet, 2 inches
Draft:	23 feet, 3 inches
Propulsion:	2 steam turbines; 2 shafts
Reactor:	2 VM-A pressurized-water
Speed:	15 knots surface
	26 knots submerged
Crew:	100
Torpedo tubes:	4 21-inch (533-mm) (bow)
	4 15¾-inch (400-mm) (2 bow, 2 stern)
Missiles:	6 P-5 (SS-N-3c Shaddock), removed in 1960s

Project 675 (*NATO*: Echo II)

Number:	29
Builder:	Severodvinsk (16 units)
	Komsomolsk-on-Amur (13 units)
Completed:	1963–1968

Displacement:	4,500 tons surface
	5,760 tons submerged
Length:	378 feet, 6 inches
Beam:	30 feet, 6 inches
Draft:	22 feet
Propulsion:	2 steam turbines; 2 shafts
Reactors:	2 VM-A pressurized-water
Speed:	14 knots surface
	23 knots submerged
Crew:	100
Torpedo tubes:	4 21-inch (533-mm) (bow)
	2 15¾-inch (400-mm) (stern)
Missiles:	8 P-5 (SS-N-3c Shaddock)
	after 1965: 8 P-5D (SS-N-3a Shaddock)

Project 651 (*NATO:* Juliett)

Number:	16
Builder:	Baltic Shipyard, Leningrad (2 units)
	Krosnoe Sormovo, Gor'kiy (14 units)
Completed:	1963–1968
Displacement:	3,140 tons surface
	4,132 tons submerged
Length:	281 feet, 9 inches
Beam:	31 feet, 10 inches
Draft:	22 feet, 8 inches
Propulsion:	2 diesel engines; 8,000 horsepower; 2 shafts
	2 electric motors; 4,000 horsepower
Speed:	16 knots surface
	18 knots submerged
Crew:	83
Torpedo tubes:	6 21-inch (533-mm) (bow)
	4 15¾-inch (400-mm) (stern)
Missiles:	4 P-5 (SS-N-3c Shaddock)
	after 1965: 4 P-5D (SS-N-3a Shaddock)

Project 949 (*NATO:* Oscar)

In the post-Soviet period several of these submarines have been modified to launch Kalibr-series missiles in place of the P-700/SS-N-19 weapons.★

Number:	13 (2 Project 949; 11 Project 949A)
Builder:	Severodvinsk
Completed:	1980–1996

★ Characteristics for Project 949A/Oscar II series

Displacement:	14,700 tons surface
	19,400 tons submerged
Length:	508 feet, 4 inches
Beam:	59 feet, 9 inches
Draft:	29 feet, 6 inches
Propulsion:	2 steam turbines; approx. 100,000 shp; 2 shafts
Reactor:	2 OK–650 pressurized–water
Speed:	15 knots surface
	30 knots submerged
Crew:	107
Torpedo tubes:	4 21-inch (533-mm) (bow)
	4 26½ –inch (650-mm) (bow)
Missiles:	24 P-700 Granit (SS–N–19 Shipwreck)

Project 949 (*Severodvinsk*)

The *Severodvinsk*-class submarines are believed to be the world's deepest diving combat undersea craft, with an operating depth in excess of 3,280 feet (i.e., 1,000 meters); they have steel pressure hulls. ★★

Number:	ongoing program
Builder:	Severodvinsk
Completed:	2014–
Displacement:	approx. 9,500 tons surface
	approx. 13,800 tons submerged
Length:	390 feet
Beam:	49 feet
Draft:	28 feet
Propulsion:	2 steam turbines; approx. 40,000 shp; 2 shafts
Reactor:	1 pressurized–water
Speed:	20 knots surface
	30+ knots submerged
Crew:	approx. 65
Torpedo tubes:	8 21-inch (533-mm) (bow)
Missiles:	32 Kalibr

★★ No NATO known to be assigned. The Russian class name is *Yasen* (ash).

Notes

Chapter 1. Bombardment from the Sea

1. Don Everitt, *The K Boats: A Dramatic First Report on the World's Most Calamitous Submarines* (New York: Holt, Rinehart and Winston, 1963), 160. The Royal Navy commissioned 17 K-class submarines in 1916–1918. These were *steam-driven* on the surface and by any criteria were failures; they were involved in 16 major accidents; one was lost on trials, three sank in collisions, and one disappeared.

2. The three *Formidable*-class battleships were completed in 1901. Each mounted four 12-inch guns and 12 6-inch (152-mm) guns. Two were sunk in World War I.

3. Vice Adm. James Jungius, RN, letter to N. Polmar, 3 February 1977. Details of the M-class boats—laid down as units of the K Class—are found in Everitt, *K Boats*.

4. See Robert Branfill-Cook, *X-1: The Royal Navy's Mystery Submarine* (Yorkshire, U.K.: Pen & Sword/Seaforth, 2012).

5. The USS *Argonaut*, commissioned in 1928, initially was designated as a submarine minelayer (SM 1); on 22 September 1942, she was changed to transport submarine (APS 1). Her submarine linear number was SS 166, although that designation was never officially assigned.

6. See N. Polmar, *Atomic Submarines* (Princeton, N.J.: D. Van Nostrand, 1963), 183–84; based on Ernest A. Steinhoff letter to N. Polmar, 11 April 1962, and discussions with Steinhoff in 1962. The commanding officer of *U-511* at the time was Steinhoff's brother, *Kapitanleutnant* Friedrich "Fritz" Steinhoff.

7. During World War I the German Army had employed the "Paris gun"—a 238-mm weapon—to bombard the city of Paris from a range of 70 miles.

8. The attack on Fort McHenry occurred during the British-American War of 1812.

9. The V-2 ballistic missile's development began earlier than that of the V-1 cruise missile, but it entered operational service only after the Flying Bomb, which thus became known as the V-1.

10. The British air defense system included fixed early warning radars (known as Chain Home), command and plotting centers, fighter aircraft, and anti-aircraft artillery.

11. The German Army had long-range guns that could just reach the English coast at Dover from firing positions along the French coast, a distance of about 20 miles. The fall of shot at that range is not very accurate.

12. There were four experimental ballistic missiles: A-1, A-2, A-3, and A-5. The designation A-4 was reserved for the planned operational missile, thus when it proved necessary to develop one more experimental missile after the A-3 it became the A-5.

13. Anthony L. Kay, *Fieseler Fi 103 Buzz Bomb* (Sturbridge, Mass.: Monogram Aviation, 1977), 2.
14. Ibid., 2–3.
15. The Meteor became operational in July 1944.
16. Kay, *Fieseler Fi 103*, 3.
17. Peter G. Cooksley, *Flying Bomb: The Story of Hitler's V-Weapons in World War II* (New York: Charles Scribner's Sons, 1979), 25–26.
18. The USAF Matador cruise missile also was designed with a chemical warfare delivery capability, although it was only deployed with the W5 nuclear warhead.
19. Steven Zaloga, *V-1 Flying Bomb* (Oxford, U.K.: Osprey, 2005), 12.
20. Benjamin King and Timothy J. Kutta, *Impact: The History of Germany's V-weapons in World War II* (Cambridge, Mass.: Da Capo, 1998), 97.
21. Cooksley, *Flying Bomb*, 28.
22. Kay, *Fieseler Fi 103*, 7.
23. King and Kutta, *Impact*, 191.
24. Kay, *Fieseler Fi 103*, 8–9. See also Michael J. Neufeld, *The Rocket and the Reich* (New York: Free Press, 1995), 230.
25. Seth W. Carus, *Cruise Missile Proliferation in the 1990s* (Washington, D.C.: Center for Strategic and International Studies, 1992), 100.
26. Neufeld, *Rocket and the Reich*, 274.
27. Anthony Beevor, *D-Day: The Battle for Normandy* (New York: Viking, 2009), 224–26. The bunker had been prepared at Margival, near Soissons, for use by Hitler during the invasion of Britain; it was in a deep railway cutting near a tunnel for the Führer's train.
28. Kay, *Fieseler Fi 103*, 9.
29. Cooksley, *Flying Bomb*, 101.
30. Zaloga, *V-1 Flying Bomb*, 20–21.
31. Otto Skorzeny, *Skorzeny's Special Missions* (London: Greenhill Books, 1957), 152–54.
32. John Gordon, "German Kamikazes?," letter to the editor, *Air and Space* (December 2004 / January 2005), 6.
33. Skorzeny, *Skorzeny's Special Missions*, 152–54.

Chapter 2. Loon Goes to Sea

1. There had been a "JB-1," an earlier, unsuccessful attempt by the Army Air Forces to produce a flying bomb. The French also experimented with the V-1, under the designation Arsenal 5.501. See Cooksley, *Flying Bomb*, 143.
2. George Mindling and Robert Bolton, *U.S. Air Force Tactical Missiles, 1949–1961* (Morrisville, N.C.: LuLu.Com, 2008), 29.
3. Muroc Army Airfield was renamed Edwards Air Force Base in 1949.
4. Cooksley, *Flying Bomb*, 141–42.
5. Mindling and Bolton, *U.S. Air Force Tactical Missiles*, 30.
6. Kenneth P. Werrell, *The Evolution of the Cruise Missile* (Maxwell Air Force Base, Ala.: Air University Press, 1985), 67. For early cruise missiles the size of the CEP was directly related to the range from missile launch to target: the longer the range the larger the CEP. In conventional bombing, the CEP is directly related to bombing altitude, the higher the altitude the greater the CEP. Precision-guided bombs and missiles have changed those equations.

7. At that time the Navy had more than 100 escort carriers in service and under construction.

8. Quoted in Malcolm Muir Jr., "A Stillborn System: The Sub-Launched Cruise Missile," *MHQ* [Military History Quarterly] (Winter 1994), 80.

9. Mark L. Evans and Roy A. Grossnick, *United States Naval Aviation, 1910–2010,* vol. 1, *Chronology* (Washington, D.C.: Naval History and Heritage Command, 2015), 228.

10. The *Norton Sound* subsequently was engaged in missile, radar, and gunnery trials; she was redesignated AVM 1 on 8 August 1951. See N. Polmar, "USS *Norton Sound*: The Newest Old Ship," U.S. Naval Institute *Proceedings* (April 1979), 70–83.

11. BuAer designated the Loon as first the KGW-1, then KUW-1 (both indicating target drone), and later LTV-N-2.

12. John H. Bothwell, USN (Ret.), "The Barnstorming Days of Submarine Missiles," U.S. Naval Institute *Proceedings* (December 1990), 54.

13. Ibid.

14. Evans and Grossnick, *United States Naval Aviation,* 1:240.

15. David K. Stumpf, *Regulus: The Forgotten Weapon* (Paducah, Ky.: Turner, 1996), 14–15.

16. Kay, *Buzz Bomb,* 14, 30.

17. Stumpf, *Regulus,* 14–15. Cdr. John McCain Jr., USN, went on to become a full admiral and served as Commander-in-Chief Pacific during the Vietnam War. His son, who served as a captain in the Navy, became a U.S. senator from Arizona.

18. Bothwell, "Barnstorming Days of Submarine Missiles," 53.

19. Electronic Countermeasures (ECM) are designed to interfere with enemy electronic devices such as radar. Electronic Counter-Countermeasures (ECCM) are a defense against ECM.

20. Evans and Grossnick, *United States Naval Aviation,* 1:272.

21. Berend Derk Bruins, "U.S. Naval Bombardment Missiles, 1940–1958: A Study of the Weapons Innovation Process," PhD thesis, Columbia University, Ann Arbor, Michigan, 1981, 187–88 (University Microfilms International).

22. N. Polmar and Robert S. Norris, *The U.S. Nuclear Arsenal: A History of Weapons and Delivery Systems since 1945* (Annapolis, Md.: Naval Institute Press, 2009), 42.

23. USS *Caiman* (SS 323) took part in a SLAMEX in 1957, and USS *Pickerel* (SS 524) was similarly employed in a SLAMEX in 1963. Both submarines reached their designated launch sites undetected and simulated firing their missiles. Coauthor O'Connell was assigned to those submarines during their respective exercises.

24. Early concepts of Regulus employment in a deterrent role called for an SSG to launch at a range of about 150 nautical miles from the target and guide the missile during the first part of its flight. Then an SS/SSN with guidance radar, operating submerged and closer to the target, would take over and provide guidance for the last leg of the flight. However, during the 1959–1964 periods of SSG/SSGN deterrent patrols only the launching SSG/SSGN was on station.

25. Although the system was called Jet-Assisted Takeoff (JATO), the devices were in fact rockets.

26. All of these aircraft were redesignated on 1 October 1962, in the all-service system:

   AD   > A-1   A4D > A-4
   AJ   > A-2   A3J > A-5
   A3D > A-3

   Also, the P2V Neptune became the P-2 series in the new system.

Chapter 3. The Regulus Missile

1. In 1948 the U.S. Air Force fitted a ramjet engine in an F-80 Shooting Star, the first time that a ramjet was fitted to a piloted aircraft.
2. Stumpf, *Regulus,* 20–21.
3. The Submarine Officer Conferences began in 1926 as a means to provide a submarine perspective to the General Board of admirals. It also served to educate senior submarine officers about new developments and to get general consensus in the submarine officer community about avenues of improvement to submarine design.
4. Stumpf, *Regulus,* 21.
5. For a discussion of Japanese ASW efforts see N. Polmar and Edward Whitman, *Hunters and Killers,* vol. 2, *Anti-Submarine Warfare from 1943* (Annapolis, Md.: Naval Institute Press, 2016), 45, 46, 49–56.
6. The Navy flew the P-80C as the TO-1 and, subsequently, TV-1 Shooting Star. The Air Force two-seat T-33 variant was the Navy's TO-2/TV-2.
7. Stumpf, *Regulus,* 21.
8. Ibid., 21–22.
9. Bruins, *U.S. Naval Bombardment Missiles,* 165. The author refers to several JCS documents as sources but does not list the other three missiles.
10. Ibid., 201.
11. The *Princeton,* an *Essex*-class carrier, originally was commissioned in 1945 as the CV 37; she was redesignated as an attack carrier (CVA 37) on 1 October 1952. (All fleet carriers—CV and CVB—were changed to CVA on that date.)
12. Bruins, *U.S. Naval Bombardment Missiles,* 201.
13. Stumpf, *Regulus,* 16–17.
14. Bruins, *U.S. Naval Bombardment Missiles,* 204.

Chapter 4. The Regulus Submarines

1. Bruins, *U.S. Naval Bombardment Missiles,* 161–62.
2. See Stumpf, *Regulus,* 173, for a drawing of the submarine's hangar.
3. John D. Alden, *The Fleet Submarine in the U.S. Navy: A Design and Construction History* (Annapolis, Md.: Naval Institute Press, 1979), 136.
4. Coauthor O'Connell, then a lieutenant on the Submarine Squadron 1 staff, was at the Submarine Base when he heard a loud bang. He saw a 25-foot column of fire pulsating from the after torpedo room hatch of the *Sargo.* He went back to Submarine Flotilla 5 headquarters to assist the duty officer in what was turning into a very hectic day and was a witness to the exchange related between Lt. Cdr. Crawford and the flag lieutenant that evening.
5. Holifield was elected as a Democrat to 16 congresses, serving from 3 January 1943 until his resignation on 31 December 1974; he was not a candidate for reelection to Congress in November 1974.
6. Bruins, *U.S. Naval Bombardment Missiles,* 296–97.
7. U.S. Navy, "The Navy of the 1970s Era," Op93G/ac ser 04P93, Washington, D.C., 13 January 1958, 7. In the event, 41 Polaris SSBNs were completed through 1967.

Chapter 5. Regulus in Surface Ships

1. The *Essex*-class aircraft carrier *Princeton* was completed in 1945 as CV 37; she was redesignated as an attack aircraft carrier (CVA) on 1 October 1952. At that time all CV/CVB-type carriers were changed to CVA.

2. The airfield, originally named East Field in honor of Maj. Whitten J. East, U.S. Army, was opened in 1918 when the Army established an aerial gunnery and aerobatics school on the site. In 1943, the U.S. Navy took over the airfield and changed the name to Naval Auxiliary Air Station Otay Mesa; later that year the name was changed again to NAAS Brown Field, in honor of Melville S. Brown, who was killed in a plane crash in 1936. Between 1943 and 1946, the Army and Navy used Brown Field for training. In 1946, the Navy decommissioned the field and turned it over to San Diego County. The county ended up renting portions of the former base for use as a chicken farm; elsewhere on the airport property, the Chula Vista High School was established in 1946. In 1951, the Navy reopened Brown Field because of the Korean War; in 1954 it was once again commissioned, primarily to provide support for ASW and utility squadrons. On 1 September 1962, the Navy transferred ownership of Brown Field to the City of San Diego.

3. The Douglas-built Skyhawk, designed by the brilliant Ed Heinemann, was the world's smallest aircraft to carry a nuclear weapon and the smallest turbojet aircraft to operate from U.S. aircraft carriers during the Cold War.

4. George Fielding Elliot, *Victory Without War: 1958–1961* (Annapolis, Md.: U.S. Naval Institute, 1958), 66.

5. Floatplanes—primarily for gunnery spotting—were carried by U.S. battleships and cruisers until shortly after World War II. Most ships thereafter carried helicopters for rescue, VIP transport, and other roles.

6. Stumpf, *Regulus,* 95–99.

7. The world's first nuclear-propelled surface ship was the Soviet icebreaker *Lenin*, completed in 1959.

8. As converted and built as CG/CGNs, these ships had no gun armament; subsequently two 5-inch/38-caliber, single-mount guns were added to deter small-boat attacks.

9. The battleship *Mississippi* (BB 41) was employed as a gunnery training and missile development ship after World War II; in that role she was redesignated AG 128 in 1946. She was stricken in 1956.

10. Stumpf, *Regulus,* 167.

Chapter 6. Training for War

1. In 1973 the U.S. submarine flotillas became "groups"; at the same time submarine divisions were eliminated.

2. Most type commanders were not operational commanders, having only administrative and training control over units assigned to them. However both the Atlantic and Pacific submarine force commanders also were operational commanders.

3. *Medregal* (SS 480) was the first submarine to be equipped with the BPQ-2 missile guidance radar.

Chapter 7. Deployments and Patrols

1. Deputy Chief of Naval Operations (Air), Op-005/cdr Memorandum for the Secretary of Defense, ser 00209700, 5 July 1960, Naval History and Heritage Command, Washington, D.C.

2. Polmar and Norris, *U.S. Nuclear Arsenal*, 40–70, 75–76.

3. Ibid, 40–70, 77–78.

4. President Dwight D. Eisenhower himself is credited with having directed that the Polaris submarines be named for famous Americans.

5. The SSG/SSGN deterrent patrols fell under the "special operations" category of submarine operations conducted by the Commander, Submarine Force Pacific. The normal special operations patrol focused on intelligence collection missions. The Regulus SSG/SSGN patrols included that tasking along with readiness to launch nuclear-warhead missiles.

6. During World War I, Count von Luckner, commanding a German sailing raider that was at sea for months at a time, instituted that practice for his crew. The "leave section" was only called for duty if the raider encountered a ship to be boarded.

7. A similar casualty on board the USS *Gudgeon* (SS 567) in 1957 during a surveillance patrol off Vladivostok led to her being forced to the surface by Soviet ASW ships after a lengthy pursuit. See Sherry Sontag and Christopher Drew, *Blind Man's Bluff: The Untold Story of American Submarine Espionage* (New York: PublicAffairs, New York, 1998), 25–39.

8. The missile guidance computer's flight plan for a missile strike, started at the launch reference point and ended at the target "dump" point, where the missile began its downward trajectory. Offsets from the reference point allowed the computer to maintain an accurate track of the missile along its projected path.

9. The duty officer was then-Lt. John O'Connell, one of the authors of this book.

10. Robert Blount completed the nuclear power program, commanded the USS *Permit* (SSN 594) and subsequently an SSBN, and retired as a rear admiral after commanding the Operational Test and Evaluation Force.

11. N. Polmar, "Regulus: Missile Now on Station Manned by Hard Workers," *Navy Times* (10 March 1962), M4. Data provided by the ComSubPac plans officer, Cdr. D. A. Paolucci, USN.

Chapter 8. Regulus Aftermath

1. Established in 1962 as Navy special forces, SEAL originally indicated Sea-Air-Land.

2. Chief, Bureau of Ships, memorandum to Chief of Naval Operations (Chairman, Ship Characteristics Board), "USS *Grayback* (SSG 574) and USS *Growler* (SSG 577); Feasibility studies for converting to attack submarines, report of," C-SSG/S1(440) ser 440-0125, 14 August 1959.

3. The transport submarine designation periodically changed. It began after World War II as APS, then became APSS, and later LPSS.

4. During her conversion to an LPSS, *Grayback's* sea suction openings were relocated up from her bottom, allowing her to sit on the bottom but still operate essential machinery like air conditioning that required cooling water.

5. Information based on discussions by Capt. John O'Connell with Cdr. John Chamberlain, USN, commanding officer of *Grayback*, and Capt. Charles Cullen, USN, commanding officer of *Harold E. Holt* (FF 1074).

6. Four ex–ballistic missile submarines were reconfigured to transport special operations forces: the *John Marshall* (SSBN 611) and *Sam Houston* (SSBN 609) were extensively converted in 1984–1986 to transport SEALs or other special forces; they were decommissioned in 1991–1992. They were replaced by the *James K. Polk* (SSBN 645) and *Kamehameha* (SSBN 642), converted in 1992–1993; they were decommissioned in 1999 and 2002, respectively. (The *Kamehameha* was in commission for more than 36 years, longer than any other U.S. nuclear-propelled submarine.) Subsequently, four former Trident strategic missile submarines were extensively modified to cruise missile/special operations configurations (SSGN); see chapter 12.

7. *Permit* was the second submarine of the *Thresher* (SSN 593) class; these submarines generally were referred to as the "*Permit* class" after the loss of *Thresher* in 1963.

8. The Deep Submergence Systems Project was established in response to the 1963 loss of the submarine *Thresher*. Details of the *Halibut's* conversion and special-mission operations are found in John Pina Craven, *The Silent War: The Cold War Battle beneath the Sea* (New York: Simon & Schuster, 2001), and N. Polmar and Michael White, *Project Azorian: The CIA and the Raising of the K-129* (Annapolis, Md.: Naval Institute Press, 2010).

9. The thruster device was never used; it was found to be too noisy and was not needed.

10. Lt. Philip V. H. L. Duckett, USN, quoted in Polmar, "Regulus: Missile Now on Station," M5.

11. See Polmar and White, *Project Azorian,* 55.

12. This concept of "saturation diving" had been developed by the Navy's Deep Submergence Systems Project under the direction of Capt. George Bond, USN.

13. A former employee of the National Security Agency, Ronald Pelton, revealed the Pacific cable tap program to the Soviet KGB beginning in January 1980. That put an end to the Sea of Okhotsk cable tap missions. Pelton was tried and convicted of espionage in 1986 and was sentenced to life imprisonment. Subsequently one of *Halibut's* listening devices was recovered by Soviet authorities; after minute examination, it was placed on display at the KGB headquarters museum (the Lubyanka) in Moscow—where it was seen by one of the authors of this book.

14. ComSubLant press release, 17 April 1997.

Chapter 9. Supersonic Cruise Missiles

1. Werrell, *Evolution of the Cruise Missile,* 117–19.

2. Grumman had produced the highly successful F4F Wildcat and F6F Hellcat fighters during World War II, and the F9F Panther/Cougar series during the early jet age. The firm's F-14 Tomcat was one of the outstanding fighter-attack aircraft of the Cold War.

3. Bruins, *U.S. Naval Bombardment Missiles,* 238–39.

4. Committee on Appropriations, House of Representatives, hearings, *Department of Defense Appropriations for 1960: Part 1 Policy Statements* (Washington, D.C.: 23 January 1959), 637.

5. The *King County* was constructed as the landing ship *LST 857,* commissioned on 29 December 1944. After extensive service as an LST she was converted, from October 1957 to November 1958, to a Regulus II test ship at the Mare Island Naval Shipyard and reclassified as a miscellaneous auxiliary (AG 157) on 17 May 1958.

6. U.S. Navy, "Navy of the 1970s Era," 7. Adm. Burke, in office from August 1955 to August 1961, was the longest-serving U.S. Chief of Naval Operations.

7. Funds for the P6M Seamaster flying boat and three missile cruiser conversions (CA to CG) also were shifted to the Polaris effort, canceling those projects.

8. See N. Polmar, *Aircraft Carriers: A History of Carrier Aviation and Its Influence on World Events,* vol. 2, *1946–2006* (Washington, D.C.: Potomac Books, 2008), 11–13.

9. The "heavy" aircraft carrier *United States* was laid down on 18 April 1947 and cancelled on 23 April 1949. The carrier–versus–B-36 debate is described in Dr. Jeffrey G. Barlow's excellent account *Revolt of the Admirals: The Fight for Naval Aviation, 1945–1950* (Washington, D.C.: Naval Historical Center, 1994).

10. Bruins, *U.S. Naval Bombardment Missiles,* 296–97.

11. In the event, only three of these heavy cruisers were converted to anti-air warfare missile cruisers (CGs 10–12, ex-CA 123, 136, and 74, respectively); as noted above, funding for additional conversions were shifted to the Polaris missile project. .

12. Bruins, *U.S. Naval Bombardment Missiles,* 300.

13. Ibid., 330–31.

14. U.S. Congress, Subcommittee of the Committee on Appropriations, House of Representatives, hearings, *Department of Defense Appropriations for 1960,* Part 1, *Policy Statements* (23 January 1959), 7.

15. L. Edgar Prina, "France Bids for Regulus II," *The Evening Star* (Washington, D.C.), (8 February 1959).

16. That last Regulus II missile was recovered and now resides at the Frontiers of Flight Museum at Love Field, Dallas, Texas, on loan from the National Museum of Naval Aviation at Pensacola, Florida.

17. Werrell, *Evolution of the Cruise Missile,* 119.

Chapter 10. Air Force Strategic Cruise Missiles

1. This chapter is based largely on Werrell, *Evolution of the Cruise Missile*; Polmar and Norris, *U.S. Nuclear Arsenal*; and U.S. Air Force, *A History of Strategic Arms Competition, 1945–1972,* vol. 2, *A Handbook of Selected U.S. Weapon Systems* (Washington, D.C., June 1976). The last-listed contains characteristic sheets on U.S. Air Force strategic aircraft and missile systems.

2. Werrell, *Evolution of the Cruise Missile,* 97; also see James N. Gibson, *The Navaho Missile Project* (Atglen, Pa.: Schiffer Military/Aviation History, 1996), 11–12, 80–81.

3. The missile's name alludes to the fictional animal species in Lewis Carroll's *The Hunting of the Snark* (1876).

4. Werrell, *Evolution of the Cruise Missile,* 85–86

5. The J57 engine was also used in several manned aircraft, including the B-52 Stratofortress, the F-102 Delta Dagger, the Lockheed U-2 spyplane, the B-57 Canberra, the F-100 Super Sabre, and the F-8 Crusader.

6. Werrell, *Evolution of the Cruise Missile,* 89–95. Inertial guidance systems suffered a loss of accuracy as time progressed due to precession of the system gyroscopes. Stellar (star) observations were made to update the guidance system and maintain its accuracy.

7. Ibid., 95–96. Werrell does not state the range in his book. The distance from launch point (Cape Canaveral) to the usual target (Ascension Island) is about 5,070 miles.

8. Ibid., 95–97.

9. Mindling and Bolton, *U.S. Air Force Tactical Missiles,* 114, 160–61; also see Lt. Col. Raddall L. Lanning, USAF, *United States Air Force Cruise Missiles: A Study in Technology, Concepts, and Deterrence* (Research Report, Air War College, Maxwell Air Force Base, Ala., 15 April 1992).

10. Werrell, *Evolution of the Cruise Missile,* 109–11.

11. Mindling and Bolton, *U.S. Air Force Tactical Missiles,* 149.

12. Gregg Herken, "The Flying Crowbar," *Air & Space Magazine* (April/May 1990), 28.

13. The acronym SLAM later was used for "Standoff Land-Attack Missile" and "Submarine-Launched Assault Missile"; the former comprised the AGM-84H/K variants of the Harpoon missile.

Chapter 11. The Soviet Perspective I

1. Near the end of World War II, three U.S. B-29s had landed in Soviet Siberia after bombing the Japanese home islands. At the time the Soviet Union was not at war with Japan. The bomber crews were repatriated, but the aircraft were retained. Aviation genius Andrei Tupolev,

directed to copy the bombers, produced the near-duplicative Tu-4 Bull. A total of 847 Tu-4s had been built when production ended in 1952; a few aircraft were transferred to China.

2. The ministry was established on 26 June 1953; on 11 September 1989, it was renamed the Ministry of Atomic Energy and Industry of the USSR.

3. S. Bystrov, "A Reactor for Submarines," *Krasnaya zvezdochka* (21 October 1989).

4. The first November-class submarine, the *K-3,* was commissioned in July 1958.

5. See James Hartford, *Korolev: How One Man Masterminded the Soviet Drive to Beat America to the Moon* (New York: John Wiley & Sons, 1997), 75.

6. MiG = Artem Mikoyan and Mikhail Gurevich.

7. Central Intelligence Agency, *Soviet Delivery Capabilities to Undertake an Attack on the United States* (Washington, D.C., 4 June 1953). The document was released on 23 March 1999, with heavy redactions.

8. Available sources differ on the deployment of the 10X. Steven J. Zaloga, in *Target America: The Soviet Union and the Strategic Arms Race, 1945–1964* (Novato, Calif.: Presidio, 1993), 183, states that the 10X missile was fired from ground launchers and aircraft as early as 1945 but did not enter production. Leningrad had been founded as St. Petersburg in 1703 so called until 1914, when renamed Petrograd; it changed to Leningrad in 1924 and back to St. Petersburg in 1991.

9. That Mikoyan's design bureau employed Sergei Beria, the son of Stalin's security chief, was obviously a key factor in Mikoyan's influence.

10. In September 1940, Korolev was moved from a brutal gulag camp to a prison aviation design bureau. He was released in June 1944 and his prior convictions expunged. A year later he was commissioned as a colonel in the Soviet Army and was sent to Germany that September to collect material on German missile programs. See Hartford, *Korolev,* 57–63.

11. Zaloga, *Target America,* 133.

12. Hartford, *Korolev,* 102.

13. Zaloga, *Target America,* 133. Lavochkin's bureau continued designing aircraft until 1950, his last conventional-aircraft efforts being the La-200 fighter and a drone—Object 201—in 1951; the latter was produced with the designation La-17. He had produced several highly successful piston-engine fighters during World War II.

14. Central Intelligence Agency, *The Soviet Titanium Industry and Its Role in the Military Buildup,* SOV 85–10052 (Washington, D.C.: March 1985), iii.

15. Igor Shevalyov and Alexei Fomichev, " 'Storm' in Midair," *Military Parade,* March–April 1996, 87.

16. Steven Zaloga, *The Kremlin's Nuclear Sword: The Rise and Fall of Russia's Strategic Nuclear Forces* (Washington, D.C.: Smithsonian Institution Press, 2002), 51. A modified version of the R-7 missile (8K71PS) placed the *Sputnik 1*—the earth's first artificial satellite—in orbit from the Baikonur (Kazakhstan) cosmodrome on 4 October 1957.

17. The name "Buran" subsequently was assigned to the Soviet space shuttle.

18. Zaloga, *Kremlin's Nuclear Sword,* 51.

19. The concept of a submarine-towed launch container had been developed by the Germans in World War II for the V-2 ballistic missile for attacks against the United States. Several launch containers were produced, but no launches were attempted. See Norman Polmar and K. J. Moore, *Cold War Submarines: The Design and Construction of U.S. and Soviet Submarines* (Washington, D.C.: Brassey's, 2004), 103–4.

20. TsKB-18 was named "Rubin" in 1966.

21. The development of the first cruise missile submarines is described in I. D. Spassky, ed., *Istoriya Otechestvennogo Sudostroeniya* [The History of Indigenous Shipbuilding], vol. 5, *1946–1991* (St. Petersburg: Sudostroenie, 1996), 146–53. See also Capt. 1/R V. P. Kuzin and Capt. 1/R V. I. Nikol'skiy, *Voyenno-morskoy Flot SSR, 1945–1991* [The Navy of the USSR, 1945–1991] (St. Petersburg: Historical Oceanic Society, 1996).

22. The Shaddock SS-N-3a anti-ship missile also was fitted in eight surface ships: the four Kynda-class "rocket cruisers" had eight launch canisters plus eight reloads, and the four Kresta I cruisers had four canisters (NATO ship code names). Beginning with the first Kynda, which was commissioned in 1962, these ships regularly appeared on the world's oceans, especially in the Mediterranean, and often trailed U.S. warships, especially aircraft carriers.

23. The number of twin-cylinder SSGs (four) is derived from several Russian sources, especially Spassky, *History of Indigenous Shipbuilding*, vol. 5, 147. U.S. sources for Soviet submarine numbers include: Central Intelligence Agency, *Intelligence Handbook: Soviet Submarines*, SR 1H 69–5 (Washington, D.C., December 1969), 8–9; and Defense Intelligence Agency, *Soviet Submarine Order of Battle: 1950–1974* (Washington, D.C., November 1978), various issues of the latter publication beginning with March 1964. The DIA reports provided a month-by-month accounting of Soviet submarines by fleet assignment.

24. *K* designation indicated *kreyser* (cruiser) submarine.

25. See Hartford, *Korolev*, 259–60.

Chapter 12. The Soviet Perspective II

1. Spassky, *History of Indigenous Shipbuilding*, 5:150.

2. Unlike the U.S. Strategic Air Command, which controlled both manned bombers and land-based strategic missiles, the Soviet Strategic Rocket Forces had no influence over the strategic bombers of the Soviet Air Forces.

3. F. G. Dergachev, "World's First Titanium High Speed Submarine, Design 661," *Gangut* (no. 14 1998), 58.

4. Project 651 and 675 submarines fitted with the satellite receiver system were given the designation suffix *K*.

5. The Tu-20/95/120 Bear aircraft program—in almost continuous production since 1952—included conventional bomber, missile carrier, reconnaissance, and anti-submarine variants. The original military designation for the aircraft was Tu-20; however, the Tupolev bureau designation Tu-95 has been universally accepted for the aircraft.

6. The smaller S-band Front Piece was the data-link guidance antenna; the larger UHF Front Door was the target acquisition antenna.

7. Central Intelligence Agency, *The Soviet Attack Submarine Force: Evolution and Operations,* SR IM 71–11-S (Washington, D.C., September 1971), 12.

8. Submarines constructed at Gor'kiy and Komsomol'sk were transported via the inland waterway system of rivers and canals to Severodvinsk or to yards in the Black Sea area for completion.

9. One submarine of this class was leased to the Indian Navy from 1988 to 1992—the first nuclear submarine ever transferred to another nation.

10. Central Intelligence Agency, "Strategic Employment of Soviet Cruise Missile Submarines," memorandum, 19 November 1968, 1.

11. Central Intelligence Agency, *The Soviet and East European General Forces,* NIE 11–14–67 (Washington, D.C., 16 November 1967), 47.

12. Rear Adm. G. H. Miller, USN, Memorandum for Assistant Chief of Naval Operations (Intelligence), subj: "Cruise Missile Threat," OP-97/aaa, ser 000115P97, 28 October 1968, 1–2.

13. Soviet coastal missile and artillery troops are described in Kuzin and Nikol'skiy, *Navy of the USSR,* 786–89 (trans.).

14. The AS-1 Kennel was carried by the Tupolev Tu-4 Bull and Tu-16 Badger bombers.

15. Gen. Anatoli I. Gribkov, Soviet Army, and Gen. William Y. Smith, U.S. Army, *Operation Anadyr: U.S. and Soviet Generals Recount the Cuban Missile Crisis* (Chicago: edition q, 1994), 4, 45. The *Indigirka* arrived in Cuba on 22 October 1962, after an uneventful 18-day voyage from Severomorsk. President John F. Kennedy authorized a "quarantine" (blockade) of Cuba the following day.

16. Unknown to the American leadership, the Soviets had 128 nuclear warheads for missiles and six nuclear aircraft bombs in Cuba at that time.

17. The lead Oscar SSGN, the *K-525,* had only two 650-mm torpedo tubes in addition to the 533-mm tubes.

18. The only two-reactor submarine produced in the West was the USS *Triton* (SSRN 586), a radar picket submarine completed in 1960. Her two S4G reactors produced an estimated 34,000 horsepower.

19. The submarine was renamed *Arkhangelsk* in 1991, following the breakup of the Soviet Union, when Minsk became the capital of independent Belarus.

20. I. D. Spassky conversation with N. Polmar, St. Petersburg (Russia), 10 May 1994.

21. The carrier *Admiral Kuznetsov* displaces some 55,000 tons standard and 59,000 tons full load.

22. Kuzin and Nikol'skiy, *Navy of the USSR,* 69.

23. The previous Soviet nuclear-propelled submarine losses were:

Project	Type	NATO codename
627A	SSN	November
667A	SSBN	Yankee
670	SSGN	Charlie
685	SSN	Mike

24. The 118 men consisted of 5 personnel from the staff of the 7th Submarine Division, 2 torpedo specialists, and a crew of 43 officers and 68 enlisted men. USS *Thresher* was lost with all 129 men on board on 10 April 1963.

25. The underwater detonations were detected by the U.S. submarine *Memphis* (SSN 691), possibly also by a second SSN; both were conducting routine surveillance in the exercise area. Initially some Russian sources cited a collision between *Kursk* and *Memphis* as the cause of the former's loss.

26. C. A. Prins, *Kursk Submarine Sinking: An Assessment of Potential Nuclear Hazards* (St. Petersburg: Kursk Foundation, 25 July 2001), 7. These explosive amounts are based on Richter scale measurements.

27. Kuzin and Nikol'skiy, *Navy of the USSR,* 478.

28. Under the INF treaty the Soviets destroyed 80 missiles.

29. See Michael R. Gordon, "Russia Deploys Missile, Violating Treaty and Challenging Trump," *The New York Times* (14 February 2017), 1.

30. The ships were a Gepard-class frigate and three Buyan M–class corvettes.

31. The original Project 885 design provided for four 26½-inch and four 21-inch torpedo tubes.

32. Since the fall of the Soviet Union in 1991, all nuclear-propelled submarine construction has been concentrated at the Severodvinsk shipyard.

33. The U.S. Navy lists the crews of current nuclear-propelled attack submarines as:

SSN 688 *Los Angeles*	143
SSN 21 *Seawolf*	140
SSN 774 *Virginia*	132

Chapter 13. U.S. Cruise Missile Rebirth

1. Henry Kissinger, *Years of Renewal* (New York: Simon & Schuster, 1999), 853–61.

2. Ibid., 856.

3. Ibid., 856–57.

4. Adm. Holloway served as Chief of Naval Operations from June 1974 to June 1978.

5. The film *Thunderball* (1965) starred Sean Connery as James Bond—British agent 007.

6. Walter Andrews, "Naval Aviators Rap Tomahawk Missile's Speed, Survivability," *Navy Times,* 6 August 1982, 23.

7. Adm. Zumwalt discussion with N. Polmar, Washington, D.C., 29 May 1990. *Dewey*'s anti-ship capability consisted of a single 5-inch/54-caliber dual-purpose gun.

8. Adm. Elmo R. Zumwalt, USN (Ret.), *On Watch* (New York: Quadrangle, 1976), 81. The CNOs during this period were Adm. David L. McDonald (1963–1967) and Adm. Thomas H. Moorer (1967–1970), both naval aviators. Moorer then served as Chairman of the Joint Chiefs of Staff (1970–1974).

9. "Laird Says U.S. Plans Ship-Hunting A-Subs," *The Evening Star* (6 June 1971), 14. Secretary of Defense Laird revealed the program at the keel laying ceremony of the submarine *Glenard P. Lipscomb* (SSN 685).

10. Vice Adm. Rickover, prepared statement in testimony to Committee on Appropriations, Senate, 10 May 1972.

11. The Harpoon became operational in 1977 on U.S. surface ships and submarines, in 1979 on land-based aircraft (P-3C Orions), and in 1981 on carrier-based aircraft (A-6E Intruders). The Harpoon also was used by the U.S. Air Force and by 24 other countries.

12. See Capt. Robert F. Fox, USN (Ret.), "Build It & They Will Come," U.S. Naval Institute *Proceedings* (April 2001), 44–47.

13. The TASM range was given as 250 n.miles in "Tomahawk Ready for the Warpath in the '80s," *Surface Warfare* (March 1980), 15. The magazine is published by Commander, Naval Surface Forces, Pacific Fleet.

14. Testimony of Secretary Lehman before Committee on Appropriations, Senate, hearings, *Department of Defense Appropriations for Fiscal Year 1982: Part 1 Posture Statements* (Washington, D.C., 6 April 1981), 464.

15. The four *Ohio*-class submarines, SSBNs 726–729, were reclassified as SSGNs during their cruise missile conversion. A passionate justification for the SSBN/SSGN conversions is

Capt. Charles D. Sykora, USN, "SSGN: A Transformation Limited by Legacy Command and Control," *Naval War College Review* (Winter 2006), 41–62.

16. See N. Polmar, "The Submarine Arsenal Ship," *The Submarine Review* (January 1997), 7–12. The article was based on a Polmar memo to Adm. J. M. Boorda, USN, then Chief of Naval Operations, on 3 April 1996.

17. See U.S. Navy Fact File, "Attack Submarines—SSN," http://www.navy.mil/navydata/fact_display.asp?cid=4100&tid=100&ct=4.

18. The Block V submarines began with hull SSN 803, with planned delivery in 2026. See Capt. Edward Lundquist, USN (Ret.), "Building *Virginia* class Submarines More Efficiently and with Greater Capability," *Naval Forces* (3, 2017), 26–27; also General Dynamics/Electric Boat data sheet "Virginia Payload Module (VPM)," October 2016.

19. Stanley W. Kandebo, "U.S. Fires Over 25% of Its Conventional Land Attack Tomahawks in the First Week of War," *Aviation Week & Space Technology* (28 January 1991), 29.

20. U.S. Department of Defense, *Conduct of the Persian Gulf War: Final Report to Congress* (Washington, D.C.: April 1992), 244.

21. Al-Shayrat was the base for three Syrian fighter squadrons—two with Su-22s and one with MiG-23s—plus helicopters.

22. Secretary of Defense Gen. James Mattis, USMC (Ret.), Pentagon press conference, Washington, D.C., 11 April 2017.

23. See, for example, Walter Pincus, "Cruise Missiles May Get Chemical Warheads," *The Washington Star* (16 January 1982), A5.

24. Two each of the Soviet SS-20 ballistic missiles and of the Pershing missiles were retained for display in Moscow and Washington, D.C. Those in Washington are on exhibit at the National Air and Space Museum on the National Mall.

25. The six *Dolphin*-class submarines are of two similar designs, the three later boats being the largest submarines constructed in Germany since World War II. They were completed from 1999 through 2018.

26. The air-launched Popeye was purchased by the United States for use by B-52 Stratofortress bombers.

27. The TLAM(N) was the first non-strategic nuclear weapon to enter the U.S. Navy inventory since 1964.

28. Commo. Roger Bacon, USN (later vice admiral), prepared statement in testimony before the Committee on Armed Services, Senate, 8 March 1985.

29. The ballistic missile option for the *Virginia*-VPM submarines is described in detail in Elaine M. Grossman, "Pentagon, Lawmakers Deal Blows to Navy Fast-Strike Missile Effort," Global Security Newswire produced by the *National Journal* (31 July 2013); http://www.nti.org/gsn/article/pentagon-lawmakers-deal-blows-navy-fast-strike-missile-effort/.

Chapter 14. Is There a Better Cruise Missile in Your Future?

1. See Polmar and Moore, *Cold War Submarines*.
2. See James Drew and Lara Seligman, "Bold Action?," *Aviation Week & Space Technology* (17 April 2017), 26–27.
3. Vladimir Putin, state of the union address, Moscow, 1 March 2018.
4. Vladimir Putin, press conference, Sochi, 18 May 2018.

5. "Trump Announces Plans to Pull Out of INF Treaty Due to Russian Violations," *The Wall Street Journal* (22 October 2018).

6. Paul Sonne, "Mattis: No Alternative to Leaving Arms Pact," *The Washington Post* (29 October 2018), A2.

7. "Putin Says Missiles' Hosts Will Be Targeted," *The Washington Post* (25 October 2018), A8.

8. "New Cruise Missile More Widely Deployed than Thought," *Radio Free Europe/Radio Liberty* (11 February 2019).

9. Quoted in Aaron Gregg, "Defense Pushes for Production of Hypersonic Weaponry," *The Washington Post* (31 December 2018), A12.

10. Ibid.

11. Quoted in Missy Ryan, "U.S. Tests 1st Missile after Ending Pact with Russia," *The Washington Post* (20 August 2019), A3.

12. Department of Defense press release, "Pentagon Test-Fires Ground-Launched Cruise Missile," 20 August 2019, quoted in Ryan, "U.S. Tests 1st Missile after Ending Pact with Russia," A3.

Bibliography

Books in English

Alden, John D. *The Fleet Submarine in the U.S. Navy: A Design and Construction History.* Annapolis, Md.: Naval Institute Press, 1979.

Beevor, Anthony. *D-Day: The Battle for Normandy.* New York: Viking, 2009.

Betts, Richard K., ed. *Cruise Missiles: Technology, Strategy, Politics.* Washington, D.C.: Brookings Institution, 1981.

Brown, Anthony Cave, and Charles B. MacDonald, eds. *The Secret History of the Atomic Bomb.* New York: Dell, 1977.

Carus, Seth W. *Cruise Missile Proliferation in the 1990s.* Washington, D.C.: Center for Strategic and International Studies, 1992.

Cooksley, Peter G. *Flying Bomb: The Story of Hitler's V-Weapons in World War II.* New York: Charles Scribner's Sons, 1979.

Elliot, George Fielding. *Victory Without War: 1958–1961.* Annapolis, Md.: U.S. Naval Institute, 1958.

Evans, Mark L., and Roy A. Grossnick. *United States Naval Aviation, 1910–2010.* Vol. 1, *Chronology.* Washington, D.C.: Naval History and Heritage Command, 2015.

Everitt, Don. *The K Boats: A Dramatic First Report on the World's Most Calamitous Submarines.* New York: Rinehart and Winston, 1963.

Ford, Roger. *Germany's Secret Weapons of World War II.* New York: Chartwell, 2013.

Gibson, James N. *The History of the U.S. Nuclear Arsenal.* Greenwich, Conn.: Brompton Books, 1989.

———. *The Navaho Missile Project.* Atglen, Pa.: Schiffer Military / Aviation History, 1996.

———. *Nuclear Weapons of the United States.* Atglen, Pa.: Schiffer Military / Aviation History, 1996.

Gribkov, Gen. Anatoli I., Soviet Army, and Gen. William Y. Smith, U.S. Army. *Operation Anadyr: U.S. and Soviet Generals Recount the Cuban Missile Crisis.* Chicago: Edition q, 1994.

Hansen, Chuck. *U.S. Nuclear Weapons: The Secret History.* Arlington, Tex.: Aerofax, 1988.

Hartford, James. *Korolev: How One Man Masterminded the Soviet Drive to Beat America to the Moon.* New York: John Wiley & Sons, 1997.

Hewlett, Richard G., and Francis Duncan. *Nuclear Navy, 1946–1962.* Chicago: University of Chicago Press, 1974.

Kay, Anthony L. *Fieseler Fi 103 Buzz Bomb.* Sturbridge, Mass.: Monogram Aviation, 1977.

Kennedy, Gregory P. *Vengeance Weapon 2.* Washington, D.C.: Smithsonian Institution Press, 1983.

King, Benjamin, and Timothy Kutta. *Impact: The History of Germany's V-weapons in World War II.* Cambridge, Mass.: Da Capo, 1998.

Kissinger, Henry. *Years of Renewal*. New York: Simon & Schuster, 1999.

Miller, Vice Adm. Jerry, USN (Ret.). *Nuclear Weapons and Aircraft Carriers: How the Bomb Saved Carrier Aviation*. Washington, D.C.: Smithsonian Institution Press, 2001.

Mindling, George, and Robert Bolton. *U.S. Air Force Tactical Missiles, 1949–1961*. Morrisville, N.C.: Lulu.Com, 2008.

Muir, Malcolm, Jr. *Black Shoes and Blue Water: Surface Warfare in the United States Navy, 1945–1975*. Honolulu, Hawaii: University Press of the Pacific, 2005.

Neufeld, Michael J. *The Rocket and the Reich*. New York: Free Press, 1995.

Nicklas, Brian D. *American Missiles*. Yorkshire, U.K.: Frontline Books, 2012.

Ordway, Frederick I., III, and Mitchell R. Sharpe. *The Rocket Team*. Burlington, Ont.: Apogee Books, 1979.

Podvig, Pavel, ed. *Russian Strategic Nuclear Forces*. Cambridge, Mass.: Massachusetts Institute of Technology, 2001. Originally published in Russian by the Center for Arms Control, Energy and Environmental Studies, Moscow.

Polmar, Norman. *Atomic Submarines*. Princeton, N.J.: D. Van Nostrand, 1963.

———. *Guide to the Soviet Navy*. Annapolis, Md.: Naval Institute Press (various editions).

———. *Ships and Aircraft of the U.S. Fleet*. Annapolis, Md.: Naval Institute Press (various editions).

———. *Strategic Air Command: People, Aircraft, and Missiles*. Annapolis, Md.: Nautical & Aviation, 1979.

Polmar, Norman, and K. J. Moore. *Cold War Submarines: The Design and Construction of U.S. and Soviet Submarines*. Washington, D.C.: Brassey's, 2004.

Polmar, Norman, and Robert S. Norris. *The U.S. Nuclear Arsenal: A History of Weapons and Delivery Systems since 1945*. Annapolis, Md.: Naval Institute Press, 2009.

Polmar, Norman, and Edward Whitman. *Hunters and Killers*. Vol. 2, *Anti-Submarine Warfare from 1943*. Annapolis, Md.: Naval Institute Press, 2016.

Refuto, George J. *Evolution of the U.S. Sea-Based Nuclear Missile Deterrent*. Bloomington, Ind.: Xlibris, 2011.

Skorzeny, Otto. *Skorzeny's Special Missions*. London: Greenhill Books, 1957.

Sontag, Sherry, and Christopher Drew. *Blind Man's Bluff: The Untold Story of American Submarine Espionage*. New York: PublicAffairs, 1998.

Sorrels, Charles A. *U.S. Cruise Missile Programs*. New York: McGraw-Hill, 1983.

Spassky, Nikolai. *Russia's Arms Catalog*. Vol. 3, *Navy*. Moscow: Military Parade, 1996.

Spinardi, Graham. *From Polaris to Trident*. Cambridge, U.K.: Cambridge University Press, 1994.

Stumpf, David K. *Regulus: The Forgotten Weapon*. Paducah, Ky.: Turner, 1996.

Werrell, Kenneth P. *The Evolution of the Cruise Missile*. Maxwell Air Force Base, Ala.: Air University Press, 1985.

Zaloga, Steven. *Flying Bomb*. Oxford, U.K.: Osprey, 2005.

———. *The Kremlin's Nuclear Sword: The Rise and Fall of Russia's Strategic Nuclear Forces, 1945–2000*. Washington, D.C.: Smithsonian Institution, 2002.

———. *Target America: The Soviet Union and the Strategic Arms Race, 1945–1964*. Novato, Calif.: Presidio, 1993.

Zumwalt, Adm. Elmo R., USN (Ret.). *On Watch*. New York: Quadrangle, 1976.

Books in Russian

Kuzin, Capt. 1/R V. P., and Capt. 1/R V. I. Nikol'skiy, Russian Navy. *Voyenno-Morskoy Flot SSR, 1945–1991* [The Navy of the USSR, 1945–1991]. St. Petersburg: Historical Oceanic Society, 1996.

Spassky, I. D., ed. *Istoriya Otechestvennogo Sudostroeniya* [The History of Indigenous Shipbuilding]. Vol. 5, *1946–1991*. St. Petersburg: Sudostroenie, 1996.

Articles

The articles listed below are in addition to those cited in chapter endnotes. In addition to the citations listed below, the authors have reviewed numerous articles in the following periodicals:

Air & Space Magazine
Aviation Week & Space Technology
The Bulletin of the Atomic Scientists
Gangut [Russian]
Military Parade
Morskoy sbornik [Russian]
Naval War College Review
Navy Times
Ships of the World [Japanese]
The Submarine Review
Surface Warfare
Undersea Warfare
U.S. Naval Institute *Proceedings*

Bothwell, Cdr. John H., USN (Ret.). "The Barnstorming Days of Submarine Missiles." U.S. Naval Institute *Proceedings* (December 1990).

Carey, Merrick, and Loren Thompson. "Defense Panel Pushes Trident Conversion." *Submarine Review* (January 1998).

"Cruise Missile Upkeep Start at $1 Billion." *Aviation Week & Space Technology* (27 June 1983).

Dergachev, F. G. "World's First Titanium High Speed Submarine, Design 661." *Gangut,* no. 14 (1998).

Drew, James, and Lara Seligman. "Bold Action?" *Aviation Week & Space Technology* (17 April 2017).

Estes, Kenneth W. Comment: "U-Boat with Wings." U.S. Naval Institute *Proceedings* (August 1968).

Fox, Capt. Robert F., USN (Ret.). "Build It & They Will Come." U.S. Naval Institute *Proceedings* (April 2001).

Fullinwider, Capt. Peter L., USN (Ret.). "Recollections of Regulus." *Submarine Review* (October 2009).

Herken, Gregg. "The Flying Crowbar." *Air & Space Magazine* (April/May 1990).

Muir, Malcolm, Jr. "A Stillborn System: The Sub-Launched Cruise Missile." *MHQ* [Military History Quarterly] (Winter 1994).

Oster, Patrick. "Missile Crisis, and How We Got There." *The Chicago Sun-Times* (29 November 1981).

Paine, Christopher. "Pershing II: The Army's Strategic Weapon." *Bulletin of the Atomic Scientists* (October 1980).

Philpott, Tom. "Cruise Missile's War Debut Hailed as Outstanding Performance." *Navy Times* (28 January 1991).

Polmar, Norman. "Regulus from Surface Ships." *Undersea Warfare* (Winter 2008).

————. "Regulus: Missile Now on Station Manned by Hard Workers." *Navy Times* (10 March 1962).

————. "The Submarine Arsenal Ship." *Submarine Review* (January 1997).

————. "USS *Norton Sound*: The Newest Old Ship." U.S. Naval Institute *Proceedings* (April 1979).

Prina, L. Edgar. "France Bids for Regulus II." *The Evening Star* (Washington, D.C.) (8 February 1959).

"Regulus Crews Get Deterrent Patrol Pin Nod." *Submarine Review* (July 1977).

Shevalyov, Igor, and Alexei Fomichev. "'Storm' in Midair." *Military Parade* (March–April 1996).

Spark, Nick T. "Battle Stations Missile!" *Naval History* (August 2003).

Stumpf, David K. "Blasts from the Past." U.S. Naval Institute *Proceedings* (April 1993).

"Ten Carriers Equipped for Regulus Is Report." *Navy Times* (2 March 1957).

"Tomahawk Ready for the Warpath in the '80s." *Surface Warfare* (March 1980).

Tsipis, Kosta. "Cruise Missiles." *Scientific American* (February 1977).

Weiler, Lawrence. "Strategic Cruise Missiles and the Future of SALT." *Arms Control Today* (October 1975).

Whitman, Edward C. "Regulus: America's First Sea-Borne Nuclear Deterrent." *Undersea Warfare* (Spring 2001).

Official Documents

U.S. Air Force. *A History of Strategic Arms Competition, 1945–1972*. Vol. 2, *A Handbook of Selected U.S. Weapon Systems*. Washington, D.C. (June 1976).

U.S. Central Intelligence Agency. *Intelligence Handbook: Soviet Guided Missiles*, SR IH 69-2. Washington, D.C. (May 1969).

————. *Intelligence Handbook: Soviet Submarines,* SR IH 69-5. Washington, D.C. (December 1969).

————. *Intelligence Report: The Soviet Naval Cruise Missile Force: Development and Operational Employment*, SR IR 71–19. Washington, D.C. (December 1971).

————. *Soviet Submarine Warfare Trends,* SNIE 11-20-84JX. Washington, D.C. (January 1987).

U.S. Department of Defense. *Conduct of the Persian Gulf War: Final Report to Congress.* Washington, D.C. (April 1992).

U.S. National Photographic Interpretation Center. *SSC-1b Shaddock Missile/Equipment Deployment USSR*, PIR-012/74. Washington, D.C. (March 1974).

U.S. Navy. *Handbook, Servicing and Launching Instructions: SSM-N-8 Guided Missile Regulus*, NAVWEPS 01–45JAD-501. Washington, D.C.: Bureau of Naval Weapons (1 January 1962); repr. Periscope Film LLC, 2009.

———. "The Navy of the 1970 Era," Op93G/ac ser 04P93. Washington, D.C.: Office of the Chief of Naval Operations, 13 January 1958.

———. *Standard Aircraft Characteristics SSM-N-9 "Regulus."* Washington, D.C.: Naval Air Systems Command, 10 February 1958.

Miscellaneous

Antonov, Alexandr M., Vladimir I. Barantsev, Boris F. Dronov, and Antoly V. Kuteinikov. "40 Years of Nuclear Submarines Development: A View of a Designer." Warship '96 Symposium, London, 12 June 1996.

Bruins, Berend Derk. *Naval Bombardment Missiles, 1940–1958: A Study of the Weapons Innovation Process.* PhD thesis, Columbia University, Ann Arbor, Mich., 1981, University Microfilms International.

Kuteinikov, A. V., L. Y. Khudiakov, and K. J. Moore. "Emerging Technology and Submarines of the 21st Century." Warship '96 Symposium, London, 12 June 1996.

Lanning, Lt. Col. Randall L., USAF. *United States Air Force Ground Launched Cruise Missiles: A Study in Technology, Concepts, and Deterrence.* Research Report, Air University, Maxwell Air Force Base, Ala., 15 April 1992.

Manthorpe, William H. J., Jr. "The Submarine Threat of the Future." Naval Submarine League meeting, Falls Church, Va., 14 June 1990.

Spassky, I. D. "The Role and Missions of Soviet Navy Submarines in the Cold War." Naval History Symposium, U.S. Naval Academy, Annapolis, Md., 23 October 1993.

Submarine History Seminar "Submarines in Land Attack," Navy Memorial, Washington, D.C., 15 April 2009. The speakers were Rear Adm. Walter M. Locke, USN (Ret.); Capt. Peter L. Fullinwider, USN (Ret.); and Ambassador Linton F. Brooks.

Also, the published hearings of the Appropriations and Armed Services Committees of the House of Representatives and Senate, U.S. Congress, and various issues of *Military Balance* published by the International Institute of Strategic Studies (London).

General Index

Ship and Submarine Index

Note: U.S. Navy ships are identified by hull number. Hull designations are listed on page xvi.

Missile Index

About the Authors

Norman Polmar has written or coauthored more than 50 published books, including four editions of *Guide to the Soviet Navy* and nine editions of *The Naval Institute Guide to Ships and Aircraft of the U.S. Fleet*. He has served as a consultant/advisor on naval matters to three U.S. Senators, the Speaker of the House, three Secretaries of the Navy, and two Chiefs of Naval Operations. For ten years he was a member of the Secretary of the Navy's Research Advisory Committee, and then served as chairman of the Science and Technology Advisory Committee of the Department of Homeland Security.

Capt. John O'Connell, USN (Ret.) (1930–2018), served in surface ships and submarines, having commanded a submarine as well as a submarine division. He served as the U.S. Defense and Naval Attaché in Japan from 1978 to 1981. In retirement he served as a docent at the National Air and Space Museum, and wrote three books on air power and two books on submarines as well as articles on these subjects.

The Naval Institute Press is the book-publishing arm of the U.S. Naval Institute, a private, nonprofit, membership society for sea service professionals and others who share an interest in naval and maritime affairs. Established in 1873 at the U.S. Naval Academy in Annapolis, Maryland, where its offices remain today, the Naval Institute has members worldwide.

Members of the Naval Institute support the education programs of the society and receive the influential monthly magazine *Proceedings* or the colorful bimonthly magazine *Naval History* and discounts on fine nautical prints and on ship and aircraft photos. They also have access to the transcripts of the Institute's Oral History Program and get discounted admission to any of the Institute-sponsored seminars offered around the country.

The Naval Institute's book-publishing program, begun in 1898 with basic guides to naval practices, has broadened its scope to include books of more general interest. Now the Naval Institute Press publishes about seventy titles each year, ranging from how-to books on boating and navigation to battle histories, biographies, ship and aircraft guides, and novels. Institute members receive significant discounts on the Press' more than eight hundred books in print.

Full-time students are eligible for special half-price membership rates. Life memberships are also available.

For a free catalog describing Naval Institute Press books currently available, and for further information about joining the U.S. Naval Institute, please write to:

Member Services
U.S. Naval Institute
291 Wood Road
Annapolis, MD 21402-5034
Telephone: (800) 233-8764
Fax: (410) 571-1703
Web address: www.usni.org